The Atheist's Survival Guide

35 Ways to Combat Religious Intolerance

By
Martin Johnson

First edition 2024

ISBN: 9798218421625

This book is dedicated to my beautiful and talented wife, Jelveh, and my beloved dog, Mooshi Bella.

Table of Contents

Preface

"I Found It" to "He Gets Us"

WITH SOME TREPIDATION, my mother and I took a deep breath and entered the packed church. We shuffled quickly past the black-suited ushers, who seemed to have been strategically placed like Secret Service agents to keep the large congregation in rather than interlopers out and slid inconspicuously into one of the back pews. Given my secular upbringing, I was fascinated by the strangeness of religious rituals at age nine, so when my mother asked me to accompany her to our neighbors' evangelical service, I jumped at the chance.

I was initially disappointed. The service began with a languid and uninspiring fire-and-brimstone sermon that neither captured my interest nor struck me with fear or awe. It just lumbered on, and I soon began to drift off, thinking about how I was wasting yet another day of my precious summer vacation. Roughly twenty minutes in, however, my stupor was shattered when the choir members slipped out of the shadows one by one and took the stage, weeping and swaying to the preacher's call-and-response.

"Who clothed you when you were naked?" he belted out, startling me to attention. *My parents?* I found myself pondering.

"*Jesusss!*" they wailed in response, their voices growing increasingly melodramatic with each passing moment. *Ah, now we're getting somewhere.* I suddenly perked up.

"Who fed you when you were hungry?" he cried out again. "McDonald's?" I mumbled with a hint of sarcasm, much to my mother's chagrin. She nudged me, if only half-heartedly. Her eyes were as full of bemusement as my own.

The real kicker came when the entire congregation sprang to their feet after this display and launched into a pop hymn that, to my young ears, rang with a disquieting note of masochism and creepiness.

> *"Wasn't it a wonderful thing for Jesus to do-hoo?*
> *to suffer pain and loss,*
> *and die on the sinner's cross,*
> *wasn't it a wonderful thing for Jesus to do-hoo?"*

Wonderful, my ass, I thought. Weird, more like it, and not in a good way. I slowly slumped onto my mother's shoulder pleadingly and whispered, "Boy, it's getting pretty thick in here." She snorted and squeezed my arm as we fumbled out of the pew and tiptoed past the ushers at the door well before the end of the service, busting out in peals of laughter in the parking lot. It was a good Sunday.

All that summer of 1977, the *Campus Crusade for Christ* had been making waves with their *I Found It* ad campaign. I still recall the bumper stickers and billboards peppered across Colorado, each bearing that enigmatic phrase. My inquisitive nature was piqued, especially after spotting an ad featuring a chiseled, vacant-eyed man with perfect hair and a white smile that could rival the entire Osmond family. He seemed to be leering down at me as our car hurtled down the highway toward Denver, a calculated effect, no doubt, designed to ensnare unsuspecting heathens like us.

My parents must have sensed my profound confusion. They tried to explain it to my brother and me from the front seat for several minutes. Evangelicals around the country were using these surreptitious tactics to sneak their way into everyday conversations, smugly asking strangers, "I've found it (Christ). Have you?"

The evangelical wave washed over us soon after when our religious neighbors, friendly to a fault, set their sights on us. For weeks through the spring, they had hounded my mother in particular, relentlessly pestering her to "find it" at their church. Not wanting to offend, she eventually relented and reluctantly agreed to attend a Sunday service they had billed as a "special event about love and kindness," dragging me along as her partner in crime.

I was lucky compared to most children. It had been only the second or third time I had been to a religious event, typically as a gesture of courtesy to my parent's friends and my father's military colleagues. My parents hadn't dragged me to church every Sunday, as many of my playmates had been. As almost anyone can attest, mainline services are usually excruciatingly dull and baffling to a child and lack any spark of inspiration. The story of Jonah trapped in the belly of a whale may make for a charming Sunday school picture book, but it tends to leave a child, especially one raised without religion, highly perplexed and not a little incredulous. The fictitious Christian deity, to me at the time, seemed more obsessed with dominance and obedience and, as I would later learn, with what other people do with their genitalia than ethics, tolerance, or even good citizenship.

To provide some context, as far as I could tell, we were the only "nones" in our social group, although no such term at the time described those of us who were unaffiliated with any organized religion but may or may not have a belief in a deity. Perhaps lapsed Christians was the best way to describe my parents. They had gradually fallen away from their respective religious communities, my mother an ex-Methodist and recovering born-again Christian, my father a nominal ex-American Baptist. So, my brother and I were never much exposed to religion beyond a commercialized Christmas of beautifully flocked and tinseled trees and panoramic sugar eggs for Easter. Even then, we were only vaguely aware of the mythical origins of these traditions and symbols. So we were a ripe target for the endless parade of proselytizers, doe-eyed door knockers, and concerned friends.

My brother and I were fortunate to grow up in a home that allowed us to view religion with a healthy dose of skepticism and even irreverence. My maternal grandfather, a former Catholic, held a deep-seated resentment and white-hot rage toward the Church. My parents, on the other hand, were mainly indifferent to religion, with occasional sarcastic jabs at the dinner table on the illogic of certain religious beliefs, particularly those that veered toward the bizarrely charismatic, or how Christianity, in particular, perpetuated the mistreatment of women. The latter was one of the primary reasons why my progressive and feminist mother rejected organized religion, though, as I would only find out much later, she and my father still quietly maintained a spiritual bent that I lacked.

In addition to my parents' antipathy toward religion, I was also a neurodivergent kid who had no capacity for *teleological thinking* or much of a verbal filter, for that matter. The notion that everything in the material world has a cosmic purpose was, and continues to be, entirely beyond my grasp. Instead, from the start, I found the concept of religion to be a dusty, though sometimes beautiful, cultural artifact that I could study, like my mounted bug or coin collections, and at times, to serve as a source of amusement. Naturally, I was intrigued to attend the church service with my mother, hoping to find it educational or at least entertaining.

Not to say that I wasn't apprehensive as well. Most military communities in which we had grown up were of the Stepford variety: conformist, patriarchal, and oppressive, but not overtly religious. Our upbringing had hardly prepared us for Colorado Springs in the 1970s. Before my father transferred to Fort Carson, we had visions of snow-topped mountain ranges and endless cross-country ski and biking trails but no idea that the area was politically and religiously conservative. Today, the city is relatively diverse, if still quite conservative but at that time, its heavily white evangelical and Catholic populations held sway, given several military bases surrounded the city. These included Cheyenne Mountain, Peterson Air Force Base, and the U.S. Air Force Academy, a festering hotbed of evangelical zeal even then. A 1977 Academy graduate later filed a lawsuit in 2005, claiming academy leaders had fostered an environment of religious intolerance for years. Many others have since alleged extreme religious bias is rampant at the school, but the graduate put the problem most succinctly, saying that it wasn't only a matter of "Christian versus Jew" at the Academy but "evangelical Christians against everybody else."[1]

That religious chauvinism was very real for us. On the street where we lived, there was a Jewish family next door to a house with handmade signs dotting its lawn, bearing messages like "Jews stay off our property" and "The Jews killed Christ." Likewise, the owners planted other signs with disturbing biblical verses that sprouted like noxious weeds everywhere. For the three years we lived there, the family's young son was subjected to physical and verbal harassment and exclusion by other kids on the block. Even adults who may have taken exception to this behavior remained passive.

You wouldn't know it now, but I was raised in old-school fashion, never to talk about religion or politics in public, so my family sought to avoid religious confrontation and raise as few eyebrows as possible. Only my best friend's stepmother, an excommunicated former nun who had overheard me casually mention my godlessness, would remind me, occasionally and without apparent malice or irony, that my entire family was destined for the eternal torment of hell.

The *I Found It* campaign, like the church service with my mother, turned out to be all emotion, virtue signaling, and manipulation and eventually fizzled out like a damp fuse. It marked, however, a point at which white American evangelicals began to fully emerge from their Southern revival tents and conservative Catholics from their moldering church pews to discover a new social and political voice and were determined to use it. This shift was disconcerting for those unaccustomed to such brazen attempts to breach the wall between church and state. My family took solace in the fact that, to our knowledge, minimal overt hostility or repressive politics was at play at the time.

Figures like Richard Viguerie, Phillis Schlafly, and Anita Bryant immersed themselves in malicious political and religious scheming at the time. Yet, their machinations broadly unfolded outside the Overton Window and out of mind among those in polite society. In this sense, we could maintain our distance from the more insidious aspects of the movement, even as we navigated the discomfiting landscape of ever more fervent religious expression.

Fast forward ten years.

As I drove an hour daily on Highway One from our family home in Monterey, California, to the University of California at Santa Cruz, I found myself in a world far different from Colorado Springs. The campus was alive with hippies, drum circles, and the heady scent of progressive politics. It was also a far cry from the controlled intellectual environment I endured as a military brat.

Despite my newfound intellectual liberation, for almost two years, I tuned in religiously, no pun intended, to a local Christian radio station, *880AM KKMC*, with their anesthetizing jingle that went something like, "KKMC, isn't it nice for you and me?" I don't remember how I first stumbled on it, but its strangeness compelled me to listen day after day during my interminable commute.

The channel's highlight was a syndicated program by James Dobson, who founded the fundamentalist Christian organization *Focus on the Family,* coincidentally, the same year as my trip to the evangelical church service with my mother. He also eventually moved its headquarters from Southern California to Colorado Springs in 1991. I listened mesmerized, amused, and not a little horrified by the pseudo-academic discussions on the horrors of abortion, the cultural decay from the lack of organized prayer in schools, the scientific impossibility of evolution, and, of course, the depravity of the so-called, "homosexual lifestyle choice." On its surface, it sounded like a naive quest to reclaim an idealized vision of the wholesome Christian goodness of the 1950s — paradise only if we ignored the rampant racism, antisemitism, homophobia, and misogyny of the era — but just beneath the surface, I could feel the more sinister pulse of brewing resentment and a need to regain control by white Christian men and their submissive wives over a fast-changing world.

Unlike my earlier experience at our neighbors' church, I was no longer laughing. I had begun to recognize the potential threat posed by a politicized, authoritarian version of the extremist Christianity that we had taken so lightly during my childhood. And yet, it all still seemed like an abstract threat. Our Constitution was supposed to protect us from such un-American, anti-democratic ideologies, wasn't it? Television evangelists Jim and Tammy Faye Bakker, with his infidelity and graft and her runny mascara and big hair, were the butt of jokes, weren't they?[2] I held fast to that belief, even as groups like the *Moral Majority* and *Concerned Women For America* were aiming at every aspect of our secular society, my female and gay friends, and the rights of my non-religious family members. They were gaining more and more power, driving the Conservative Christian social agenda and shifting the Overton Window inexorably to the religious right.[3]

The thought that politicized religious extremism would ever be more than a fringe movement still seemed far-fetched to me, a product of our ever-optimistic American psyche. So, as a college student with a heavy load of coursework and a future career fast bearing down on me, I just continued to keep my head down and out of the brewing religio-political fray.

This brings us to today.

I now live within the atheist kingdom, Silicon Valley, California, working in the "anti-Christian" citadel of high tech. From within our fortified walls and lofty parapets, we think ourselves protected from Luddism and religious radicalism as we build the digital world of tomorrow. But just outside on the horizon, we can see the religio-fascist armies arrayed, a radical force led by Christian Dominionists, or the Dominionist-adjacent perhaps, judging by some theocratically-oriented religious and political leaders bent on making Margaret Atwood's fictional *The Handmaid's Tale* a reality.[4] It is still out of view for many Americans, but we know the siege is coming, beginning with the few skirmishes we've had but with the potential for a massive attack on the fortress of science and reason.

Religio-fascism, as we will explore in more depth, is not a fixed or delineated social or political end-state. We can observe it in its most advanced and conspicuous form in theocratic republics like Iran or Saudi Arabia, where religious diversity and acceptance of atheists are virtually nonexistent. Less apparent, however, are the creeping, more subtle forms and nascent versions of religious intolerance that are taking root today in the West. One needs only turn to the so-called "religious freedom" legislation, a peculiarly American phenomenon. On the surface, this appears to champion the rights of all faiths, a seeming beacon of our commitment to religious liberty and equality. Yet, a somewhat different picture emerges when we peer beneath this façade and look at how it is applied and by whom. This legislation is cunningly designed to disproportionately favor radical Christians (note that I don't call them conservative as they are anything but), conveniently granting them the legal authority to discriminate against out-groups and ignore laws that conflict with their beliefs.

The rapid rise of anti-"woke" legislation, now a catch-all for anything the extreme religious right doesn't like, the troubling resurgence of book banning, and the bold suppression of free speech, particularly by those who cannot bear to have themselves or their children face up to our racist and religiously intolerant past, these are not unrelated phenomena. Instead, they are the predictable outcomes, the inevitable next steps, once religious legislators redefine religious freedom to include the freedom to discriminate under the banner of spiritual conviction and dogma.[5]

The fabricated Supreme Court case of a gay man who

turned out to be married and straight and had never spoken to the plaintiff but who had supposedly requested a website be designed by a Christian web designer commemorating his gay marriage is a prime example.[6] The staunch Christian conservative majority on the Supreme Court forced a 7-3 decision in the case *303 Creative LLC v. Elenis* with the specious argument that it violated the designer's First Amendment rights. This case was just the latest example of the court's increased willingness to allow Christian businesses to openly discriminate and deny service based on their religious beliefs, even if it deviates, as in this case, from the teachings attributed to a man named Jesus.[7]

Moreover, this case came on the heels of the decision in the case of Groff v. DeJoy during the same *Supreme Court* session. Gerald Groff, a white evangelical Christian, sued the United States Postal Service for religious discrimination when he got in trouble for refusing to work Sunday shifts. In a unanimous decision, justices refined the law forbidding employer discrimination based on religion, necessitating that they accommodate workers' religious beliefs unless it inflicts an "undue hardship on the employer's business."[8] The unanimity of that decision, if nothing else, points to a more systemic pro-Christian bias in our legal system that trumps all other rights, even according to some on the left. While the law takes into account hardship on the business, it neglects whether such accommodations impose undue hardship on other more secular workers who must then pick up the slack of religionists. A Muslim checkout clerk doesn't want to sell pork or alcohol to a customer? Another employee must step in, or the customer must go elsewhere to buy his food, even if it's the only store nearby. A Christian pharmacist doesn't want to fill a prescription for birth control? Again, another employee must step in, assuming they are allowed, or the prescription goes unfilled. The Supreme Court is heading down this slippery slope at full tilt. They are taking advantage of the ambiguity of our laws and systemic biases that remain deeply embedded in the U.S. legal system, casting a long and ominous shadow over our purported universal values of tolerance, acceptance, and equality.

Europe also finds itself witnessing a pernicious resurgence of religious intolerance, though, in their case, brazenly masquerading as secular nationalist and civilizationist fervor. Religious prejudices against those perceived as "others" might be considered an archaic relic by Europeans who deem themselves too sophisticated to succumb to them. However, they are still part of their secular present day. For instance, a French colleague of mine, the very model of a secular, burn-it-all-down type radical and social justice warrior, still trots out ancient religious tropes about devious Jewish cabals that control events around the globe and are the cause of all wars, inequality, injustice, and misery. Unfortunately, his is not a singular perspective.

Xenophobia, homophobia, anti-semitism, and misogyny, of course, trace their roots to the dusty, time-weathered pages of books scribbled by the less enlightened men of Middle Eastern antiquity. Yet, they've proved remarkably robust, persisting through the ages, and still potent enough to be harnessed by modern secular authoritarians such as Marie La Pen's National Front in France and Giorgia Meloni's Vox party in Spain, who know how to repackage their brand of religious chauvinism for European audiences, and their popularity is growing.[9] They artfully shroud it in the garb of secular parlance, ultra-nationalism, and even neo-fascism, obscuring the medieval religious sentiments beneath. The essence remains unaltered: a profoundly ingrained intolerance that, regrettably, has yet to be consigned to the dustbin of history.

As I reflect on the current state of affairs, I can't help but feel a sense of déjà vu. The same old tactics, wrapped in a shiny new package, are being used to ensnare the unsuspecting masses into the grasping clutches of the religio-fascist MAGA cult. The $100 Million *He Gets Us* ad campaign burst onto our TV screens during the 2023 Super Bowl and returned like severe acid reflux in 2024. Developed by the *Servant Foundation*, it is partly funded by ultra-conservative Christian donor David Green of Hobby Lobby, though it claims to be nonpartisan. Still, its insidious agenda to lure the unchurched with slick emotional videos of a "real" Jesus who is "just like us," a veritable Buddy Christ for Gen Z, cannot be ignored. Unlike its more rudimentary *I Found It* predecessor over four decades ago, this campaign has the potential to feed the unsuspecting through increasingly politicized churches into the well-oiled machine of radicalized and politicized Christianity, transforming them into unwitting soldiers in a dominionist cause they may not fully understand.

We atheists have been asleep at the wheel for too long, content to play nice, to be polite, and to fly under the radar. But it's clear now that religionists have violated this cozy arrangement. The siege on the U.S. Capitol under the twin banners of flag and cross and the systematic implementation of anti-LGBTQ+ legislation, book banning, school board takeovers, and extreme abortion bans are just the tip of the iceberg. Religio-fascists use fear-mongering tactics, riling up the faithful by perverting the meanings of originally favorable terms like *DEI* and *Woke* or promoting and normalizing dangerous buzzwords and concepts like *Christian Nationalism*, *grooming*, and *great replacement theory* to instill paranoia and anger in their followers. They've even managed to convince a disturbing number of Americans that Christian law should rule our country rather than the principles of democracy that we hold dear.[10] Yes, the population of nones is growing, but virulent Religio-fascism is growing even faster, at least in terms of its political power, if not the ranks of the religious. We atheists are now at risk of ostracization, persecution, or worse.

Like Donald Trump surveying his inaugural crowd, these religio-fascists absurdly believe they are the majority against all evidence or, worse, style themselves as a select minority ordained by their deity to uphold divine laws that should supersede those of our secular government and the popular will of the majority. By exploiting loopholes in our sclerotic political and legal systems, amplifying their voices through hate speech on social media and news outlets, and leveraging their disproportionate representation, they have been punching far above their weight politically. The dystopian, religio-fascist vision they have been working toward for decades is now within their grasp, and it is up to us to resist and fight back.

Until Now, a Weak Defense

As an atheist, I must confess that I, like many of my non-believing peers, have been guilty of prioritizing the refutation of religious fallacies, which have little bearing on us day-to-day, over the more practical challenge of addressing the societal impact of religious fanaticism. This error is now having a deleterious effect on our lives as atheists, especially those of us who may also be members of an ethnic, racial, or sexual minority who receive a double dose of religious intolerance.

I should have been faster off the mark due to my academic background in history and life experiences, which should have made me more aggressive in addressing the threat but instead entangled me more in its esoteric implications. Throughout my life, I've had the privilege of studying and experiencing religions around the world, as well as their followers, in all their beauty and charity, as well as their narrow-mindedness and brutality. However, I was guilty of the "sin" of complacency, lulled into a false sense of security by our constitutional rights. I foolishly treated the religious threat as an annoying mosquito in my ear that could be handled by a well-timed rhetorical swat.

Only after working in high-tech for years and heavily using social media was I entirely awakened to the realization that the threat is here now. Say what you will about the dangers and inanity of *X* and *TikTok*. Social media can be a great eye-opener regarding human thought and behavior if only sometimes an accurate news source or a good educator.

It broadly exposes how the cancer of Religio-fascism is metastasizing throughout our society, amplified and spread by the power of the internet. It is now striding confidently in broad daylight where once it had skulked around in the shadows, despite religious affiliation being on the wane for decades.[11]

A few months ago, I was propped up in bed late at night, scratching my dog's ears and waiting for my melatonin gummy to kick in, when I found myself browsing comments on *X* posts by the *Lincoln Project*, a group of never-Trump Republicans dedicated to defeating Right-wing fanaticism. I eventually, and by eventually, of course, I mean within seconds, found a particularly inane comment by a religionist just begging for a particularly witty and sarcastic response. Drunk with my cleverness, I quickly began typing, then suddenly stopped and set my iPhone aside. This is the type of thing on which I, and millions of atheists dedicated to democracy and freedom from religious oppression, are wasting our time? Are we constantly begging for a few passing thumbs-ups and likes without changing a single mind? Even my dozing dog at my feet sees the futility in that.

On social media, atheists like myself have been quick to share and highlight Biblical contradictions and scientific and historical fallacies, denounce the rampant hypocrisy and immorality in the Bible and Koran and their followers, or scoff at clergy covering up, let's just say, bizarre methods for providing spiritual healing and mentoring to male youths. Our banter and sarcasm online can offer a needed intellectual challenge and emotional catharsis for those on society's religious margins. It's anonymous fun, and it's relatively safe for now, but as I've come to admit, it's also impotent in confronting the religious intolerance looming before us in any meaningful way.

What has become most disturbing for me, and became the genesis of this guide, is that merely espousing a more scientific approach to problem-solving, voting against the latest legislative outrages, or raging against judicial decisions that inappropriately advance religion isn't enough. We atheists often find ourselves at a loss when attempting to either elicit help or dispense practical knowledge to another atheist in distress, leaving ourselves and fellow atheists vulnerable in our times of greatest need. Confronting issues as local and personal as how to deal with hostile religious neighbors or protecting our atheist children from harassment in school over their lack of faith can be a challenge.

For newcomers to atheism, those of us who currently live surrounded by extreme religionists, including in the Middle East and the rural areas of the United States and other Western countries, or those who simply don't have a support system of nonbelievers, this lack of practical guidance can leave many of us feeling alienated, perplexed, and disoriented. This feeling will only continue to grow as religious extremists insinuate themselves and their retrograde vision for society into our lives and politics, not to mention schools.

Ultimately, I am optimistic that we can find effective methods for combating religious intolerance or at least endure their onslaughts, if not eliminate it, given that, by all measures, religion, and religious extremism are here to stay. But to achieve the future we want, we must understand ourselves and our oppressors, help our fellow atheists and allies in times of need, remain vigilant against the encroachment of undemocratic, extremist religious movements, and above all, not be afraid to fight back.

Introduction

This guide attempts to provide practical advice to my fellow atheists facing hostile religious environments. It does not presume to teach them how to deliver withering rebuttals to religious arguments using clever scientific proofs, deep insights into theological inconsistencies, or even cutting wit. Nor is it a cogent refutation of the various philosophical arguments devised over the centuries to convince the gullible to believe in the existence of an omnipotent deity without evidence. If that is what you are looking for, read no further. These topics have already been discussed extensively and competently throughout history by numerous atheist minds much more acute than my own, from the Greek poet and sophist Diagoras, "the Atheist" of Melos, who fled a death sentence 2,500 years ago for being a "godless person" to the New Atheists Richard Dawkins, Sam Harris, Daniel Dennett and Christopher Hitchens whose works are currently leading us, religion-free, into the future.

These thinkers, not to mention atheist comedians like George Carlin, Bill Maher, and Ricky Gervais, have thankfully delivered many of us to our current state of skepticism regarding the existence of a deity and, hopefully, evidence-free arguments in general, even if they have yet to diminish the intolerance and ignorance of our antagonists after more than two millennia of intellectual discourse. Their works will continue as they always have to enlighten and emancipate with or without my contributions.

No, this guide is about something that tangibly matters right here and now — our very survival or, at minimum, the maintenance of our rights, freedoms, and even opportunities in a religiously repressive environment.

I am not trying to speak for all atheists who may have different views and approaches to these challenges. I hope to spark further dialogue and effective resistance among them by sharing my practical knowledge and experience and providing insight and valuable advice to nonbelievers. If that is the case, then this guide has done its job.

Why Now?

We are currently witnessing a breathtaking pace of change, stretching across all facets of human society, from advancements in artificial intelligence (AI) and quantum computing, which look to radically transform the high-tech world that I inhabit, to the economic convulsions that technology and globalization bring forth, to the hastened march of social justice. The sheer velocity of this transformation is dizzying, outstripping the ability of the average person to keep up. Even being in cybersecurity, which exists on the bleeding edge of high-tech, I sometimes count myself as a member of the clueless if I stay off my *iPhone* for more than five minutes or take more than a day off from work.

This transformative whirlwind directly challenges the mid-twentieth-century optimism that grew out of the unique post-WWII era of protracted stability, peace, and prosperity that became entrenched mainly in the hearts of white, male, blue-collar Americans and Europeans. It was one of the few times in history when the future promised to burn brighter for them and their offspring. That optimism now faces an onslaught of grim realities. These include the insidious toll of ecological degradation and global climate change that threaten our lives and livelihoods. They also encompass fundamental economic shifts that are creating gaping chasms between educated and highly compensated knowledge workers like myself and those precariously teetering on the brink of poverty, resentful of the growing equality of women and minorities, who they believe are inching them toward irrelevance, economic disaster, homelessness, and often the scourge of opioid addiction. In this turbulent environment, individuals once basking in privilege and prosperity now find themselves unsteady, bewildered, and continually seeking a scapegoat for their social and financial diminishment.

Concurrently, amidst these upheavals, another significant societal shift is simultaneously unfolding — a type of awakening that has thankfully been nudging us toward a semblance of parity in rights, if not opportunities, between those who have historically enjoyed the privileges promised by the American Dream and those who have sat outside of it. This long overdue shakeup of traditional roles and hierarchies, typically buttressed by religious dogma, has inevitably spurred a nasty backlash.

Harking back to the familiarity of religion and conventional social hierarchies that augmented their status post WWII, many disoriented Americans and Europeans are venting their frustrations on those they perceive as "interlopers" through biased anti-pluralistic legislation, a disturbing trend swiftly spreading across the Bible Belt and a large swath of red and blue state America alike. Like kudzu slowly smothering the natural environment, this rage is throttling the very life from our commitment to liberal democracy.

Many beneficiaries of the old *status quo,* especially religious troglodytes (again, I'm reluctant to grant them the mantle of conservative or traditionalist given their perception of tradition and the past is typically distorted), have yearned to return to a simpler and often more religious way of life that never really was. The recently coined *tradwife* movement is one example. Some politically extremist millennial and Gen Z women look to an idealized version of the 1950s for inspiration, where men were the leaders and providers and women were disempowered homemakers, hopefully minus the Valium needed by their post-war role models to weather the daily monotony and lack of agency. Dozens of happy, shiny ultra-Christian women on *TikTok* in retro house frocks and mid-century hairdos sharing their meatloaf recipes revel in their newfound liberation through submissiveness.[12] Similarly, masculinist Right-wing media stars like Tucker Carlson,[13] Andrew Tate,[14] and Nick Adams (the first two have had their comeuppance — Carlson by being canceled from *Fox News*, Andrew Tate for being arrested for rape) decry the feminization of males, gay rights, and the decline of patriarchal, divinely-ordained hierarchies. In response, these insecure men and intellectual incels promote, among other things, unfettered gun ownership, sex without consent, "alpha-male" worship, and even testicular tanning to boost their flagging manhood.[15]

Ignoring the political and economic elites who are actively driving the devolution of society into an oligarchy that disempowers all but the .01%, the disgruntled misdirect their ire at what they perceive as the architects of this unwelcome change and the breakdown of traditional gender and racial roles — namely, irreligious educated liberal elites (i.e., godless atheists) and the so-called "social and sexual deviants" to whom we have often offered allyship, if not always actively worked to liberate. Yet, despite the propaganda of religionists, most of us atheists do not hate people of faith or want to deny them the right to worship, believe, or live as they choose, even if it's in their own private *Father Knows Best* fantasy. Typically, most of us are concerned only with organized and politicized faith, weaponized to aggressively impinge on our lives and body politic in ways that violate our right to live our lives unshackled from subjective religious dictates. Yes, I ashamedly admit that this includes much of my now MAGA-voting white Christian Gen X cohort, whom I thought would be iconoclasts but regretfully took Pink Floyd's *Brick in the Wall* as a call to conformity and authoritarianism rather than the rebel anthem it is.

At a minimum, most atheists like me wish to avoid being harangued by proselytizers knocking on our doors at all hours or trolling our social media accounts. Most of us who lean toward tolerance detest the normalization of the imposition of faith in the public sphere. We also want to maintain relationships and live unmolested in ways that may not conform to traditional religious and sexual strictures. We want to freely create and consume art, literature, and scientific knowledge that religionists may find objectionable because they challenge their delicate religious sensibilities. But above all, we don't want to be economically, socially, or politically disadvantaged, persecuted, or even killed, as occurs in multiple countries across the Middle East and Africa today, for our refusal to genuflect to a man-made deity. Unfortunately, our request to be left unmolested is a threat to the religionists' proselytizing lifestyle, their god's command to violate our personal and intellectual boundaries, and their right to discriminate as an article of faith.

The resulting reactionary response has empowered religious zealots and the 25% of Americans with authoritarian tendencies to seize the moment by promising to return society to a morally unambiguous time with which many are more comfortable and familiar, even as the pace of change continues to accelerate beyond any attempts at control and the rest of us find such acceleration exhilarating.[16] In the United States, those in out-groups or some intersectional mixture of multiple out-groups are bearing the brunt of religionists' fear and wrath. As a result, nations in the West are currently teetering precariously between growing secular segments of society led by millennials and Gen Z on one hand and many older, often rural religionists and their politicians promoting religious intolerance, resistance to modernity, and authoritarianism on the other.

Ultimately, I aim not to indict faith here or cast individual believers as an impending existential threat to nonbelievers. That would insult good friends and beloved members of my extended family. Instead, I hope to raise our defenses against the power and growing threat of extremist religious groups and their radicalized political movements and regimes. These movements go by many designations in their respective societies and nations — Christian Nationalists, Dominionists, Hindu Nationalists, Islamic fundamentalists, etc. — but I will refer to them collectively here as religio-fascists.

You may be skeptical that full-blown religio-fascist regimes could potentially descend on the United States, Western Europe, and other advanced democracies and may even perceive my perspective to be a bit hyperbolic and sensationalist. Given the rise of the religiously unaffiliated nones across the Western world in the last decade and continuing majoritarian support for maintaining the separation between church and state, that is understandable and, I admit, quite possible. Or you may agree that an alarming wave of religious nationalism is building. Yet, while it may eventually place atheists at some social discomfort or even economic and political disadvantage, it would never result in an overt religio-fascist state that could pose an actual threat to life and limb. In this, I sincerely hope you are correct, though to be honest, I'd wager many atheists who are awake to the threat have no intention of giving up one *iota* of our liberty or being forced into second-class citizenship without a fight. For minority, gay, and female atheists who have already been there due to their color, orientation, and gender, the threat is even more visceral and real.

It is not unreasonable to contemplate and prepare for any eventuality, even as we maintain our optimism. Whether religious intolerance or pluralism will win out is anyone's guess. The need to detect the signs of creeping religious authoritarianism, know our antagonists, and understand the best way for us to address threats from hostile religionists, however, is necessary to prevent it from becoming a certainty.

Religio-fascism Is Already Here

As atheists, we must recognize that not all of us are fortunate enough to reside in the currently pluralistic regions of the United States or Western Europe. Religio-fascist regimes, displaying varying degrees of repression and animosity toward minority groups, are spreading all around us. Modern nations like Turkey and Russia, as well as traditional theocratic strongholds like Iran and Saudi Arabia, continue to cling to their anachronistic traditions and medieval moral codes. The limitations of secular liberal democracies in curbing the growing tide of economic disparity and societal upheaval, exacerbated by globalization and shifting demographics, provide a breeding ground for the emergence of such autocratic alternatives.

In the United States, religion, unfortunately, continues to hold a significant influence in society compared to other advanced nations, and a segment of the population is now looking to authoritarianism and religion for easy answers.[17] The sobering reality is that the zealots have already fired the first shots against religious and non-religious minorities worldwide. A 2023 Pew Research report paints a dire picture. The year 2020 alone saw a ninefold increase in the number of countries actively harassing the non-religious, with twenty-seven countries now implicated. Such harassment can take many forms, from verbal abuse to physical violence and even killings committed by governments, groups, or individuals.[18]

The United States is among those twenty-seven countries due to reports specifically of social harassment. Unfortunately, the report fails to include legislation that advantages Christians in the United States, which can also constitute governmental harassment by violating our First Amendment rights to freedom from religion and 14th Amendment right to privacy, precarious as both are under today's politicized Supreme Court. These laws prevent the non-religious from living according to their moral principles and interpretations of individual rights, which are often far more rigorous and humane than the rules followed by religionists. Moreover, since atheism is frequently associated with liberal ideology, as well as specific groups that are usually assumed by the ignorant to be non- or anti-Christian, an attack on a synagogue, an Asian-American elder, or a drag show is effectively an assault on the values of pluralism and tolerance that protect atheists as well. Not to mention that many of those targeted are themselves, in fact, atheists.

The report also notes that religious minorities, our potential allies under the right circumstances, have seen a rise in harassment in recent years. In the United States, anti-Semitic attacks have surged with multiple synagogue bombings and assaults, including the deadliest such attack in U.S. history at a synagogue in Pittsburgh in 2018 that claimed eleven Jewish lives.[19] The heinous terrorist atrocities committed by Hamas in Israel that claimed the lives of around 1,200 Israelis and others on October 7, 2023, only accelerated such antisemitic attacks in the United States and globally, in addition to renewing attacks on Muslims.[20] In India, the Hindu nationalist BJP has been extra-judicially punishing Muslims, including demolishing their homes and properties and publicly flogging Muslim men, all without due process. Hindu mobs, incited by the rhetoric of *Hindutva*-minded nationalist politicians, regularly destroy mosques and assault and even murder Muslims.[21]

Similarly, a steady stream of vigilante attacks and judicially imposed punishments on those accused of apostasy in the Middle East and Africa have persisted since the inception of that faith and have only accelerated over the last thirty years with the spread of neo-medieval Muslim groups such as Al Qaeda, The Taliban, Boko Haram, and Isis, among others.[22]

In Hungary[23], Poland[24], and Turkey,[25] we are currently witnessing religious authorities and the state forming neo-medieval alliances, with the clergy often lending their legitimacy to the bigotry of politicians. In every case, these leaders are driven by a quest for absolute control over their citizens and the ballot box, legal impunity for immoral and unethical behavior, and greed, all justified by their claims of religious sanction.

Intolerance has become socially normalized more broadly, particularly on social media and mainstream news outlets, with anti-Semitic, anti-Muslim, and anti-secular rhetoric going virtually unchecked, even on once respectable news outlets. This vitriol comes from political leaders, celebrities, and others who we would have expected to model acceptable behavior as recently as ten years ago. Now celebrity has-beens like Kid Rock, Ted Nugent, Randy Quaid, and Kevin Sorbo are lending legitimacy to fringe religious and extreme Right-wing ideas, giving the United States, among other things, Donald Trump, MAGA, and a surge in white Christian nationalism.

In these times of global instability, the norms that once made secularism and pluralism possible in liberal democracies are breaking down.[26] The question arises: how long until the virulent anti-outgroup rhetoric boils over into full-blown persecution and physical violence? As atheists, we are equally despised and distrusted as immoral societal misfits, blasphemers, and destroyers of religion and the foundations of Western culture by virtually every theological tradition. Conservatives regularly blame us for the moral decay of society and the scourge of "woke" media and social media.

For historical reference, atheists and intellectuals were, in fact, among the first targeted by the Nazis. In 1933, Hitler decreed that no National Socialist would suffer if he made no religious profession at all, but then went on to ban all of Germany's atheist and freethought organizations, including the 500,000 members of the *German Freethinkers League.* On October 24th of that year, Hitler claimed to have "stamped out" the atheistic movement:

> *"We were convinced that the people need and require this faith. We have therefore undertaken the fight against the atheistic movement, and that not merely with a few theoretical declarations; we have stamped it out."*[27]

The common belief that Nazism was itself atheistic is a misnomer. They did believe that Christianity, mixed with Teutonic myths of German superiority, could be effectively co-opted by the state to glorify the Reich. The Catholic Church in Germany was frequently prodded into complicity or at least silence since it couldn't be allowed to coexist as an autonomous rival power center to the Nazi regime. The unholy alliance between MAGA and white evangelicals and paleo-Catholics in the United States sounds eerily similar.

The recent rise of Right-wing politics driven by extreme religiosity is a cause for concern. Religio-fascist movements strive for ever stricter moral or at least loyalty purity tests and anti-democratic political forms once they have gained momentum if not outright control. The Hindu Nationalist, Muslim extremist, and Christian right movements have grown to become serious populist threats to democracy and pluralism whose extremism only grows, never retreats. This self-reinforcing cycle could spell trouble for us atheists, who are grease for the gears that power religio-fascist crackdowns.

Few religionists of any tradition would, in all probability, complain if we were among the first to draw the religious authoritarians' ire.

Where does the end point of religious extremism lie? Does it become recognized as the destructive and incompetent theater of the absurd that it is and simply fade away? Does it become just an abusively intolerant yet semi-functional regime like that in Hungary under Viktor Orban that most people will detest but grudgingly grow to accept because they are too demoralized or complacent to fight? Or does it devolve into a paranoiac witch hunt or *pogrom* made all the more horrific, efficient, and persistent by modern technology? Again, only time will tell.

For those who favor preparation over panic, this guide is for you. Atheists who live alone, afraid, and surrounded by religious authorities, neighbors, and family members who would, with little provocation, ostracize or even hurt you for your disbelief will find it the most helpful.

Do not be afraid. We more seasoned secularists are here to embrace and guide you, and we're growing in number.

This Guide Is Not Anti-religion

There are a few practical points to note as you read this guide. Religion and its adherents may not have earned my unconditional respect, but I owe their followers my courteousness. As an atheist, I, like many others, have no qualms with those who privately adhere to a particular faith.

I appreciate much of what some religious organizations

have done in the name of charity and care for the poor, sick, and oppressed. I am also overjoyed when someone finds solace and comfort in their religious community. Many of my friends and family members have. Belonging and a sense of security are rarities that we should seek wherever we can. The beauty of living in a Western pluralistic society, especially one with a strong socially libertarian inclination, is that people can say or do whatever they want as long as they do not infringe on the rights and freedoms of others.[28] However, getting everyone to realize those ideals is challenging when that sense of belonging comes with self-righteousness and a need to exclude and abuse out-group members.

The problem lies in the fact that some radicalized and politicized religionists are currently denying the rights and freedoms of nonbelievers, from Tallahassee to Istanbul to Budapest, as core tenets of their faith. This guide does not condemn religion or religionists as a whole but rather the radical religionist movements that claim a divine mandate to rule and oppress and insist on forcing their religious expression into the public sphere and ultimately into legislation that restricts the rights of atheists. It is their bullying condescension and denial of our fundamental human rights that necessitates a guide such as this.

Moreover, I refrain from discussing deities, using clever religious terminology, or delving into theology or religious differences. As a historian, I have studied these subjects extensively and find contemplating religion and spiritual matters both nonsensical and tedious despite their destructive power. Ruminating on theology or the existence of a fictitious creator does not deserve any more of my precious time on Earth, nor should it demand yours. While many have known me to treat religion with sarcastic derision and humor frequently, this guide requires a more disciplined approach to the tangible negative impacts of extremist and politicized religion.

Although trained as an academic, I also endeavor to avoid academese and neologisms or dainty classroom concepts like *microaggressions* and *victimology* that are best left, as I have done, in the lofty realm of university humanities departments or, better yet, forgotten altogether. Most atheists are inured to criticism and view ourselves as anything but victims, as we arrived here by choice. Instead, most of the topics and terms I introduce here have been experienced and practiced in my real life as an atheist, and I refer back to my personal experiences often to establish context. I borrow useful albeit controversial academic frameworks like *Critical Theory* and *intersectionality,* which is understandable as I have based this guide on the controversial notion that atheism is a viable worldview struggling against religion as a destructive, hegemonic force that permeates every corner of society.

While this guide applies equally to Islamic fundamentalism, Hindutva, and Christian nationalism, among other extremist religio-political movements, I speak predominantly from my experience that lies mainly in the majority-Christian United States and Europe. I have also traveled and lived extensively in the Middle East, India, and the Far East, which has influenced much of my thinking. Still, all radicalized religions draw sustenance from the same poisoned well of fear, oppression, and intolerance that fuels the desire to seize control and dominate, putting atheists and our allies at risk. They are all religio-fascist movements.

Finally, this guide intends to raise awareness about religious enablers as much as extremist zealots themselves. This approach is deliberate, as it remains laser-focused on the common existential threats of any powerful religious movement, which is typically composed of both rabid acolytes and complicit moderates. We must avoid falling into the linguistic traps set by religionists to obscure the culpability of moderates and the actual end goal of religious authoritarians — the resurrection of some degree of neo-medieval, neo-puritan, or neo-caliphate style autocracy, depending on the prevailing traditions in our respective host countries.

You may perceive it as naive to generalize about extreme religionists, as they are not all the same, and not all have a hidden agenda for world domination and a will to power. However, as this is my guide, I will keep the discussion focused on their commonalities and dangers, as defending religionists, even the moderate ones coerced into complicity, dilutes the central message here: Religio-fascism is dangerous. It has the power to co-opt even the most moderate believer and could if we are not careful, plunge nations like the United States into a new Dark Age of religious chauvinism and outright persecution of atheists.

Thirty-Five Ways To Combat Religious Intolerance

In today's world, where religious extremism and Right-wing political fanaticism are becoming increasingly intertwined, the challenges faced by atheists can be daunting, but merely identifying them and bemoaning the creeping confiscation of our rights is pointless. Whether it's simply overcoming impediments to pursuing lives unencumbered by religious nonsense or fighting back against threats to our lives and livelihoods, we must take decisive action to analyze our situation and strike back against the increasing social pressure to conform to religious dictates.

As an essential guide to navigating this tumultuous landscape, I have compiled thirty-five ways to help fellow atheists combat religious intolerance and extremism, each with an actionable checklist at the end. This compilation seeks to equip nonbelievers with insights, strategies, and tactics to maintain their well-being, dignity, and autonomy, even when confronted by oppressive religious forces. In the following observations, you will find a comprehensive array of advice, from subtle social navigation to fierce advocacy, ensuring that atheists' unique needs and aspirations are met with understanding and support.

These observations, grounded in the spirit of humanism, rationalism, and empathy, do not aim to antagonize or belittle those who hold religious beliefs. Instead, they serve as a tool for mutual understanding and respect, promoting peaceful coexistence amid diversity — and encourage going into full survivalist or combat mode when necessary. They highlight the importance of embracing individuality, fostering open communication, and cultivating resilience. In essence, this collection empowers atheists to survive and thrive, reaffirming the inherent value of every person's right to freedom of conscience and self-expression.

SECTION I
ATHEIST, KNOW THYSELF

The more you know yourself, the more patience you have for what you see in others.

ERIK ERIKSON

WHEN UNDERSTANDING OURSELVES, people of faith of all denominations and traditions have it relatively easy compared to atheists. I have been trying for over half a century and have yet to understand even a tiny portion of what goes on in my own hyperactive, idiosyncratic, and skeptical mind. Religion, however, provides a ready-made identity to many who follow it, regardless of denomination, making it simple for them to define themselves and their beliefs if they choose to do so. The devout, in particular, may find every aspect of their daily lives circumscribed by their faith, from their daily routines to their moral values and political beliefs. Followers can adopt such worldviews without much personal reflection or introspection in constrictive religious environments. I, and I'm sure many other atheists, know plenty of religious people who are faithful because their parents were devout, and "the Bible told them so." End of story.

Many radical religious parents insist on indoctrinating their children from an early age. To them, parenting is often not about raising an adaptable free thinker but more akin to pressing a blank piece of metal with a die press, hoping to produce a coin permanently stamped with a specific denomination — a child forever obedient to the deity of their parents, religious authorities, and if a woman, to the patriarchy. Atheists, in contrast, must come to know ourselves, either from birth or through religious deprogramming, by daily coming to grips with our unique but small place in a vast and chaotic universe. Without the guiding force of religion, we must forge our identities and understanding of the world we live in through careful self-reflection and critical thinking.

Of course, membership in any group, whether we're diehard Manchester United football (soccer) fans in the UK, drunkenly brawling and chanting on the train home from a match, or members of the Mar-a-Lago resort, expert at pairing a petite Syrah with an anti-gay tirade, carries with it some of the same identity-defining dynamics as religion such as a shared set of interests, traditions, and in-group biases. All of us, religionists and atheists, like well-ordered schizophrenics, have multiple overlapping identities adopted throughout our lives that go partially toward defining us, including our national identity, ethnicity, career, gender identity, and so on.

Yet, while membership in any of these groups can give

us a partial sense of self, only religion offers something more profound and all-encompassing. It purports to provide a complete and unambiguous understanding of one's place in a divinely constructed universe without any evidence or intellectual rigor required by its adherents. Even the most illiterate person can be a model Christian or Muslim; we've all met them. It's just a matter of obedience to religious authorities and depth of conviction. Such religionists predicate this understanding on the existence of a paternalistic creator who governs everything in the universe according to a set of inerrant moral principles, which are then routinely violated by that same creator in a capricious display of cruelty to terrorize humanity into obedience. The fatherly Christian and Muslim god is the belt-wielding patron deity of do as I say, not as I do school of parenting; powerful stuff compared to a fan's subjective belief that Christiano Ronaldo is the greatest footballer of modern times rather than Lionel Messi. Religion offers a level of authority and surety that can be truly awe-inspiring. It's no wonder that those who believe in it feel a deep sense of connection to their religious community and often view outsiders who threaten to rob them of it with suspicion and hostility.

In addition, the degree to which the faithful of any denomination believe in every nonsensical tenet or participate in every obsessive-compulsive ritual may call into question the depth of their commitment or their designation as a "virtuous Christian" or "good Muslim." A Christian may struggle with the mental contortions necessary to believe in the Virgin Birth or understand the nature of the Trinity, or a Muslim may consider whether to force their wives into the hijab or to eat pork and shellfish. However, as long as individuals adhere to the fundamental principles of their faith and don't challenge religious authorities, their spiritual standing remains secure.

In the Arab quarter of Jerusalem's Old City, a Muslim proprietor of a spice shop asked me about my religious affiliation. When I replied that I was an atheist, he seemed perplexed and inquired about my parents' and grandparents' religious backgrounds. Upon learning that they were ex-Christians, his brow suddenly unfurrowed, and he declared, "Oh, so you're Christian!" This observation may seem naive or wrongheaded, but it was quite incisive. For many, religious identity is more about communal, familial, and cultural identity than adherence to a particular dogma. Even as a fervent atheist, since Christians and their traditions surround me, I am, to some extent, a cultural Christian. This may equally hold for a Jewish or Muslim person living in the United States, given that Christianity and its language and customs are so ubiquitous in almost every aspect of American life. Atheists often give gifts during Christmas or hide painted eggs for their children at Easter. Hanukkah bushes have become alternatives to Christmas trees in some Jewish homes but still borrow from the Christian tradition, complete with feasts, gifts, and lights. Though this syncretism does not protect atheists or the Jewish community from persecution by extremist Christians, it does speak to the power of religious acculturation and the persistence of religious identity across generations.

One might contend that religious group identity takes precedence over actual religious tenets or practices in numerous instances. As communal beings, we tend to internalize social norms, including the ethics, traditions, and mores of our social groups and the society in which we reside. These are conveyed by parents, religious authorities, and even the media.[29] This situational and ethical flexibility is indispensable in enduring unexpected societal shifts and maintaining social harmony. We yearn most for social affirmation and to have our understanding of the world corroborated by others, as much as any adolescent in the throes of peer pressure and an overweening need to be accepted.[30] At its extreme, that is how cults, populist political movements, and mob-ocracies are born.

I've often encountered friends and family members who, during personal crises, joined a conservative religious group, party, or movement due to its deceptively welcoming and supportive outreach. A friend had alcoholism, and AA saved her; a homeless acquaintance went to a church kitchen that fed him. Similarly, I've known politically and socially moderate friends who, due to their conspiratorial proclivities, found comfort in aligning themselves with the MAGA or QAnon crowd, segueing from *chemtrail* and *anti-vax* tropes to the *Big Steal* and *lizard people*, ultimately modifying or even abandoning their previous beliefs to embrace hard-right political positions, including their often religious trappings. It is sad to say that they are no longer friends.

Such groups scratch the itch of the malcontents in our midst, offering scapegoats for their life's failures and targets for their outrage while at the same time providing a like-minded community. Over time, they may begin to see us on the outside as despicable or evil, their former friends and associates, particularly those in California like myself, who are now viewed as irreligious left-coast elitists. It's worth noting that the same transformation may occur among those who have gravitated toward extremist progressive stances, though it happens less frequently. At least at this moment in history, conspiracy theories and perpetual moral outrage seem to burn brightest on the political and religious right.

We atheists don't have it so easy. There is no Church of Atheism or absolute cosmic organizational principle to embrace readily, nor a common set of beliefs or traditions that we all share and can latch onto beyond the simple designation "atheist." Even that definition is fungible to many. For instance, some may reject the notion of a god yet still believe in spirits, aliens, or other faith-based fantasies. In contrast, others dismiss any idea that is not backed by scientifically verifiable evidence. Still others, myself included, believe that a practical atheist not only rejects a belief in a deity and non-scientific notions but also fights to dismantle the social and political institutions and mental and linguistic constructs underpinned by religion that oppress us.

So we atheists don't have the luxury of simply defining ourselves by membership in a group with a pre-packaged worldview or set of all-encompassing beliefs, nor, as narcissistic religionists would have us believe, simply by defining ourselves in opposition to them. We must think for ourselves and construct our own personal belief systems.[31] This requires nuance and an understanding that identities and beliefs are not always black and white.

Even if we do manage to clearly define ourselves with our atheism at our identity's core, the resulting definition provides little clear or consistent guidance on how to live or think. While many like myself may follow the principles of reciprocity and empathy that are essential to maintaining a civil society, there is still a risk of absorbing the cultural biases and taboos of our religion-steeped society. As a result, there are both conservative and liberal, gun-owning and pacifist, pro-LGBTQ+ and homophobic, and pro-immigration and xenophobic atheists, even though most of us do admittedly lean to the left. Yes, as a group, we are a frustratingly diverse but wonderful mess.[32]

Unless we are surrounded by other nonbelievers or are born into a non-religious family, as I was, we typically come to our nonbelief through a personal process of self-reflection, internal struggle, and often substantial research into religion. The path of disbelief is not taken lightly. It is traversed only by fighting against the colossal weight of cultural indoctrination, tradition, and, in the case of ex-religionists, our family and friends pressuring us to remain within the fold with promises of belonging or threats of excommunication. Even those like me who are sperm-to-worm nonbelievers must, through constant self-evaluation and introspection, resist the tremendous group and societal expectations to conform to or at least respect a dominant religious paradigm that we often find so horrifyingly immoral and malicious.

Ultimately, the only thing that we, as atheists, really have in common is our skepticism regarding religious arguments claiming the existence of a deity. That is not to say that some of us, like any religionist or ideologue, don't wear our atheism on our sleeves and see it as a core part of our identity, but it isn't universal or group-defined. We all know, or are ourselves, militant atheists, with clever atheist memes emblazoned across our tee shirts, ready to verbally spar with anyone who deigns to mention religion in public or private. The last admittedly describes myself. Yet, as a whole, all the ways we conceive and articulate our skepticism are as diverse and numerous as we are.

Since atheists are an out-group that can be readily ostracized for our rejection of our larger community's worldview, the ancient Greek aphorism *know thyself* has particular relevance to us given our well-being and even survival may depend on it, so it is entirely incumbent on us to put considerable effort into understanding ourselves. Ask yourself, since you decided to reject religion or faith, do you now consider yourself a proud die-hard atheist and Anti-religionist, an ambivalent agnostic, or something in between? Are you uncomfortable with calling yourself a nonbeliever altogether, despite your convictions, and would instead present yourself as a humanist or pantheist to avoid social opprobrium? Or maybe you just wish to remain in the closet altogether for fear of losing your job teaching art at a Christian private school.

In addition, if you aren't a lifelong atheist, did you become a de-convert because you are unconvinced by arguments for the existence of a deity, because you resent the nonsensical social and intellectual strictures of religion, or were you abused by a member of the clergy and bear deep animosity toward the religious organization that enabled them? I know it is a bit jarring to hear me throw in the last point since trauma as a primary cause of atheism is a common trope amongst religionists, enabling them to deny the fact that most of us came to our atheism intellectually. Nevertheless, we cannot ignore the fact that a number of us do come to atheism, in part, via abuse and are equally legitimate and welcome within the fold. Ultimately, there is no right or wrong answer to any of these questions, as there are more types of skeptics, rationales for disbelief, and de-conversion stories than nonbelievers. No kind of atheist is better or worse than another, and getting to know what type you are is a critical part of self-discovery.

It is interesting to note that when it comes to practically navigating and thriving in a religiously hostile environment, none of these minutiae matter from a practical standpoint except to understand the depth of our conviction or non-conviction in our case. Ultimately, all that boils down to is knowing whether we are the kind of atheist willing to fight for our right to be unmolested by religious authorities or not.

Way #1

Determine What Type of Atheist You Are

To everything there is a season. Yes. A time to break down, and a time to build up. Yes. A time to keep silence and a time to speak. Yes, all that.[33]

Ray Bradbury, Fahrenheit 451

MY VOICE HAS always been a loose cannon, booming through the air with impolitic candor that often offends or lands me in open verbal warfare. There are rules hammered into our heads by our parents that hold that politics, religion, and anything else that makes our adrenaline pump or arguments more heated should be kept under lock and key like gunpowder. But me? That lock was never fastened, despite my parent's best attempts to encourage me to be more discreet and diplomatic. Plus, I admit, I relish the verbal sparring. And so, my thoughts on these topics, especially religion, come blasting forth. I show no favoritism, whether we're talking about Islam, Christianity, Judaism, or Hinduism; I like to think I'm an equal-opportunity offender.

As a white man, I occupy, both in the physical and metaphorical sense, considerable space, a privilege I can't ignore. It allows me the audacity to be outspoken, to offend, and to wear my atheism on my sleeve in ways that women and racial and sexual minorities cannot. There's often pushback, yes, but it's pushback I can handle, and nothing yet that has threatened to erase my existence.

I understand not all atheists are so privileged by size, geography, gender, race, or otherwise. Some of us live in places where speaking our mind can quite literally cost us our lives, as in many corners of the Middle East. This also occurs in rural America, where questioning religion can cut us off from our kin and community. This social exile can be unbearably harsh in its own right. We may be female nonbelievers in societies where the patriarchy holds unquestioned sway or non-religious people of color in societies that don't fully embrace racial equality regardless of creed. Then there are those of us who can't be bothered to explain ourselves to the closed, dogmatic minds of the religionists around us.

To make some sense of this mosaic of atheism, perhaps it helps to see ourselves in three basic shades: crypto atheists, who are the silent nonbelievers; diplomat atheists, who walk this tightrope with a certain grace and diplomacy; and firebrand atheists, the ones who speak up and punch back. This is an oversimplification, of course, since we may exhibit the characteristics of any of these types depending on circumstances. Still, maybe it's a beginning, a starting point to understanding how we navigate a world so thoroughly steeped in religion.

Crypto Atheists

Crypto atheists are those of us who, for any number of reasons, prefer to keep our lack of faith private, either as a general principle or only in extreme circumstances. With the latter, I'm referring to those of us who may be out with our like-minded friends in progressive Austin, Texas, but remain silent when we take a road trip to religious Lubbock, the buckle of the Bible Belt. Although not broken out statistically, we can assume that, like any other out-group, crypto atheists comprise a substantial cohort of nonbelievers. No wonder, given the extent of contempt, slander, and even violence projected toward atheists throughout time and across much of the world. Furthermore, it's essential to recognize that acts of prejudice and violence against LGBTQ+ individuals, women, and racial and religious minorities also indirectly target atheists. This is due to the significant overlap and shared values between many atheists and these marginalized groups, making such acts a proxy for aggression against atheists as well.

From a survival standpoint, one thing in our favor as atheists is our ability to maintain free will when it comes to hiding or promoting our nonbelief. Unlike Jewish or Black Americans, who are frequently persecuted solely based on their immutable racial or ethnic characteristics and therefore do not have the luxury of hiding their otherness when in peril, we atheists can at least blend in. No matter how steadfast in our convictions, we all came to our current atheistic state as a matter of choice. In any case, atheism doesn't leave an indelible mark unless perhaps we were so committed to the cause as to get a tattoo of an atheist logo in a prominent place or crazy enough to have written a book about it. Otherwise, for most of us, avoiding responding to inquiries into our convictions is just another choice away.

Obviously, in many ways, public rejection of our atheism would be the easiest route to avoiding harassment by a casual inquirer and the safest move when facing a rise in religious intolerance. It would not pose much of an intellectual or moral conundrum. I could ostensibly drop down and pray with my ass in the air in a Turkish mosque five times a day or go to church daily in Alabama right now, spending hours on my knees like some Red Light District sex worker. It wouldn't change the basic fact that there is currently no evidence for the existence of a deity, let alone proof that might persuade me to believe. Nor would aping religionist behavior call into question my atheist *bona fides* if I embraced it as a merely performative act of virtue signaling to save my hide. Only when authorities develop a way to perform a Vulcan mind-meld can they ascertain my duplicitousness with any surety.

Members of the Jewish community who converted to Catholicism to avoid expulsion or death in 14th and 15th century Spain and Portugal, known as *conversos* (converts), did this somewhat successfully, though *23andMe* and *Ancestry.com* would make the same almost impossible today. The same goes for Muslims forced to convert in Spain, known as *moriscos* (Spanish Moors), during the same period. Yet, while many *conversos* and *moriscos* found forced conversion to be culturally and religiously unbearable and continued to practice their faiths and traditions secretly, we atheists don't have a singular culture we would lament losing nor a vindictive deity we would fear betraying.[34] We are cosmic free agents.

If a powerful, religiously driven event or movement arises, realize that denial can be a legitimate choice, especially if self-preservation or protecting our family is a top priority. For those of us who would choose this route, know that no confirmed atheist could fault us for it. It is a very logical, if self-centered, choice. The only substantial negative to consider is that we could potentially become passively complicit in the perpetuation of religious intolerance and the persecution of other atheists. One way to mitigate this to some degree would be to consciously avoid doing anything that might materially support the oppression not only of other atheists but of other out-groups. This might include acts as simple as opposing discriminatory legislation. Even better would be to aid any future resistance movement covertly or indirectly. Look the other way or misdirect authorities when they inquire about another atheist or persecuted minority. Openly extol the virtues of mercy and kindness generally to foster a kinder society for everyone. The point is to do anything we can to counteract the religious poison and break the fever of their irrational hatred and zeal. Remember that authoritarians will eventually use any tactic or mechanism devised to disadvantage one out-group on atheists as well. We must stop these efforts before they engulf us.

History has shown us that regimes like the Nazis in

Germany were not always universally supported by their populations but instead came to power through a combination of tactics like intimidation and cowing the opposition into silence. Massive crowd size does not necessarily translate to overwhelming popular support, whether they are Nazi or MAGA rallies. We must be careful not to be engulfed by the crowd.

Diplomat Atheists

Whenever dialog is still possible with religious opponents, unbending militancy on any contentious topic can breed greater resistance and backlash, even if we hold the moral high ground. We have seen several noble movements many of us atheists have championed, from LGBTQ+ rights to pro-choice advocacy, that have faced setbacks and backlash recently because a tradition-bound segment of society at least perceived us as being uncompromising or pushing too aggressively. Of course, given the often absolutist stance of many religionists, I might argue that any mutual understanding has been and will remain impossible on some contentious topics, no matter the level of diplomacy applied. Still, militant opposition does nothing to mitigate hostility.

Although religious zealots, if not increasing in number, are gaining political and social power beyond their numerical strength, I am optimistic that most believers in the advanced world who aren't too far gone down the MAGA/QAnon/white Christian nationalist rathole are receptive to reasoned discussion, at least regarding the issue of religious pluralism.

Americans, in particular, still have a strong "live and let live" streak that runs through our entire culture. Europeans are no slouches in espousing liberty, equality, and, as the French say, *laïcité* (secularism). The opportunity to leverage and nurture this independence and tolerance makes diplomatic atheists indispensable in turning the tide against rising religious intolerance and potentially advancing the atheist worldview.

One caveat: of the types of atheists, diplomatic atheism demands the most self-reflection. Most people like to believe they are open-minded, but, in reality, few have the tact, emotional intelligence, and ability to see an argument from the other person's viewpoint to be a successful diplomat. I often fall short in these respects. Devolving into aggressive diatribes is always a risk for most of us. Accepting a compromise between a cause that we believe to be righteous and the seemingly unreasonable or even immoral needs of our tormentors requires an unusually high degree of emotional control and acceptance of some degree of cognitive dissonance.

As diplomats, we may also be at odds with the ideological purists in our midst. Some of us are unwilling to give an inch and will view diplomats with contempt as milquetoast nonbelievers. At some point, diplomats will need to work some rhetorical magic to convince stalwarts that we cannot achieve ultimate victory against overwhelming opposition by perpetually inflaming the passions and convictions of our adversaries, especially when they are in thrall to a force as powerfully emotional and hypnotic as religion.

Yet, if we determine that we are suited to walking the path of the diplomat atheist, it can open several doors of opportunity and understanding. Chief among these is the refutation of the misconceptions surrounding atheists and atheism. Despite what conspiracy theorists say in the alternative media, we don't eat babies. We don't condone pedophilia. We didn't adopt atheism to give us license to conduct ourselves immorally. As much as can be generalized about any group, most of us maintain a solid moral compass and sense of civic duty. Despite the ridiculousness of many of the claims against us, convincing our detractors of the truth of our worldview is easier said than done. In addition to fostering dialog, living our values is paramount in proving to religionists that we are ethical and trustworthy members of society.

Maintaining a diplomatic attitude allows us to sustain and nurture relationships with our friends, family, and colleagues, especially those who may be inclined toward religious intolerance if society takes a turn in that direction. Our angry Christian nationalist grandpa Bill, who constantly spouts QAnon conspiracies and votes MAGA, or our Muslim uncle Hamid, who rages in defense of honor killing for apostasy or female disobedience, may be exceptions. But with most people, there is usually an opportunity to achieve, if nothing else, a peaceful *détente*. We can then inform and influence discussions surrounding secularism, freedom of belief, and the proper role of religion in public life.

Before engaging in heated and controversial religious topics, we should be mindful that diplomacy can be a dangerous game. We are constantly at the mercy of unpredictable religious zealots in our communities and the government. The rewards of success are high, but so are the potential penalties. Firebrand atheists may figuratively or even literally fall in battle, but our opponents can also mercilessly drag diplomats through the reputational mud, the law courts, and the court of popular opinion.

Martin Luther King, for instance, was not an overt militant like Malcolm X, but believed in passive resistance and often spoke about the dream of achieving a brotherhood of man, ultimately bringing about the liberation of Black Americans. Despite this, he was jailed, investigated by the FBI, and finally assassinated for his efforts. Being a moderate, a peacemaker, and a diplomat is not for the faint of heart. Nothing empowers an authoritarian movement more than publicly taking down high-profile opposition members, especially moderates, as it deters compromise and contributes to the extreme polarization that drives their movements.

Firebrand Atheists

When trapped in a foxhole fighting an intractable enemy, there is no one we would rather have beside us than a fire-breathing combatant with an unwavering commitment to their secularism and freedom from religious coercion.

In the late 1950s, Steven Engel, a founding member of the New York Civil Liberties Union who was Jewish, and several other parents of multiple religious and non-religious backgrounds heroically challenged an officially sponsored prayer prescribed by The Union Free School District in New Hyde Park, N.Y., as a violation of the First Amendment. After years of battling in court, they ultimately won in the 1962

Supreme Court ruling *Engel v. Vitale.* Yet, even though Engel had no intent to call into question others' religious faith or right to worship freely, he later said that he and his family members nevertheless suffered irate phone calls, taunts, and ostracism for their conviction.[35] Though not atheist, Engel's stalwart defense of secularism and separation of church and state is a model to which firebrand atheists should aspire, fighting not only for our right to be free of religious coercion but for the rights of minority religionists as well.

A firebrand atheist is someone who, at minimum, is unabashedly passionate and outspoken in their commitment to pluralism and secularism like Engel, and may go as far as to use confrontational language and tactics to challenge religious beliefs and institutions that resist these values. On the other end of the spectrum, radical atheist firebrands may see religion as a destructive and irrational force in society and aggressively seek to persuade others to abandon their beliefs.

The challenge, however, is that though we may wish to pull up all religions root and branch, given the zeal and fecundity of religionists, reports of the death of religion to bastardize a phrase are greatly exaggerated.

No matter on which end of the spectrum a firebrand atheist sits, we risk alienating people who might otherwise be receptive to our message. We may also reinforce negative stereotypes about atheists being intolerant or disrespectful of religious beliefs. This perception further exacerbates tensions between religious and non-religious communities and makes it more difficult for atheists to gain acceptance or find common ground on important issues. But if diplomacy fails, we are the indispensable last line of defense against religious extremism.

As a firebrand atheist myself, I find it's essential to enter into the decision to speak out aggressively or fight with a clear-eyed understanding of the risks and potential personal ramifications, which is no easy decision. My life and those of the ones I care about are more precious, knowing they are the only lives we know with certainty that we have, and all too short ones at that. Potentially risking those lives for the greater good of a society free from religious coercion would be an incredibly heart-wrenching decision. No afterlife will repay me or my family for our sacrifice. We should, therefore, enter into this decision both clear-eyed and rational.

In addition, we must make sure we're not risking dragging our friends and family down with us unwillingly. We must ensure they're equally committed to the cause and fully aware of the risks. Otherwise, we are deciding for them. The repercussions for them could be job loss, doxing, police harassment, or worse. Authoritarians frequently exact vengeance on the families of their enemies as a matter of course, especially when they cannot punish their enemies directly, such as when resistance fighters remain at large. Regardless of social class, collective punishment happens under all authoritarian regimes, whether they are religio-fascist or not.

There is no right atheist path, but we must know the rewards and risks. During our self-analysis, we should ask ourselves several questions when determining whether we should hide, negotiate, or fight:

1. **Am I fundamentally selfish or selfless?** In analyzing our reasons for wanting to fight for atheism and pluralism, we must determine if it is born out of an altruistic and principled commitment or an unhealthy desire for self-aggrandizement and a need to prove something to ourselves or others. We must be honest about the depth of our reasons and only fight out of principle.
2. **Are there others whose welfare I need to consider?** If we have children, a spouse, or other important people in our lives, we probably have considerations beyond our idealism. If we do need to consider others, we need to ask ourselves: is preserving their lives and reputations paramount, or is ensuring that they live in a world free of religio-fascist coercion? Have we consulted with them, and are they on board with our decision?
3. **What is my tolerance for stress and hardship?** Fighting for a cause like atheism, which may be one where the odds are stacked against us, can wreak havoc on our health and stress levels. Some people are thick-skinned, others not. If we are prone to stress, we should consider whether we would be an asset or a hindrance to the effort. If still intent on fighting, we should look at opportunities to contribute to the cause of pluralism that are meaningful but less stressful, such as writing or organizing programs rather than being on the front lines of resistance.

4. **Are my principles enough?** Fighting solely for a principle such as atheism can, by itself, be hard to sustain over time without a tangible reason. It is not an ideology or an all-embracing community that supports us through our trials and tribulations. If we would otherwise be facing persecution for our gender or sexual orientation, or our children would be forced into a school environment of political indoctrination and religious brainwashing, the fight may be more likely to have sustained resonance. Otherwise, remaining steadfast will take an act of sheer will and conviction in the long term.
5. **How have I handled conflict in the past?** Have we successfully fought for our beliefs or values, or have we found that avoiding conflict has worked better for us in the past? Reflecting on previous instances of conflict resolution can provide insight into our tendency toward one approach or the other.
6. **Do I have other atheists or allies who can support me during conflict?** It's essential to consider our support system and whether fighting for our beliefs or values will be more manageable with the help of allies. Most people have little experience in resistance or survival, so going it alone can be foolhardy, not to mention lonely. Fortunately, those who are feeling alone and ostracized realize that there are plenty of other atheists out there, and our numbers are growing. We just need to seek them out.

Way #2
Understand Gender Differences In Religious Belief

A woman does not possess the image of God in herself but only when taken together with the male who is her head, so that the whole substance is one image.

Saint Augustine,
Bishop of Hippo Regius
(354-430) *On the Trinity*

HAVING WORKED IN the high-tech industry in Silicon Valley for longer than I sometimes like to contemplate, I've known far more atheists and nones than vocal religionists, and it's no wonder. By and large, urban, highly educated, often socially liberal, and belonging to the millennial and Gen Z cohorts, my colleagues from engineering to marketing have been much less religious on average than the rest of the nation, save for the Muslims, Hindus, and members of the Israeli

Jewish community with whom I've also worked. Those who are practicing Christians keep their faith private. Admittedly, there does tend to be a bias in the valley against overt Christian expression specifically, and extreme religiosity in general, as a mark of ignorance, poor education, and intolerance.

There is something else atheists in tech have in common: we are overwhelmingly male. Of course, much of this severe gender imbalance in tech is due to the historical domination by men of the STEM fields of study, though much of it is also due to systemic sexism. It is a microcosm of the broader society, casting into sharp relief the preponderance of male atheists worldwide. A 2016 Pew Research poll found that, even in the United States as a whole, 68% of all atheists are men. This finding is surprising since men and women tend to identify as non-religious at more similar rates, with 55% of nones being men and 45% women.[36]

To many men, it might spark confusion, this notion that fewer women openly claim the mantle of atheism, especially given the burden of subjugation that countless religious traditions have imposed upon them. Yet, male privilege, characterized by a license to question and even defy authority often with impunity, a mark etched into the very essence of their gender role, is blinding them to a crucial understanding. Women, perennially crushed under the colossal weight of religious patriarchy and restrictive societal roles, have been inordinately saddled with the burden of religious doctrine, yet paradoxically valued for their submission to it, to the religious authorities who concocted it, and to their husbands who often abuse it. For millennia, their identity has been tied, consciously or unconsciously, to their role as the bulwark of faith within the family, tasked with nurturing the succeeding generation of devout, compliant offspring. Amid the intricate dance of defiance and conformity, the narrative of female atheism is often lost, casting a nebulous shadow over their silent rebellion.

Just over 100 years separate feminists Susan B. Anthony and Zarah Sultana, and only sixty years separate the time when women could only aspire to become a court stenographer from now when four women sit on the Supreme Court; truly remarkable, even if later than anyone should have hoped. The fact that women, in a relatively short period, have come as far as they have in breaking that programming is nothing short of heroic but has yet to tip them fully toward our atheist ranks. Indeed, it's men who more frequently declare themselves estranged from religion even as they are empowered by it. It is as though the echoes of ancient sermons and social expectations, reverberating through centuries, have instilled an immutable sense of duty, or a profound case of *Stockholm Syndrome* compelling women to linger within the strictures of religion, even as they propagate women's subjugation.

Throughout history, men have built their identities around their careers, triumphs on the battlefield, political and social status, and intellectual and artistic success. I know mine has been. I partly define my self-worth on what I do at work, at home, or as a husband, not on the degree to which I obey temporal or religious authorities. I've often been well rewarded by bucking convention and charting my path at work. This self-definition has been made possible by men's dominant place in the religious hierarchy and has been perpetuated by secular society, which has internalized its sexual inequality without its clerical trappings. In modern secular societies, the promotion of rugged male individualism, unfettered by piousness or religiosity, has continued to be reinforced, even to the point where men often violate biblical prohibitions against adultery and the like with impunity. Boys, after all, will be boys.

In addition, men throughout history have been the only ones free to pursue careers in science, philosophy, and other fields that have often directly challenged religious beliefs. Indeed, being a "real man" has demanded it. Men, in general, have claimed greater latitude in questioning authority and established institutions, including religious ones. Charles Darwin only had to face religious authorities when his theory of evolution cast doubt on literal creationist beliefs. At the same time, his wife would have had to face the wrath of her husband, her minister, and her entire community if she were to have merely questioned her role as a wife and mother. To bastardize Sigmund Freud, we might say her only choice was to be either the Madonna (a good Christian wife) or whore (really, anything else); there was no in-between. As much as many men have in recent decades abandoned this dualism and acknowledged female equality, the ghosts of women's second-class status haunt the deep recesses of even the most enlightened men's and women's minds.

Only in the past two hundred years have women participated in religious movements that have afforded them the only means to assert their moral authority and shape the values of their communities, yet still without challenging the patriarchy. Limited female empowerment was particularly evident in the ill-conceived temperance and anti-abortion movements, where women were at the forefront of advocating for moral and social change and, in the case of the latter, their oppression. Recent religiously driven movements, such as school board takeovers and classroom book bans, have often allowed women to assert their political power while maintaining their identity as subservient, morally righteous women. For every step forward toward female inclusion in religious decision-making, however, there is a step back, as evidenced by the recent ban on female pastors in the Southern Baptist Convention, with other traditions looking to follow suit.[37]

Even today, in our modern secular world, in which women in many places can pursue careers and lives just as men do, the pressure on women to continue to define themselves as moral and godly has been internalized to the point that they often enforce morality on each other. I've personally seen religious women in Turkey and throughout the Middle East do this by guilting others into wearing the *hijab*, and situations in the United States where "pious" women have judged each other for being sexually promiscuous or flaunting their sexuality, unbidden to do so by men.

Though women are slightly more likely than men to be religious, they are nevertheless like men, trending away from religion as education levels rise and gender equity in the home and workforce becomes more commonplace. They are perhaps more reticent about openly declaring themselves atheists, however, due to their relatively less secure place in the workplace and society where overt rejection of religion can bear serious career and financial consequences. So men who are atheists should take comfort in the fact that women are in much of the West evolving beyond religion just as they are, but also be cognizant of the fact that men, including atheist ones, are in part the reason it is not happening more quickly. Every man has absorbed the biases of the broader culture to some degree.

I started this chapter talking about the high number of atheists in tech. There are many reasons for this, including the fact that it draws a disproportionate number of introverts, intellectuals, and social misfits, the dorks and nerds from high school, who are often ill at ease with interacting with the opposite sex. It's a generalization, of course, but a stereotype held by many, including women. It doesn't help that some of the New Atheists and many atheist organizations come across as "good ole boys clubs" much as the tech world does, where members snigger with derision when a woman tries to join what amounts to their *Warhammer* and *Dungeons and Dragons* games. They often minimize the importance of fighting for the rights of women and minorities, believing it should take a back seat to other issues, such as fighting militant Islam.[38]

Ironically, women's rights play a pivotal role in challenging the dominance of religion. The control of gender roles and sexuality is a crucial tool used by religiously oppressive societies to maintain their authority, which we can observe in various contexts, such as Saudi Arabia's Wahhabi ideology, Iran's theocratic regime, and radical Christian movements in the United States. All of these groups recognize that by limiting women's rights, in addition to suppressing sexual expression and the rights of the LGBTQ+ community, they can consolidate their hold on power and push society toward more conservative and religiously oriented mindsets.

Revanchist religious authorities are, by and large, obsessed with what transpires in the bedroom and which set of genitalia occupies the boardroom and other seats of power because they realize that sexual repression and gender inequity are crucial to maintaining religious hierarchies and patriarchy. Break that, and the coercive power of religion will be little more than a faint memory. It may seem like liberal claptrap to atheists on the right, but the more we support conservative politicians who believe in traditional gender roles and women's inferior position in society and who vote against women's interests, such as equal pay and bodily autonomy, the more we are propping up the mental constructs and institutions that relegate atheists as a whole to second class citizenship.

It is essential to recognize that achieving true religious tolerance requires an intersectional approach addressing the overlapping forms of oppression faced by different marginalized groups, especially women, who constitute 50% of the population. By standing up for women's rights and advocating for equality, we are advancing justice for women and fostering an environment where diverse beliefs and identities coexist peacefully.

There are several guidelines atheists should follow to promote gender parity within our ranks:

1. **Fight our misogyny, which is core to religious oppression**: Women can be the most powerful champions in the movement against Religio-fascism since they have suffered more than men under religion's bootheel and have more reason to overthrow it. Men can have plenty of legitimate qualms with religion. Still, they also have blind spots that women don't since they cannot deny that they have benefitted from religion-backed patriarchy. Every man has had the luxury of believing that no matter how far he has tumbled off the social ladder, there will always be a woman below him to break his fall. We can never escape the unequal and abusive chains of religion that shackle society without the co-equal engagement of 100% of our atheist cohort. We are too small in number to afford to exclude any nonbelievers, so all male atheists need to listen to and incorporate women's voices to confront the conscious and subconscious misogyny within their ranks.
2. **We must include women in the leadership of any resistance movement if we are to be effective:** Atheism isn't an ideology, movement, or organization and has no leaders as such, but men dominate many of the organizations founded to defend us and have often insisted women's equality take a back seat to broader social equality and religious freedom goals. Such an arrangement is highly counterproductive and plays by the same religiously dictated hierarchies, albeit in secularized and sanitized language. Think of it this

way: what incentive is there for a woman to jettison a religion that treats her unequally and excludes her from leadership positions for a male-dominated atheism that does the same? At least religionists have a familiar, well-defined, and broadly accepted doctrine to justify such second-class treatment and offer the consolation of a community that provides women a recognized place in it. As atheists, we can only explain the oppression of women by using flawed logic and perverted science. Male atheists need to make room so that atheist women can take their place equally beside them, just as if they were looking to diversify the boardroom in business.

3. **Build a sense of community that welcomes all genders:** We humans are social creatures with a deep need to be part of an in-group with shared beliefs, values, and goals. Religion provides that and a sense of our place in the universe. Historically, women have valued such social connections more than men since society has tied their role to their communal responsibilities, such as collectively protecting and raising children. Although gender roles have become much less rigid, the high value placed on community by women remains. Unless we, as atheists, can provide a similar sense of belonging, we will find less success in making atheism equally relevant for both sexes.
4. **Atheist women can teach male atheists a lot about oppression:** If you are female and an atheist, you experience multiple dimensions of oppression as

women, atheists, and more if you are also of color, LGBTQ+, neurodivergent, etc. Those men who are atheists and heteros may have experienced limited discrimination, especially if they, like me, live in a tolerant community. Sexism is ubiquitous and has been persistent, so while it isn't a female atheist's responsibility to educate her male counterparts, men can learn much from them about what to expect if Religio-fascism rises and how to combat it.

5. **Atheist women, please bear with us. We are trying:** Even male atheists can mansplain, swing their thing, and otherwise say idiotic shit. I want to believe they are trying more than others, but they are also run-of-the-mill human males with millennia of indoctrination within them. We need you to better fight for a more secular, pluralistic society. So please don't be put off by the tech bro stereotype of atheists. You have earned the right to reject religion, loudly and proudly, without validation from the comic book guy.

WAY #3

ADMIT YOU ARE A LIBERAL

You'll be pleased to hear, Christopher, that I am no longer a Muslim liberal but an atheist...I find that it obviates the necessity for any cognitive dissonance.[39]

AYAAN HIRSI ALI

YOU'VE VOTED A straight Republican ticket in every election since you were 18. You believe in traditional marriage and never-ending tax cuts for the wealthy and are leery of gender fluidity and gay marriage. Anyone to the left of Ted Cruz is a communist in your book.

The trouble is, you are also an atheist, and in the eyes of many traditionalists, you're as radically liberal as Alexandria Ocasio-Cortez and the rest of *The Squad*, as libertine as a stripper at a Miami nightclub, and as undermining of religion as Stalin.

Ok, so this may be an exaggeration. Of course, several atheists stand out for their conservative leanings; respected figures like George Will, S.E. Cupp, and the late Charles Krauthammer spring to mind.[40] These atheists are, however, more anomalies than the norm among the right wing at the moment since they are currently out of power, perceived as RHINOs, and condemned as collaborators with the godless left. Deep trenches of disagreement are being dug across the American landscape, resulting in a stark portrayal of our political parties as stereotypes with no room for those who don't fit them.

Consider today's Republican party. It cloaks itself in a mantle of unwavering "conservatism" and views itself as a sentinel of time-honored traditions, capitalism, family values, and Christianity, whether true or not. But the same party is also portrayed by the left-of-center as a MAGA sanctuary for those harboring misogynistic, homophobic, xenophobic, and racist views, obsessed with controlling sexuality, espousing a so-called law and order agenda that punishes the poor and minorities, and serving the interests of crony capitalists. Liberals often perceive them as using patriotism and religion as camouflage, making their unpopular, reactionary beliefs and policies more palatable to a gullible electorate.

Conversely, the Democratic party brands itself as the champion of individual rights, the protector of the working classes, and the gatekeeper of civil liberties and freedom from religious coercion. However, the right often caricatures them as socialist foes of capitalism, appeasers of sexual deviants, champions of the shiftless poor and "undeserving" immigrants and racial minorities, and proponents of a flexible moral compass with an extreme antipathy toward Christianity.

The propensity of the human mind to seek clarity, to crave defined boundaries and clear labels, plays into this political polarization. We are a binary-thinking species. We often find comfort in such simplifications as right-left, good-evil, etc., although they distort the complexity of our political and religious identities. As a result, our society, like iron filings around a magnet, increasingly aligns along these polarized lines. The picture of the chardonnay-sipping, effete coastal elites versus the beer-guzzling, hardworking "real Americans" might indeed be an exaggerated caricature, but it often drives people's impressions of and reactions to the two groups, sometimes more so than the reality.

Conservative atheists, outliers in this scenario, may find themselves caught in a storm of misunderstanding and misplaced labeling. Unfettered by religious dogma yet espousing traditional values, we can be vilified both *as* liberals and *by* liberals. This paradox underscores atheists' daunting challenge: to move beyond these entrenched lines and nurture a society that appreciates complexity and nuance.

The numbers bear out that not all atheists are liberals, and not all liberals are atheists. Pew Research has found that 15% of U.S. atheists are Republican or lean Republican.[41] It is also true, however, that there is a more significant intellectual overlap between atheists and liberals than atheists and conservatives, given that many of the values of atheism and liberalism often align and that liberal governments are less likely to pass laws that are onerous to atheists. As a result, there is a common misconception, happily amplified by conservative politicians seeking to claim the mantle of defenders of Christian values, that liberal political beliefs are closely tied to atheism and are, therefore, morally compromised because of it.

A *University of Maryland Critical Issues* poll conducted in 2022, for instance, found that 61% of Republicans would go so far as to support declaring the United States a Christian nation, whereas 83% of Democrats oppose it.[42] The assumption by Republicans is that the United States lost its moral compass and turned to liberalism when Americans began to lose their faith, ostensibly sometime after the hallowed 1950s and that we need to return to the religiosity and moral clarity of that era to reinvigorate the nation.

There are many practical reasons why the other 69% of atheists gravitate toward liberalism. While, by definition, we reject the idea of a deity or religious authorities dictating our beliefs, actions, and history, liberals similarly value the right of individuals to make their own choices independent of any authority or tradition and live their lives as they see fit. Atheists rely, for the most part, on empirical evidence, science, and reason to guide our beliefs and decisions. At the same time, liberals value evidence-based (i.e., non-faith-based) policies that help reach moral goals such as civil rights and bodily autonomy. This reality contrasts with so-called conservatives who love and rely on tradition and the authority of specific individuals and institutions to achieve their ultimate goal of group cohesion and conformity. Both atheists and liberals seek to defend diversity and pluralism.

As with any variegated group, however, there are, of course, some atheists who still align themselves with Right-wing politics for a variety of reasons, including support for conservative fiscal policy or a belief in the efficacy of traditional social structures even though those may be undergirded by religion. Right-leaning atheists need to be cautious because conservative media and social media warriors have successfully perpetuated the stereotype of the evil, woke, and socialist atheist, so right-leaning atheists can eventually be sucked into the same vortex of ostracization as their leftist compatriots.

To survive and thrive, a right-leaning atheist should consider adopting several classically liberal stances even if they could never stomach aligning with modern liberals on many items on their agenda:

1. **Unabashedly champion individual rights:** Classical liberalism, at its core, defends individual rights and freedoms, allowing people to express their beliefs and opinions and others to debate and question them. It is the bedrock that supports our ability to reject religion and isn't at odds with what we call modern, freedom-loving conservatism. We should remember this when entering the voting booth. Conservative atheists aren't obligated to embrace every out-group's beliefs or opinions. Having reservations about transgender individuals participating in female sports or the wisdom of paying reparations for slavery is everyone's choice. Adopting aspects of classical liberalism doesn't demand accepting every progressive idea or belief contrary to our conscience. What it does demand is that we all vote to ensure the dignity and human rights of everyone, even if we disagree with the way they live their lives. By doing this, we can build a society where diversity of thought and beliefs, including atheism and religion, coexist.

2. **Be rabidly intolerant of intolerance:** Don't get me wrong, liberalism dictates that even the most die-hard religious conservatives, with their fetid beliefs about women, minorities, and other out-groups, have a right to have and voice those beliefs. It doesn't mean, however, that we shouldn't, in the same breath, condemn them and fight their attempts to impinge on the rights and freedoms of others. Any thoughtful conservative should join liberals in fighting aggressively against such violations, as intolerance goes both ways for atheists. Suppose, as conservative atheists, we genuinely believe conservatism doesn't espouse racism or misogyny. In that case, we should actively work to change that perception by fighting racism and sexism, even if it pains us to think that liberals are doing likewise.
3. **Actively defend democratic values:** Classic liberalism supports democratic principles such as the rule of law, free and fair elections, and separation of powers. These principles prevent the concentration of power and ensure that the government remains responsive and accountable to all citizens, including atheists. Even the most rock-ribbed atheist conservative should find the January 6th insurrection as anti-democratic as liberals do and realize that if it had succeeded, the days in which we maintain our right to express ourselves openly as nonbelievers would be numbered.

4. **Promote social justice:** Classic liberalism aims to address inequalities and injustices in society, advocating for policies that ensure equal access to resources and opportunities for all, irrespective of one's religious or non-religious background. Such social programs contradict much of the conservative doctrine of personal responsibility, self-reliance, and limited government. However, closing the gaps between the 1% and the rest of us, between white and brown America, or between those with traditional Christian conservative values and those who don't, should be the goal of anyone who wishes to avoid ending up dangling from the gallows erected by the other 99%. It is self-preservation if nothing else.
5. **Foster critical thinking:** Classical liberalism encourages skepticism, questioning, and critical thinking, which are essential to challenging religiously dogmatic beliefs and promoting intellectual growth. Fortunately, conservative atheists typically share these values with liberals. Championing them together, especially in higher education and the media, which have drifted away from them, can help create a more informed and rational society that doesn't immediately embrace every fiction of the baby-eating, devil-worshiping atheist.

Way #4
Keep a Lookout for Atheist Quislings

Those who play with the devil's toys will be brought by degrees to wield his sword.[43]

R. Buckminster Fuller

A SMALL BUT not insubstantial number of traditionalist atheists, as mentioned in *Way #3*, align themselves with religionists, whether they admit it or not. "Craig," a colleague of mine who eventually came to his senses, had consistently voted for the Republican party ever since he turned 18, even after it made its current sharp turn toward white Christian nationalism. While admitting that the party increasingly promotes an extremist Christian agenda and has been successful in implementing it, Craig continued to vote Republican because he ran his own business and was primarily concerned with tax breaks and limited regulation. After all, he was a hetero-white male and American citizen unaffected by the threats to overturn Roe and the metastasis of anti-gay, anti-immigrant legislation across the country. Why should he, comfortably insulated in his California tennis club and gated community, have to give up any of his hard-earned income? Those who were affected by religious bigotry could fight their own battles. Only when Craig started to see MAGA extremism under Trump impinge on his friends' rights and dignity did he begin to rethink his political choices. I wish all wealthy people were as thoughtful and empathetic.

Atheists who would turn their backs on fellow nonbelievers are the *quislings* in the war for a pluralistic society, and we should approach them with caution in times of rampant religious intolerance. What would possess them to stand against their fellow atheists and their marginalized brothers in arms? Some, like members of any group, are just wealthy self-centered opportunists who recognize that maintaining the *status quo*, even if it is slouching toward Religio-fascism, is where their best chances at economic enrichment and political empowerment lie. Several studies have shown disquieting similarities between the wealthy of all stripes and psychopaths.[44]

I often see these self-absorbed, unrepentant quislings in the executive suites of high-tech. They may be nominal atheists or agnostics who give lip service to social justice for the sake of their often more progressive employees but, in actuality, embrace Right-wing politics through voting and political donations that favor Republicans despite the party's increasingly religious agenda. They do so for *laissez-faire* economic policies and access to the halls of power. Not to mention that it feeds their own Ayn Randian personal narratives that they succeeded on their own, obviously not counting the efforts of their employees, VCs, the loose monetary policy courtesy of the Fed, and the other 99% of taxpayers who are there to subsidize them if they fail.

They conveniently ignore the cultural, intellectual, and religious oppression that comes with conservative politics as irrelevant to them or perhaps hope that such a general atmosphere of oppressiveness and elitism will eventually translate into labor policies that will give them the upper hand against impudent employees demanding fair compensation and decent working conditions. It's not just blue-collar workers who should be incensed by the current state of income and political inequality, but rank-and-file tech and mind-workers.

Then there is also the belief among the wealthy that they can always buy their freedom. For those quisling atheists who believe this, look no further than Iran for a cautionary tale. Unlike secular authoritarian regimes, which often attempt to win over support within the business elites, the theocratic Iranian government, like American Christian radicals, is more concerned with ideological and moral purity and social control than economic success. Under Khomeini, the anti-government forces that eventually seized control of Iran were deeply critical of the Shah's close ties to the West, and many believed the wealthy and educated individuals who had benefited from those ties were economic collaborators and morally corrupted by Western culture. Like my Iranian-American wife's family, they were targeted for harassment, arrest, and even execution once the mullahs overthrew the Shah. Those with the means left for Europe, Los Angeles (often dubbed *Tehrangeles*), or elsewhere. Rich Iranians who prostrated themselves before the regime and stayed, always ready to party and entertain, still find ways to purchase alcohol or have clandestine gatherings that allow men and women to mingle. Yet, it is the freedom of a bird in a gilded cage living in fear under the watchful eye of the nearby government-bred Persian house cat.

Another type of atheist quisling, which shocked me when I first came across one, truly believes that traditional Judeo-Christian and, I presume, Muslim social values and power structures have proven themselves throughout history to be the best organizational principles for maintaining a civil society. These principles may include opposition to same-sex relationships and marriage, support for patriarchy and traditionally prescribed gender roles, and defense of social hierarchies. Of course, correlation does not imply causation, given that cultures with weak religious foundations, like China, have survived and thrived without threats of eternal damnation to keep their populations in line. Yet, some of these quislings believe that extricating religion and its biases from social and political power structures is a utopian pipe dream, so they will defend the religious status quo against a purely secular alternative that they believe will ultimately fail and bring about anarchy or, at minimum, an uncertain future.

Both of these perspectives are most likely to be held by those who are economically and socially vested in maintaining the *status quo* that spawned them. Still, others may live within religiously conservative areas like the Bible Belt and are just trying to be realistic about the low probability of religiosity ever subsiding. The joke is that they are nearly as expendable as the rest of us when their money and usefulness are exhausted. It is only speculation, but it makes sense that at a certain tipping point, religious extremists will discard them along with their plebeian atheist cohort. Either that or quislings will slowly shift, chameleon-like, to fully reflect the impending religio-fascist zeitgeist or use their wealth to flee the country.

But what does this mean for the rest of us when interacting with them in a religiously restrictive environment? Several risks of interacting with them include:

1. **They may betray and sabotage atheist goals for personal gain:** Atheist quislings are most likely members of the one percent. By far, most American CEOs and executives are stalwart Republicans, who are becoming religiously and socially more conservative as MAGA group-think infects the party and naked political opportunism necessitates it for those who want to influence the party or run for office. The atheists are often entrepreneurs in high-tech. Yet, many of them will jettison the socially liberal values they adopted to assuage their liberal employees in a heartbeat if their obscene wealth comes under threat.

   Newly minted Texan and anti-woke provocateur Elon Musk is a prime example. So, too, are the executives of many companies jettisoning Diversity, Equity, and Inclusion (DEI) programs or including diverse voices in their advertising the minute that a few MAGA consumers or the anti-woke zealots in Congress sneeze. In a much more extreme political environment, it is not inconceivable that they might actively work against progressive, religiously pluralistic policies and their fellow atheist. Betraying the other 99% of atheists would be no more heart-wrenching than crossing anyone else, as betrayal is almost *de rigueur* in some corners of the cutthroat world of business.

2. **Working with them may damage the reputation of atheists:** The presence of atheist quislings can harm the reputation of the atheist community insofar as there is one, especially as a sanctuary for members of other groups also facing persecution. Intersectionality demands solidarity, but that is not possible if part of the atheist community is untrustworthy or unsympathetic to those with whom we intersect. Why would a Muslim, a Jewish woman, or a Black agnostic trust a group that is already often perceived as a bastion of white male privilege if it included quislings with questionable loyalties as well?
3. **They may divulge critical information to our antagonists:** Atheist quislings may reveal confidential or sensitive information to religio-fascists to unmask atheists who are trying to keep their beliefs hidden.

Like anyone concerned with self-preservation but with the added desire to preserve one's substantial economic livelihood and power, a quisling may be more likely than average to use every means to protect themselves, including betrayal. The added fact that CEOs and corporate business leaders, in general, have a higher propensity for sociopathy and narcissism (between 4 and 12% of them) should make us pause.[45] Quislings may find it advantageous to keep the government apprised of efforts to mount legislative or legal defenses against religio-fascist authorities. Bringing the rich and influential into any resistance movement, though carrying a potential for gaining powerful allies and financial support, also risks exposure and compromise. Oskar Schindler, who protected approximately 1,100 Jewish workers from the Nazis in his munition factories during WWII, was an anomaly compared to the more significant number like Ferdinand Porsche, president of Volkswagen, who was a true believer in the Nazi Party and SS, as many German industrialists were at the time.

4. **Embracing them may decrease morale in the broader atheist community:** The unmasking of a quisling who betrays other non-religionists despite being trusted by the atheist community would be devastating. It would lower morale among atheists and reduce the minimal cohesion we have as a group.

WAY #5

APPROACH NONES WITH HEALTHY SKEPTICISM

What the rise of the "nones" shows us is not how American Christianity is declining but how it is changing.[46]

STEPHEN PROTHERO

ONE OF THE characteristics I have always admired in many non-atheist, non-agnostic nones is that they tend to be far more open to evolving their thinking than their churchgoing counterparts and, admittedly, some atheists. Leaving the comfort of their religious community and losing fellowship is no slight loss, so their commitment to rejecting organized religion, especially as it becomes more politicized, is admirable. They are not typically bound by dogma or church authority, nor are they obligated to accept any given belief or disbelief simply because their parents embraced it or it was part of their upbringing and community. Instead, they are free to form their own opinions based on evidence and reason, much like atheists. Granted, they can sometimes be open to spiritualism or alternative forms of Harry Potter wand-waving hokum, which seems strange to many atheists, but that is far preferable to the inflexibility of religious extremists or even church-going moderates. Of course, not all religious nones are the same, and there is a wide range of beliefs and attitudes among them. Still, one thing is clear: many religious nones are typically fearless in challenging the status quo and evolving in response to new ideas and evidence.

In the introduction to this guide, I categorized my family in the 1970s as just such nones, and they continue to be so today. They aren't currently members of a specific religious tradition or church, nor are they theists. Still, they have often believed in spirituality and cosmic notions bordering on deism and pantheism. They have occasionally attended New Age churches and Native American ceremonies in search of community and a sense of spiritual wonder. My brother's beliefs differ from those of my mother, whose beliefs differ again from my father's as they would in any open-minded group of more than one person not constrained by a particular religious dogma. They are also free to admire the life of Jesus without being Christian and those of the Buddha and Native American shamans without being wedded to those traditions. Not to mention that their individual beliefs have evolved with their life experiences, ages, and the *zeitgeist*.

This flexibility can often make it challenging to know where a none might land if religious intolerance were on the rise. Fortunately for me, my family is an exception, given they have always supported my nonbelief, even when I'm blunt and tactless, and the notion of equality is virtually baked into their DNA, as I suspect it is for many nones. But might another aging none parent, vulnerable in an increasingly uncivil society, confronted with financial insecurity or their imminent mortality, and discounted by our ageist society, just say "fuck it" and re-embrace the comforting bosom of religious fellowship that defined their more innocent childhood faith? Or would a sibling faced with the never-ending monotony of work and a nasty divorce who finds solace at the bottom of a bottle look for a sense of renewal, wonder, and awe in a charismatic megachurch? Each could either end up more defiant in the face of rising religious intolerance, seeing it as a perversion of free-flowing faith and spirituality, or could be nudged toward Religio-fascism by other unseen needs like fellowship, something that radicalized religion can fulfill like so much empty-calorie junk food.

In a 2019 Pew research survey, nones were the fastest-growing group on the spectrum of religious belief, making up 30% of the U.S. population.[47] (or 20%, according to Gallup.[48]) This number is considerably higher in parts of Europe and the Far East. At first blush, the numbers could lead atheists to celebrate the notion that organized religion is on the wane. And perhaps it is, albeit only in the West. In almost all other regions, religion is on the march, especially Islam and more radical strains of Christianity, such as Pentecostals that tend to out-breed the non-religious and have been rapidly displacing more mainline traditions like Catholicism in

Africa and South and Central America. It's not the meek that will inherit the Earth, but the most fertile, who sadly are usually the most radically religious and uneducated.[49]

As we have mentioned, members of the none cohort are just nones because they don't usually attend religious services, are unchurched, and often don't subscribe to a particular religious tradition. Yet, most still believe in a higher power. Think of none-ism as a way station, where members may eventually rejoin a congregation due to, say, the demands of marriage to a religious spouse, a desire to raise children in a faith community, or a strategic decision to avoid being socially ostracized by their surrounding religionist community during rising religious intolerance. Nones may also crave a perceived spiritual and social connection they were programmed to embrace as children. On the other hand, they may eventually trend toward nonbelief, with or without adopting the socially toxic atheist moniker. Which path they take depends, of course, on the individual.

Until proven otherwise, it might be prudent to assume that nones we don't know well would potentially gravitate toward greater religiosity, if only performative, in the event of coercion by religious authorities. We cannot blame them for doing so as self-preservation is an instinct, though that is little comfort to a threatened atheist. In addition, although the number of nones approaches or equals the number of Catholics and evangelicals in the United States, it is a very soft number that should not be seen as providing atheists with any degree of safety in numbers, even if their values align with ours. They are not like American Catholics, with their rigidly consistent dogma and rites, who can rely on their large numbers, robust institutions, and singular ideology for defense in the face of Protestant white nationalism.

Add to this the fact that religionists, particularly Christians, often view religious nones differently from how they view atheists and agnostics. Atheists are a lost cause, as religionists can rarely turn us from our lack of belief. Religious nones, however, are potentially redeemable as they have not necessarily rejected the notion of a god outright and may be potential converts to more radicalized variants of Christianity. In most cases, then, nones would probably be less of a target for persecution and potentially less likely to side with atheists. As with moderate religionists, we should take a zero-trust approach with nones. We should fully trust them only when we can verify their commitment to defying religio-fascist authorities.

We should be clear on the potential divergence in needs and priorities of atheists and non-atheist nones:

1. **Many nones still maintain a strong desire and respect for spiritual fellowship:** While atheists and the religiously unaffiliated nones may both value community involvement and connection, nones often retain a fondness for the social and emotional support offered by the religious communities of their upbringing, even if they no longer actively participate. Their childhood memories of spiritual fellowship tend to be positive, in contrast to atheists, who may harbor negative feelings towards religious

experiences due to adverse past encounters. The absence of a structured, supportive community for atheists can pose challenges for nones considering a stance with atheists in troubled times and turn them back to more supportive religious organizations.

2. **Nones may have less revulsion toward overt religious expression:** Those of us who are atheists see public expressions of religion as public virtue signaling and a threat to keeping ourselves and our nation free from religious domination, brainwashing, and political oppression. Equally, we may find the misogyny, homophobia, and bigotry that many spiritual traditions embrace, or at least tolerate, morally repulsive. Nones may not be bothered much by either of these things if they weren't actively driven from organized religion for these reasons and may even still retain support for them. As a result, we may have different concerns and priorities regarding protecting or limiting religious expression in public spaces or even the role of religion in politics and society.
3. **Nones may have different ethics and values from atheists:** Although atheists and non-atheist nones frequently share comparable ethical and moral principles, the values we emphasize and how we arrive at them differ significantly. We atheists typically lean on science and reason to guide our decisions, leading to an emphasis on reciprocity and being responsible citizens. In contrast, nones might place greater importance on personal experiences, spirituality, and

emotions or draw on values uniquely sourced from religious teachings. This perspective might lead them to support restrictions on sexuality and the preservation of traditional gender roles, views that are often rooted in religious doctrine many atheists oppose.

4. **Nones maintain greater diversity in political views than atheists:** As mentioned earlier, atheists and nones may have different political priorities based on differences in their approaches to morality. Therefore, a none may be more likely to be conservative than an atheist who typically views tolerance as the best protection we have and consequently lean liberal or libertarian.

WAY #6

SUPPORT NEURODIVERGENT ATHEISTS

I have Aspergers and that means I'm sometimes a bit different from the norm. And – given the right circumstances — being different is a superpower.[50]

GRETA THUNBERG

ON NUMEROUS OCCASIONS, I have found myself in situations ranging from the peculiar to the downright embarrassing. When I was around three or four, at a child's birthday party, I accidentally popped my balloon. Devastated, I ran straight home to my father, tearfully begging him to save what I believed to be a living, feeling creature. This incident was a step up from other childhood gatherings where my conspicuous absence marked my presence. Overcome with dread at the prospect of new social environments, especially in strange homes brimming with the loud chatter of unfamiliar children, their overwhelming odors, and alien interactions, or when expected to knock on strangers' doors during Halloween, I invariably implored my parents to spare me from participation. In instances where I was compelled to participate, the sensory overload would immobilize my brain, leaving me to shrink against a wall, utterly alone, feeling like a stranger in a strange land.

This wariness of large groups and unfamiliar situations, of physical touch, unpleasant textures, and food consistencies, has trailed me into adulthood. Even now, often faking a somewhat polished veneer of sociability, I find myself immobilized at social gatherings of more than two or three people. There, I linger in corners, fidgeting awkwardly, engulfed by wave after wave of voices, laughter, music, and the clang of silverware that coalesce into an unintelligible din. Retreating from the clusters of people who seem to share a secret bond and knowledge that will forever be unknown to me, I may find solace in peeling away individuals I know well for more intimate, digestible conversations. Even then, my tendency to interrupt and over-talk can cause me to irritate and offend.

More minor interactions also require a careful dance. I've lost count of the times I've told stories or attempted humor, only to be met with wide-eyed stares, a clear sign that I've veered off the acceptable path of social norms, treading instead into territories marked "weird" or "insensitive." In these moments, I become aware of my transgression of some invisible line that I fail to see.

My unshakable enthusiasm, typically when pet topics like religion or politics arise, often gets the better of me. I launch into breathless monologues, oblivious that my audience might not share my zeal or prefer to venture into less contentious conversational waters. And so, I find myself monopolizing conversations, only to end up being the one feeling unheard and misunderstood. In these moments of social exhaustion, my refuge lies in going home and retreating into the familiar world of certain movies or TV series, which I rewatch endlessly. They serve as a balm, a self-soothing ritual after the jarring cacophony of traumatic social interactions.

Those of us atheists on the autism spectrum occupy a challenging position when navigating the complex and intersecting realms of socializing and religion. The subtle art of being diplomatic, of shaping words with the precision and gentleness required in delicate, religiously charged conversations, often eludes us. Similarly, maintaining emotional equilibrium and interpreting the nuanced dynamic landscapes with religionists can be overwhelming. The ability to dissemble, lie, or remain silent at crucial moments is a skill deeply ingrained in human social interaction, often used as a shield to protect one's true beliefs or to navigate hostile ideological environments. This skill is either underdeveloped or conspicuously absent in many of us. While admirable in many contexts, our inherent inclination toward honesty and directness becomes a liability in environments where religious beliefs dominate and demand unearned respect. The act of concealing our incredulity over unfathomable beliefs, a necessity in societies where religion is ubiquitous, becomes a perilous endeavor.

As autistic atheists, we may find ourselves disproportionately exposed in societies where religious extremism reigns. Our natural disposition makes us more vulnerable to detection. This situation illuminates a broader aspect of human social evolution, the often unacknowledged struggle of those whose neurological wiring diverges from the majority, and the additional layers of complexity we face in a world where conformity, often to religious or ideological norms, is a prized and enforced attribute. In most human societies, religions have historically played a pivotal role in sculpting collective identities, typically through the constriction of thought and behavior. While effective in unifying a group, this cohesion mechanism invariably creates a rigid framework of acceptable norms. Individuals who cannot help but deviate from these standards, particularly those of us with neurodivergent conditions, find ourselves conspicuously at odds with the established order.

Our cognitive processes, characterized by different patterns of thought and emotional response, inherently resist the molds of intellectual and behavioral conformity demanded by religious dogmas. This resistance, albeit unintentional, can be perceived as a threat by adherents of religious systems. Neurodivergent people challenge, often unwittingly, the very foundations upon which these religious structures rest.

This divergence in thinking manifests as a significant asset in technology and innovation. Many atheists, particularly those within the tech industry, are found to be on the autism spectrum. These individuals, including some of the most brilliant and successful tech entrepreneurs, blend their intellectual prowess with a distinct form of social awkwardness and eccentricity. Their minds, shaped by a different neurological blueprint, allow them to "Think Different," as Steve Jobs famously encouraged. Unshackled by conventional norms, this mode of thinking often leads to groundbreaking innovations and solutions. Of course, not all individuals with autism are atheists or geniuses. Like any group, we represent a broad spectrum of intellectual and spiritual abilities.

Less well-known is that those of us on the spectrum are much more likely to embrace atheism than the neurotypical, as many of us are not wired to contemplate the divine or occult. This divergence is not born out of a lack of appreciation for the richness of religious tradition and culture; indeed, I have found myself deeply moved by the profound history, faith, and rituals that Judaism has to offer and stand in awe before the architectural grandeur of Catholic cathedrals and hidden mysteries of Tibetan Buddhist monasteries. My fascination with these religious elements is genuine and intense, reflecting a keen interest in the human quest for the divine and the myriad ways it has sought expression through art, even if I cannot join them on their journey.

When considering a deity in human-like form, a central figure in many religious doctrines, my mind hits a wall of incomprehension. The concept of an anthropomorphic god endowed with human traits, emotions, and modes of cognition governing the universe's vastness and dictating humanity's moral compass remains elusive. This is not for lack of trying; I have earnestly sought to grasp this notion, to find a foothold in the spiritual realm that captivates so many of my peers. Yet, despite my efforts and genuine appreciation for the cultural and historical impact of religion, the idea of a personal god remains beyond my reach.

Several studies, most notably one conducted in 2011 published by the University of Boston entitled *Religious Belief Systems of Persons with High Functioning Autism*, confirm our atheist leanings.[51] Individuals on the spectrum often struggle to conceptualize deities typically characterized by human-like emotions, thoughts, and biases. The anthropomorphic gods central to many religious traditions and the pursuit of cosmic truths such as "Why are we here?" or "What is the meaning of life?" often do not resonate with us. This dissonance is not due to a lack of intellectual capacity but rather a different mode of cognition. We tend to favor logical reasoning and concrete thinking over teleological or purpose-driven thought processes.

In Douglas Adams' novel *The Hitchhiker's Guide to the Galaxy*, the supercomputer *Deep Thought* was tasked by two Magrathean programmers with discovering the answer to life, the universe, and everything. After seven and a half million years of contemplation, it comes up with the answer "forty-two," a seemingly nonsensical response. Chiding the programmers that they didn't know or articulate the question, *Deep Thought*, unable to calculate the question itself, then designed a vastly superior computer known as the *Earth* to discover it. After ten million years of running the program, a Vogon constructor fleet destroyed the Earth just five minutes before the Earth could reveal the answer, but the whole story suggests to an autistic atheist like me that it, too, would have been just as meaningless as the answer.[52] The burning need to contemplate such questions, or to believe that those questions are even meaningful, is a prerequisite for belief in an anthropomorphic god and universal prime mover, yet almost incomprehensible for many neurodivergent atheists.

Even those autistic people who are religious tend to formulate their religious beliefs in a way that aligns more closely with their natural propensity for concrete reasoning, or they focus on finding comfort in rituals and traditions more than theology. Instead of embracing traditional concepts of a humanlike deity involved in the creation and moral governance of the universe, they often perceive divinity as an embodiment of universal laws, a perspective that veers toward pantheism or pandeism rather than classical deism. Their god is usually not a conscious, purposeful creator but more an expression of nature itself or the laws of physics. While intellectually coherent to some autistic people, this viewpoint may appear to others as a semantic redefinition where the supreme being becomes synonymous with the laws of the natural world.

This inclination among spiritually-inclined autistic individuals toward a non-traditional, more abstract conception of divinity carries significant social implications, particularly in environments that enforce belief in an anthropomorphic god, where the unique religious perspectives of neurodivergent believers could place them under suspicion of being *de facto* atheists or heretics.

So why not just mask it, that is, to try and pass as neurotypical (and religionist) by emulating expected emotional responses, controlling emotional outbursts when overstimulated, or hiding verbal and physical tics that are the dead giveaways of autism? As it turns out, this is much easier said than done.

Attempting to hide autism involves a deliberate modulation of behavior. However, the execution of this strategy is far from straightforward. It is not merely a matter of mimicking behaviors; it is about constantly monitoring and adjusting our natural responses in real-time, which demands considerable cognitive and emotional resources. Moreover, masking extends beyond physical behaviors into the subtler territories of social cues and communication. It involves deciphering and appropriating the often unspoken rules of social engagement, understanding when to speak or remain silent, knowing when to initiate and finish conversations, and interpreting and responding to the nuanced spectrum of human emotions. For someone like me whose neurological wiring does not intuitively align with these norms, the task can be akin to a perpetual high-wire act, with little room for error. Fortunately, I'm more empathetic and attuned to other people's feelings than most.

The toll of such sustained effort can be significant. Masking, while offering potential short-term social benefits, can lead to long-term psychological stress, identity confusion, and emotional exhaustion, especially if we must lie about our beliefs. It is akin to conducting a charade, day in and day out, without the respite of returning to one's true self. This dissonance between the outward persona and the inner reality can lead to alienation and a loss of self-identity.

Furthermore, the societal expectation that individuals on

the autism spectrum should mask their traits to fit in raises ethical and philosophical concerns that should resonate with every atheist. It implies a valuation of neurotypical traits as the standard, inadvertently perpetuating a sense of otherness among those of us who are neurodivergent and especially those who are both neurodivergent and atheist. This othering not only overlooks the rich diversity of human neurology but also negates the potential contributions that neurodivergent perspectives can bring to the collective human experience.

The upshot is neurodivergent people can't or won't mask their behavior, and rightly so. We shouldn't have to. For those familiar with the quirky, gifted Dr. Shaun Murphy on the TV show *The Good Doctor* or the penguin-obsessed Sam on *Atypical*, you have a sense of how some can have uncontrollable awkward body movements, emotional outbursts, and compulsive obsessions. Sadly, most autistic people don't get a pass but are more likely to face social ostracization than social and career success like the lead characters Shaun and Sam, even today in relatively tolerant societies.

The intensity of social rejection we meet depends on the degree to which we exhibit the more atypical social behaviors common to those with autism, such as extreme social anxiety, public meltdowns, and stimming (self-stimulating repetitive physical movements or vocalizations, thought to serve a variety of functions, such as calming and expression of feelings.) We often experience dismissiveness, condescension, and hostility when interacting with others in public, applying for jobs, etc., due to our perceived awkwardness and bluntness or the assumption that we are unintelligent. My convoluted, nonlinear communication style frequently leads to misunderstandings and dismissals of my ideas and opinions.

Societies with heightened religiosity magnify such biases. In less educated communities, where superstition holds sway, physical, emotional, and intellectual differences, including neurodivergence, are often misconstrued as moral and spiritual failings. This misinterpretation has stark consequences, ranging from hiding away the neurodivergent as mentally ill to being perceived as possessed by demons or involved in witchcraft. No one region or religion has a monopoly on such beliefs; they manifest in various forms across the globe, from certain areas in the Middle East and Asia to sub-Saharan Africa and even within devout segments of the Catholic community, where exorcism is still occasionally practiced.[53] Surprisingly, some Protestant pastors in the West, like Greg Locke, also categorize autistic people as spiritually wanting or even demon-possessed.[54]

Of course, such abuses are currently outliers in most educated, pluralistic societies. Yet, under a budding religio-fascist regime, such mistreatment and spiritual stigma could become more mainstream, primarily if it also serves a political purpose, such as social control. Religionists might persecute neurodivergent people because of the perception that our differences result from moral failure and because we often find it hard to adapt to authority, fueling a cycle of ostracism and suspicion.

The upshot is that autistic people often depend on allies, friends, and family who can act as guardians and advocates, remaining vigilant in public and religious settings where the individuals might struggle. For family members of neurodivergent individuals, there is a vested interest in offering this support. Association with a neurodivergent person can sometimes extend suspicion of being atheist to themselves.

There are a few things to consider either as an autistic person or as a neurotypical befriending neurodivergent people or caring for autistic family members when religious intolerance is on the rise:

1. **Lead the atheist charge:** Like Greta Thunberg leading the movement to stop climate change, our autistic nature often lends itself to stridence, singularity of purpose, and logical problem-solving. What better strengths to lead an atheist resistance to religious intolerance? I know I'm not all about sensory processing issues, social challenges, and odd verbal inflections – the autistic characteristics on which neurotypicals dwell. For those of us autistics who are also firebrand atheists and unafraid to speak truth to power, we should not be afraid to step into the breach. And, if anyone can think outside the box, analyze problems from a fresh perspective, and find a solution that allows religionists and non-religionists to coexist in harmony, it's us, even if diplomacy may not be our strong suit.
2. **Guide, don't control:** For those of us with low support needs, we don't need to be handled or treated like children. Think of it like assisting someone who has experienced partial vision loss. In that case, step in to help only when asked or needed. For an autistic

person who may be blind to social cues or proper comportment in some situations like religious settings, neurotypical allies can subtly provide social insights when needed, though only if they are solicited or would be well received and appreciated.

3. **Make sure to test children early:** If you suspect your child may be neurodivergent, get them tested as soon as possible, regardless of whether religious intolerance is impending. With autism, the sooner a child receives treatment, the better the outcome will be in terms of ensuring their ability to cope socially around religionists as well as manage their autism symptoms. Don't let your child's future, or your own, be compromised in the face of religious and social bias by your shame or fear. Autism is nothing to be ashamed of; it can be an atheist "superpower," just ask Greta Thunberg.
4. **Teach autistic children not to talk openly to strangers:** Autistic people are often very materialistic thinkers. It's hard to get us not to do something, like maintain verbal restraint, unless there is a tangible reason. Preventing an autistic child from divulging your family's atheism to strangers may take some extensive explanation that doing so poses genuine dangers and repercussions. It is the stranger danger talk you should have with any child, but with a perhaps more significant emphasis on "teaching" than "telling." A simple "Don't do that," which would work with a neurotypical child, would be insufficient here.

Way #7
Have the "Atheist Talk" With Your Teens

Teenage hearts are raw and new, fast and fierce, and they do not know their own strength. Neither do they know reason or restraint, and if you want to know the truth, a goodly number of grown-up hearts never learn it.[55]

Catherynne M. Valente

THE BLACK COMMUNITY in the United States has a tradition of passing down wisdom through families to its young men in the form of "the talk." This ad hoc talk, delivered by parents across the United States, provides insights and guidance, based on generations of experience of inequity and bloodshed, to sons who are mistreated by law enforcement whenever they leave the house. The *talk* provides sage advice to ensure that their sons make it home alive every night.[56]

Now, I don't dare to purport to be a font of atheist wisdom comparable to that of an entire disenfranchised community forged and tested in the fires of adversity for centuries. Nor do I wish to cheapen that tradition by drawing equivalencies, given that most atheists outside of Muslim countries are not experiencing oppression of remotely the same magnitude as people of color. We can easily pass, shrinking back into the shadows if we must, where Black people and other minorities have no such luxury. I do, however, believe in taking guidance from those who are reluctant experts on the topic of discrimination and who have discovered that an honest two-way dialog between parents and teens that is open about potential threats can be a critical tool in keeping young atheists safe.

In considering the importance of the atheist "talk," we must first acknowledge the potential for abuse that atheist teenagers may face. Atheism challenges the dominant religious paradigm, making teens, an incredibly insecure and conformist lot, especially vulnerable to stigmatization and bullying if discovered to be atheists, especially if they live in religion-bound communities. Parents must prepare their children for these challenges and equip them with strategies to handle potential discrimination and bullying by their religious peers with resilience and self-confidence.

African American men, of course, face tremendous existential risks, from street violence for those living in dangerous neighborhoods to unprovoked rogue police violence to discrimination in education, jobs, and medical care that can put their health and lives in jeopardy. For the atheist teen, the stakes aren't remotely as high in terms of the threat from authorities, at least not yet. The danger is less the potential to be shot or beaten by police when walking or driving while atheist, but in being bullied and ostracized by their peers beyond their ability to resist it emotionally. With adults, such harassment is often constrained by the legal system and the norms of social etiquette, even today when common courtesy has become frayed. Adolescents, in contrast, are frequently like feral animals with little self-restraint or sense of proper social behavior, ready to go for the jugular with little consideration of consequences. In addition, teen victims are less emotionally resilient than adults because their sense of self is not yet fully developed.

Before we dismiss this as a problem of the white and privileged, it is essential to note that atheism increasingly crosses all racial, cultural, and gender boundaries, along with bullying, especially among Gen Z. One of the prime contributors to teen suicide, which is a leading cause of death among teens in every community, is bullying and peer pressure.[57] Persistent physical and emotional bullying, cyberbullying, and social exclusion can have severe psychological effects on atheist teenagers that can exacerbate feelings of isolation and worthlessness, potentially leading to depression and suicidal ideation.

Teens are especially susceptible to pressure from adults, especially when something as emotionally charged as religion is concerned and when someone in a respected authority role, such as a teacher, athletic coach, or the community as a whole, is contributing to that pressure. We are aware that bullying can occur when a child is in the out-group due to looks, disabilities, class, race, or anything that can make them appear different. Yet we often overlook beliefs unless they go with outward material signs of alienness, such as wearing a *hijab* or a *kippah*. Laws against hate crimes and religious persecution protect minority religionists but, in practice, often fail to protect the non-religious. Authorities usually ignore bias against nonbelievers as a real threat, or they may believe free speech rights supersede those of atheists to be verbally unmolested, especially if the authorities themselves are radical religionists.

Typically unseen is bullying based on private beliefs that may be forced to the fore by both teens and adults. On June 22, 2022, the Supreme Court ruled 6-3 in *Kennedy v. Bremerton School District* that a Washington state high-school coach's First Amendment right to pray conspicuously at the fifty-yard line outweighed the teens' right to avoid pressure to participate and to be free of religious coercion. The problem with this decision was that it rejected the argument that students might have felt obligated to join the coach's prayers and have trouble resisting it. The court claimed that "learning how to tolerate speech or prayer of all kinds is 'part of learning how to live in a pluralistic society,' a trait of character essential to 'a tolerant citizenry.'"[58] That may be true in theory when it comes to adults. But adolescents aren't typically emotionally resilient enough to resist social pressure from adults; it's one of the many reasons why we have laws against statutory rape. The power differential between adults and adolescents is significant, making it impossible for teens to provide informed consent. Consent is predicated on being able to analyze a situation rationally and resist even when someone is in a position of authority, which is often difficult even for adults. As anyone with teens knows, opposing even supposedly voluntary expressions of group solidarity can provoke extreme harassment and bullying. Refusing to kneel side by side with a respected coach, inexplicably revered as a hero in many communities, is too much to expect from even the most confident teen ball player.

The atheist "talk," then, should serve as a platform for nurturing the most robust secular identity possible that can help their atheist teens develop a sense of self able to resist bullying. In addition, it can help build an understanding of when it may be prudent to keep their lack of religion private. By engaging in open discussions about atheism and secular humanism, parents can assist their teenagers in developing an effective toolset of defensive techniques. These discussions encourage critical thinking, evidence-based reasoning, and the embrace of secular values, fostering confidence and pride in their nonbelief. It can also help inoculate them against becoming religious to fit in or prevent them from fighting when it isn't prudent. Yet, these should not be one-way lectures; they must allow teens to voice their doubts and fears freely so that parents can share their wisdom without being dismissed or ignored.

To conduct a successful "talk," you should teach your teenagers to:

1. **Be aware that the dangers posed by radical religionists are real:** Most adolescents, especially those not from a traditionally marginalized racial or reli-

gious group, tend to think they are invincible. Their privilege, whether due to gender, color, or wealth, has often protected them from the harsher side of the legal system and other centers of authority, from getting let go with a warning for petty traffic infractions to avoiding suspicion for shoplifting by business owners, to receiving lighter punishments for misbehavior at school. They may then assume that they will always be untouchable, especially in the face of impending rather than immediate threats. They live for the now and dismiss potential threats as overreacting.

Sit your atheist teens down and explain that there are religious radicals, fellow students included, that take a very dim view of atheists, some who even today believe in resurrecting Old Testament punishments for nonbelief. While a minority view, it is growing in political influence and gaining an audience through social media, megachurches, and conservative media outlets. As a point of proof, educate them on the Nazis, who were able to impose their vision on a nation with only a minority of the population supporting them. Ensure they are kept abreast of advances of religious extremism on the Supreme Court and state legislatures, especially regarding anti-free speech and book-banning legislation.

2. **Be polite toward those in authority, if not respectful:** Many atheists believe that respect must be earned, not automatically granted, especially adolescents who highly value authenticity. This perspective

can cause problems for teens in a society where religions demand respect as a matter of course, no matter how ethically bankrupt or repugnant we find them. In all probability, you inadvertently passed this aversion on to your children. A teen may perceive this as a license to challenge authority in ways that invite a harsh rebuke.

Let them know that being polite to others in public doesn't automatically connote respect or approval but is a necessary social lubricant that enables civil society to exist. When dealing with those in authority, self-preservation dictates we be polite and compliant when necessary. While doing this now may merely contribute to an overall atmosphere of conviviality and coexistence, something severely strained now, it is solid training for future situations that could save your child from persecution, prosecution, or worse.

3. **Keep their own counsel both online and in real life:** In this social media age, the notion of privacy has become an antiquated concept, as peer pressure and online platforms demand overexposure and a constant flood of information and intimate details from users jockeying for "likes" and "LOLs" from peers and strangers alike. Under current conditions, the worst this can do is contribute to our communal attention deficit disorder and, for a developing mind, make children more susceptible to peer pressure and a sense of self-worth based on the perception of others. Not to belittle the resulting body dysmorphia and

suicidal ideation that can arise from this even now, under Religio-fascism, overexposure can be equally deadly for atheist teens.

My friends in the government are adamant about keeping their teens and children, including pictures of them in their social media accounts, away from these platforms altogether. They do this to protect their kids from criminals and blackmailers and because they know children tend to have no filter and could potentially harm their reputations and their parents by saying the wrong thing. While this may not be feasible for most people, avoiding online overexposure should remain at the top of their minds. Teaching your teens to minimize discussions of their atheism, politics, or anything that could be objectionable or antagonistic to religionists should be avoided online and when talking with teachers and peers. Let them know that communicating their beliefs and opinions in a way that protects them must be highly honed before they attempt to engage more freely.

4. **Choose caution over hubris:** Your teens learn by example. If you are an atheist like me, you take pride in being able to go toe-to-toe with a religionist when confronted. Intellectual sparring can be invigorating, and expressing anger at religion after experiencing clerical abuse can be cathartic, but it can also have the unintended consequence of teaching your kids to be impolitic. Instead, teach them through example that they don't need to engage with religionists when-

ever the opportunity presents itself just for sport, to dominate a conversation, or to correct an untruth. Being discerning about who they engage with and how much of their beliefs they divulge is essential for self-preservation.

5. **Be receptive to encouragement:** Remind teens they are strong and capable and, once adequately prepared, will eventually have the power to change the world. Encourage them to learn from their experiences and fight effectively for a pluralistic society when they become adults.

Way #8
Rethink Stranger Danger

Children have never been very good at listening to their elders, but they have never failed to imitate them.[59]

James Baldwin

AS ATHEISTS, WE often accuse religionists of brainwashing their children and not allowing them to choose or reject religion of their own free will when they are more intellectually and emotionally capable of making an informed decision. Yet, as atheists, some of us can be tempted to do the same thing with our children by discouraging them from contemplating religious ideas or keeping them separate from friends and family who are believers and who may try to inculcate religious notions in them. Teaching them to be free thinkers is one thing. Demanding it is the opposite of freedom. Worse yet, like a parent in the throes of a bitter divorce who psychologically damages their children by badmouthing their ex-spouse, we may spew our vitriol and hatred toward religion in our children's presence. The irony in all of this is that given that children are always looking for ways to assert their independence by defying their parents, we may be courting the very thing we are trying to avoid: a religious child.

Of course, this is not entirely analogous to what religionists do. Much of our vitriol often stems from our emotional pain and resentments toward parents who may have forced religion on us or shunned us for being gay or may be due to being sexually or physically abused by members of the clergy. This attitude is prevalent among those born into overly strict and very religious households or ones that encouraged children to remain silent concerning clerical abuse. Ideally, we want to provide our children with greater intellectual freedom and emotional support than we received. Yet, our desire to protect our children from harm can lead us to still place limits on our children's ability to explore religion freely.

Of course, all parents, religious or not, want to mold their children in their image. There is no more incredible thrill than watching them grow up to be miniature versions of themselves (though as they pass through their surly teenagehood, as most parents will attest, that's rarely the case until much later). This child-rearing approach is perhaps narcissistic to a degree but doesn't place children in harm's way in times or countries where religious freedom holds sway. When our choice of belief or nonbelief puts us at elevated risk of persecution in a religiously intolerant environment, however, we should think twice about committing our children to our fate without their informed consent, something that is impossible until they pass into adulthood.

There are two things to consider if religious intolerance is on the rise. One is that, as stated earlier regarding teenagers, children are not intellectually or emotionally mature, and the less so the younger they are. They often have little ability to maintain their parent's confidence. Although you may be able to deny your atheism if religionist neighbors or authorities inquire, are you sure that your younger children would be able to do the same? Are you confident that when on the school playground, they won't blurt out that their family doesn't believe in a deity when religious kids are gathered and are talking about their beliefs? If a teacher makes religious claims, are you sure your child won't refute them? Answering these in the negative would suggest that such situations could potentially put your child and your entire family at risk.

One option, though it requires extreme discipline, is to avoid all discussions of religion in front of your children until they are old enough to keep their counsel. Of course, you run the risk of having your child co-opted by religionists, including those in your own family. Admittedly, my sister-in-law, for example, was born in Iran into a Muslim family that never talked about religion, and her father was an atheist. When they immigrated to the United States, it came time to place her in school, and she enrolled in a Christian day school. The religious instruction, combined with not a little peer pressure and desire to fit in as an American, resulted in her suddenly declaring to the family that she was a born-again Christian while a pre-teen, an unfortunate affliction she suffers from to this day. On the plus side, not discussing religion does provide plausible deniability to your child when queried.

Given our social media obsession with perpetually announcing "our truth" and living a "genuine" life, the more difficult path is teaching them the art of discretion as you would do with your older children. Again, this is challenging, especially with loose-lipped young children, but it worked well with older generations, including my own. So, how might you raise a child who believes that discretion is the better part of valor?

1. **Reduce your rhetoric:** If you are highly animated and filter-free when discussing your atheism, you may want to curb your tendency to expound on every news article and incident to which you may take umbrage within earshot of your children. If you make a federal case out of everything relating to religion, so will your children, and the chances that it will spill over into emotionally charged exchanges with friends and acquaintances increase exponentially.
2. **Have a simplified version of "the atheist talk":** Sit them down regularly and be honest about the danger in which they could place the entire family by divulging their atheism in public. You don't need to go into graphic detail like with your teens, as fear without complete understanding is the worst educational tool. Perhaps we should teach them, as previous generations have done, but we as a society have often forgotten that it is a sign of respect and politeness to avoid conversations entailing politics or religion and that your household adheres to this practice.

3. **Do not allow them to engage with strangers unaccompanied:** This is a modified version of the stranger danger warning. Instruct your children outright that they cannot talk to adult strangers, even in your presence, without your express permission. Tell them this is a matter of courtesy, manners, and personal safety. They may feel you were overly protective or stodgy when they get older, but it is better than bearing the negative repercussions. As a result, they may even become more polite adults.
4. **Consider secular homeschooling:** Homeschooling is typically viewed as far inferior to public or private schooling in terms of quality and socialization, especially when embraced as it generally is in the United States by extreme religionists who disdain science, free thought, and socializing with outsiders. However, it may be a possible last resort in a religio-fascist society and not an intellectually crippling one if you, as parents, are highly educated and able to guide your child's education. Alternatively, if you have the financial resources, you might build an educational "pod" of like-minded parents who can pool their resources and privately engage atheist tutors. If nothing else, the COVID-19 lockdowns proved that this can be an option. Some wealthier parents did this to ensure their children didn't struggle with remote learning. Removing your child from the school environment may be a last resort, but it limits their opportunities to expose your atheist family inadvertently.

Way #9

Don't Assume You're Perceived as Ethical

But the fact that highly secular nations and states fare so well compared to religious nations and states, and the fact that many nations have seen violent crime and other social pathologies decrease over time as secularity has simultaneously increased, does prove that morality clearly doesn't hinge upon the existence of God, or require belief in God.[60]

Phil Zuckerman

WHEN I RECEIVED my acceptance letter from the University of California at Berkeley, I was ecstatic. I had studied extremely hard, taken many Advanced Placement courses, and did everything I could to prepare myself for a top college, except for one thing: I was paralyzed with a fear I had yet to master. The thought of the radical change and sensory overload of moving from my insular private school to a massive campus with a reputation for packed lecture halls and political radicalism in one of the biggest cities in the country was too much for my neurodivergent mind to contemplate when my acceptance decision got down to the wire. It sounds ridiculous, given that I moved every couple of years as an army brat, leaving behind familiar homes, friends, and family without missing a beat. Still, I always had the touchstones of my brother and parents. The comfort and security they provided allowed me to mask my social awkwardness and anxiety, at least in controlled settings. Plus, I wanted to study without being distracted by out-of-control teens.

After discussing college choices with my father and coming up with a rationale that didn't humiliate me as socially inept, I took the easy way out, or so I thought, by enrolling in a small private liberal arts college in rural Washington state instead. Everything I had heard about the campus seemed idyllic, with small classes in a self-contained campus in the middle of wheat fields. The students shared a similar background to mine, many having attended private schools. Moreover, many came from strict Catholic prep schools in Spokane and elsewhere, so I expected, even as an atheist, that their behavior would be better than that of Berkeley students.

From the moment my parents dropped me off at orientation and waved goodbye, it was mayhem. The wealthy, well-dressed students morphed into feral animals when the watchful eyes of their parents and nuns were no longer on them. It was as if they had never learned even a modicum of self-control or decorum. All-night parties rife with binge drinking, sexual predation, loud music, and drugs were constant in the dorm. I virtually stopped eating from severe anxiety and holed myself up studying in my room when I wasn't in class. I lasted only one semester.

Luckily, I applied and was accepted as a transfer student to Berkeley and the University of California at Santa Cruz near my family home. Still unprepared for Berkeley, I chose the latter. UC Santa Cruz was a large campus, and I had heard rumors of drugs, nudist dorms, undisciplined hippies, and students who practiced Wicca and New Age nonsense. However, it would enable me to live at home and develop my social skills.

Ironically, those often irreligious, tie-dyed granola eaters were anything but undisciplined. Sure, some students partied like those at any college. Still, they were mostly reasonable about it, and the environment was far more civilized than the reputation that conservatives, in particular, had perpetuated. Perhaps earlier independence and self-sufficiency had made the students more blasé about the typical vices of college life, but the lack of strict Christian morals hadn't hurt them. It was, in any case, a far more ethical environment than that of my previous private college.

The point is theists and even many atheists like my younger self have internalized the notion that religion and a more conservative lifestyle and outlook are the sole sources of morality and ethical behavior. Yet, during college and after, I have managed, like most atheists, to live a relatively virtuous life, even by the standards of the devoutly religious. I have never committed a crime, succumbed to adultery, or publicly brawled with anyone as an adult. I have given to charity and helped people in need. I am no saint and don't hold myself up as a paragon of virtue, but I am also no more given to vice than the average religionist. Perhaps less so since the allure of naughty acts of transgression, like a Catholic schoolboy's thrill at being spanked by a dominatrix in a latex nun costume when they grow up, doesn't provide a titillating thrill for me.

Like most atheists, and ironically like most of the religiously oriented, I have maintained my moral bearing not due to religion and the fear of divine retribution but to following the rules of reciprocity and having an innate sense of empathy.[61] Indeed, logic dictates that maintaining positive relationships and contributing to a well-functioning society through right action demands them. This perspective has extra resonance for nonbelievers. If we hold that life is so precious that we enjoy only a few short years of it, would we want to spend any of that time in jail, deny life to others, or constantly look over our shoulders, fearing violent payback from those we have wronged? Atheism isn't a get-out-of-jail-free card liberating us to commit all the atrocities our "evil human nature" craves but binds us to behavior that maximizes the amount of life and fulfillment allotted to us.

Despite this, all atheists are, in many religionists' minds, at least those who don't know us personally, amoral and adrift without a divine guiding hand. Several atheists have expressed to me that they were initially reluctant to embrace the atheist label due to the pervasive belief that atheists are more immoral than religionists. The publication *Nature* conducted a study in 2017 that included 3,256 survey respondents across thirteen countries to determine if anti-atheist prejudice is globally prevalent and whether it varies according to the country or an individual's level of religiosity. They asked questions based on a test scenario whereby an individual grew up to abuse animals and eventually became a serial killer. When asked whether the killer was a religionist or an atheist, most assumed that he was an atheist. Though responses varied by culture, even the majority in secular countries, including atheists, gave similar feedback.[62]

The facts belie this bias. In 2018, a study on religious belief and social well-being was published in the *Journal of Religion & Society*. Comparing eighteen prosperous democracies from the United States to New Zealand, the study cross-matched faith, measured by belief in a deity and acceptance of evolution, with homicide and sexual behavior. The result was that secular societies had lower rates of violence and teenage pregnancy than societies where many people profess belief in a deity.[63]

This disconnect makes perfect sense. No religionist wants to admit that what they know to be valid according to their holy scriptures, that only abiding by their religion makes people behave morally, is, in fact, a lie. It is perhaps the most widespread example of the *Sunk Cost Fallacy*: our tendency to continue to cling to a belief or activity against all evidence if we have already invested substantial time, effort, or money into it, whether or not the current costs outweigh the benefits. All religions hold that their faith makes one a better person than other religious traditions; otherwise, there would be no point in becoming or remaining a follower.

Conversely, anything that proves that most people, regardless of beliefs, are driven to moral behavior due to their innate empathy and appeals to philosophy and reason pulls at a very tenuous thread that can quickly unravel the entire fabric of religion. As philosopher Daniel Dennett commented, "There's simply no polite way to tell people they've dedicated their lives to an illusion."[64]

In addition, the post-WWII Cold War Era may hold some answers as to why even non-religious people think this way. Many white Baby Boomers and those who learned at their knees often look to the 1950s and 60s with nostalgia and longing. We've all heard it *ad nauseam* from our parents and grandparents. If one wasn't gay, non-white, or a member of any other out-group, the 1950s represented a halcyon decade of peace, prosperity, and polite social interaction. The root cause is debatable whether it was due to social conformity bred from the shared lived experience of the Depression and war, the relative wealth and security of the post-war peace dividend, or enjoyment of the New Deal safety net, etc. However, the perception on the right is that it was the permeation of religion into every corner of society, from prayer in schools to the addition of "Under God" to the Pledge of Allegiance and "In God We Trust" to our currency, that marks the shared beliefs of the era that made the nation a beacon of moral righteousness.

In our government's zeal to prosecute the Cold War against the "godless Soviets," Christianity became a patriotic litmus test. It was promoted as the font of all things good, wholesome, and all-American. At the same time, brutal oppression and immorality were seen to be the product of the Marxist rejection of religion. In reality, the Soviets embraced atheism not as an opportunity to reject democracy and moral principles but to seize and maintain absolute social and political control without competition from the religious authorities who had dominated Russian society for centuries. They rejected religion because the church was a rival for the hearts and minds of the people, as well as a competing oppressive force.

With the notion of a god and morality intricately intertwined in the American psyche, those today interpreting social change as decay often blame it on losing our Christocentric moral compass. Yet, if a populist leader can pull at the nostalgia thread of American society, promising to restore American values through elevating the Bible above civil law, the message could be alluring even to the moderately religious who romanticize their childhood or feel that their lives have been diminished over the past sixty years.

When it comes to the practical repercussions of the perception of atheist immorality, there are several things to consider when religious intolerance is on the rise:

1. **Moral behavior is not a panacea for avoiding bias and oppression:** Conducting oneself as an upstanding citizen and ethical person, while an absolute social good in and of itself, will not fully protect an atheist from the ire of radical religionists and reli-

gionist organizations that have a vested interest in labeling us as unequivocally evil. Be aware that the general perception of atheists as immoral even now is often more potent than the reality that we are no more unethical than the average theist. This untruth will only become more pronounced as religious intolerance grows.

2. **Antisocial and immoral behavior can reinforce stereotypes about atheists:** Like women and minorities who must work twice as hard to succeed in business as white men given the persistence of racism and sexism, atheists in a religiously intolerant environment need to work extra hard to steer clear of violating the ethics of the day if we want to avoid providing fodder for those who claim we are immoral. As mentioned before, that doesn't guarantee that religionists won't vilify us anyway, but providing additional ammo to them doesn't help.
3. **Morality is the currency of the realm in religio-fascist environments:** In a tolerant society, blackmailing or outing someone for, say, being gay is a laughable notion. Try doing that in the Bay Area with a gay man, and the sarcastic response will typically be something like, "What gave it away, my husband on my arm or the fact that we're waiting in line to see *Les Miserables*?" Blackmail loses its sting when we are not ashamed of something society no longer finds taboo. Conversely, among those who are vocally homophobic and live among the like-minded, blackmail for

closeted gay activity can still kill careers and reputations. With Religio-fascism on the rise, we need to be cognizant that we could find ourselves amidst a 1950s-type *Lavender Scare* scenario, where blackmailing anyone, atheists included, could once again come into vogue.

Way #10

Overcome Classism Among Atheists

An atheist believes that a hospital should be built instead of a church. An Atheist believes that a deed must be done instead of a prayer said. An Atheist strives for involvement in life and not escape into death. He wants disease conquered, poverty vanished, war eliminated.[65]

- **Madalyn Murray O'Hair**

DURING MY TWO years in British middle school, when my father was assigned to teach at the Royal School of Military Engineering in Kent on the south coast of England, the concept of a rigid class structure, alien to the American psyche, seemed etched into the very bones of my teachers and schoolmates. In British classrooms in the 1970s and 80s, the divisions were pronounced, with multiple forms or class levels in each grade designed ostensibly to categorize students by their abilities. Yet, in reality, they stood as proxies for social class. Rarely did the different forms mingle.

The lower-form kids were often decked in their older siblings' hand-me-down trousers and frayed black blazers and seemed to have no career aspirations beyond perhaps rubbish collection, prison, and unwed motherhood. Even their accents differed from those of my classmates in the upper form. With a stiff upper lip, they mainly seemed resigned to their meager lot in life. In contrast, the top-form students donned crisp, clean uniforms, carrying dreams of becoming doctors, businesspersons, and lawyers. The middling forms mimicked the rest of society, while the actual upper class, of course, went to boarding schools like Eton and would never deign to consort with the likes of us. Only on the sports field did anyone in the different forms mix.

When in the United States, both before and after we were in the UK, my family, like most Americans, was under the delusion that we lived in a society, for the most part, devoid of the rigid class divisions that shackled Europeans, a place where boundless opportunities for advancement awaited anyone with the audacity to reach for them. Of course, we have always had our Brahmin elites like the Kennedys and the Vanderbilts, but they have been the rare exceptions treated more like royalty or celebrities. Yet, the truth was and is far more complex. Our post-WWII self-image as a classless society was bloated from our hubris and self-delusion, just waiting to be punctured by the prick of hardship and lowered expectations that started in the 1980s. The Reagan administration ushered in four decades of sustained and successful Republican-led efforts to chip away at the safety net erected during Roosevelt's New Deal and Johnson's Great Society and the heavily progressive tax structure that had minimized wealth inequality for a generation.

The growing separation of the classes in the United States today is reflected in several measures, including the yawning gap in income and wealth inequality. In 1980, the top 10% of earners had incomes about nine times that of households in the bottom 10%. This gap reached 12.6 times in 2018, an increase of 39%, the highest among the G7 countries, including the UK.[66]

A growing spatial separation of the classes has accompanied this growing wealth gap. A recent study conducted by researchers at Harvard University and the Naval Postgraduate School using brand and location data reveals an extremely low likelihood that the wealthy and the very poor interact with those of other socio-economic groups. The tendency to shop locally within one's community explains one-third of this isolation. At the same time, differences in frequented brands, combined with distance from other social classes, account for about half the isolation of the rich. The wealthy are more likely to shop online and in local boutique businesses within their communities, buying certain high-end brands. In contrast, people experiencing poverty are mostly limited to their neighborhoods and brands, such as *Dollar Tree* and *Walmart*. Only casual restaurant chains, like *Olive Garden* and *Applebee's*, as well as public domains such as parks and libraries, seem to be the exceptions where the classes have more likelihood of mingling.[67] One might add that the classes are also less likely to mix, despite diversity efforts, at elite prep schools, colleges, and universities.

Widely divergent cultural values, especially those derived from religion, perhaps more than wealth inequality and spatial distance, define the social and political divide between classes in the United States. While all classes within British society have been drifting away from religion for decades, perhaps due to the state-sponsored Church of England rather than despite it, Americans, especially those who are economically, educationally, and socially disadvantaged, have clung much more stubbornly to their faith. As our self-delusion regarding class has slowly burst, Christianity and its associated bigotries have often become the defining features of the working classes and the fuel that now powers Right-wing populism.

Today, classism, growing class-based animosity, and an American working-class identity increasingly defined by religion and religion-adjacent ideologies can have a profound impact on the adoption of atheism. Many people see atheism as a luxury that is practical only for the financially secure and the well-educated or, as the Right-wing media would say, a mark of the coastal elites. Of course, most of us who are atheists are by no means wealthy or privileged, though it is still a widely-held perception among the working classes and those who did not attend college.

The cultural divide is also observable in communities where religion serves as the primary source of comfort in the face of adversity, where it threads its way through working-class stories and knits itself into the fabric of their identity. When Karl Marx said, "Religion is the sigh of the oppressed creature, the heart of a heartless world, and the soul of soulless conditions. It is the *opium* of the people," he meant that religion provides the illusion of happiness and succor to those who have neither in reality.[68]

I've seen this illusion in action, from the economically savaged Rust Belt in the United States, where I was born, to the Bedouin villages frozen in time in the Middle East. A universal constant holds that communities tucked away in remote rural areas or are in the throes of civil war, economic decline, famine, and ecological disaster lean toward tradition and faith. Religion often becomes an anchor, a sanctuary for those who need it most.

On the positive side, Black Americans, for instance, have taken solace in the arms of their churches, which have been refuges through the unrelenting lashes of slavery and the cruelty and injustice of Jim Crow. But it's more than just a balm for them; it's been a rallying cry, a beacon to guide them through the fog of the long struggle for civil rights and equality.

Religion plays many roles. It can be a calming potion, lulling people into an opium-like stupor and making them forget their wounds. Or it can be a firestarter, fueling the spirits of the oppressed to rise, fight, and transcend their burdens. Sometimes, it's just something to hold onto when the days are too heavy. In times of crisis, nothing drives people to the mosque or church faster than an aching stomach, the boot of oppression on their necks, or the earth heaving itself into a destructive dance of storms, floods, and fires that leave families without a home. These moments of hunger, tyranny, and tremor become magnets pulling people toward the sacred, their hands clasped in prayer, seeking refuge and maybe a glimmer of hope. Atheism is often perceived as an option only for those who are less reliant on the communal financial, emotional, and political support offered by religious institutions.

Of course, wealth also provides the time and opportunity to ponder the existential questions of "Who am I?" and "Why are we here?" and then the ultimate luxury of finding both questions nonsensical and unanswerable without the dread of tomorrow's meal gnawing at their bellies. In addition, due to their education and lack of communal thought policing in their predominantly urban and suburban enclaves that can be endemic in poorer, rural, tight-knit communities, the wealthy are not limited to looking for answers in books that have crosses, crescents, or pictures of pastor John Hagee's porcine visage on the front cover.

What is the reality? The dynamics of education, income, and self-perception of socio-economic class considerably differ among atheists, agnostics, and unattached believers. A clear pattern is apparent; the contours suggest an undeniable relationship between belief, or the absence thereof, and economic conditions. Approximately 43% of atheists and 42% of agnostics have achieved an education level of at least four years of college. This figure markedly contrasts with the 27% of all American adults, though Hindus, Unitarians, Jewish Americans, and Anglicans admittedly top the list at 77%, 67%, 59% and 59% respectively.[69]

On the economic front, a similar pattern emerges, driven primarily by educational attainment. According to the 2014 Religious Landscape Study by the Pew Research Center, 30% of atheists and 29% of agnostics possess household incomes that amount to at least $100,000 per year, which contrasts with 19% of all American adults. This percentage is only higher among Jewish Americans, Hindus, Presbyterians, and Episcopalians.[70]

There appears to be a unique intersectionality between belief structure, educational attainment, and income. Variances in socio-economic indicators influence individuals' spiritual or atheistic perspectives. For those facing economic struggles, questioning faith might be perceived as a risky luxury, especially if it leads to isolation from a supportive community. A poor atheist in a small, tightly knit Alabama town is more likely to be shunned by family and friends than one living anonymously in New York or San Francisco.

Atheism is not an inherently elitist stance. People across various socioeconomic strata can and do question religious doctrines, though they may differ in how open they are about it. Yet, the intersection of classism and religious belief does add an extra layer of complexity to the individual's journey toward atheism. It's not like people experiencing poverty can't be atheists, but when our world's falling apart, it's sometimes easier to hold onto something, anything, even if it's what we know deep down is a preposterous notion of a divine being who's got a universal plan for us. Faith and its supportive community become a survival strategy.

To grow our numbers, atheists must encourage religious skepticism among the lower and middle classes since that is where most people reside. No revolution was won solely by a small group of elitists, no matter how cohesive and committed. We must eliminate the perceived cultural, financial, and racial barriers to entry to become a worldview open to all. In the interest of inter-class solidarity among atheists, we must adjust our thinking:

1. **If you are wealthy, don't look down on financially disadvantaged religionists:** History offers a stark warning; the likes of Louis XVI and Marie Antoinette met their demise, detached from the economic reality of their subjects and displaying an air of superiority that belittled the religious and moral values of the masses. In the American context, dismissing religion and its positive effects equates to disregarding the working class, who often believe their faith serves as their moral compass. The wealthy, conservative atheist will, as they say, be the first with their back against the wall when the revolution comes unless they sensitize themselves to the plight of those less fortunate than they are.

   Our ultimate goal, to expand and diversify the ranks of atheism, requires enduring respect and understanding between social classes. The wealthy must recognize that those of lower socio-economic status, particularly cultural and racial minorities, often lack the educational advantages and financial security white men take for granted, which are vital to questioning religious beliefs. This opportunity gap is not due to circumstances of their own making but of the privileged who jealously guard the keys to the halls of power and education.

2. **Promote secular charities, scholarships, and community renewal:** While places of worship undoubtedly provide their congregants with a range of tangible resources, from food and rent subsidies to emotional support, it's vital to recognize that these institutions thrive mainly on the contributions of their believers. However, those who are atheists, particularly those of higher economic means with conservative views on welfare, find themselves at a juncture where our support can foster alternative avenues for assistance. The well-off atheist must abandon their notions of the lazy, undeserving poor (who are typically hard-working, many holding down multiple jobs) and consider their role in enabling these religious institutions to persist, especially when alternative options remain undernourished.

   Rather than perpetuating a reliance on spiritual community assistance, it's worth contemplating the virtues of secular charities and well-structured government aid programs. The broader atheist community can build a support network that aligns with its beliefs by diverting resources from faith-based institutions toward non-religious ones. It's a pivotal moment to decide whether to prioritize the preservation of personal wealth or channel it toward cultivating a thriving, inclusive, and supportive atheist community.
3. **If you are economically disadvantaged, don't question the depth of a wealthy person's commitment to atheism:** Atheism among the financially privileged

isn't typically just an affectation like a trendy jacket they put on to impress each other — a way to signal to the world that the rules, mores, or norms that the rest of us must abide by don't apply to them. Instead, it stems more often than not from a rigorous education steeped in the principles of science, augmented by worldly exposure to diverse religions and cultures, fostering a natural inclination toward atheistic beliefs. Practically speaking, science, technology, and global connectivity serve as the foundation for progress and wealth accumulation, often contradicting the limiting boundaries of religious dogma.

If you are financially disadvantaged and questioning your faith but are hesitant to embrace the notion of atheism because you perceive it as a privilege or elitist, consider for a moment that it would be more financially and socially beneficial even for the rich to hold fast to faith, or at least give it lip service. Rejection of religion may not earn an avowed wealthy atheist ostracization by their friends and neighbors or keep food from their bellies. Instead, it shuts them out of politics and many halls of power, both bastions of the at least nominally religious. It can be excruciatingly difficult for those for whom power and wealth are life's ultimate goals. Their sacrifices may not be existential, but they are significant.

SECTION II
KNOW THY RELIGIONIST ENEMY

Know thy enemy and know yourself; in a hundred battles, you will never be defeated. When you are ignorant of the enemy but know yourself, your chances of winning or losing are equal. If ignorant both of your enemy and of yourself, you are sure to be defeated in every battle.[71]

SUN TZU, ART OF WAR

WHEN DEBATING RELIGIONISTS, we must exercise vigilance and nuance. The act of falling into the seductive ease of stereotyping, deploying blanket statements such as "the problem with evangelicals is…" or "Muslims think…" is a path that can seemingly promise victory in debate. Yet, it almost always proves to be an intellectual cul-de-sac. To follow this route, one must acknowledge that it is not merely reductionist but also liable to be deemed uneducated and uninformed. This tendency, I am embarrassed to confess, has previously entrapped me in encounters with religionists, including family members, who did not fit the stereotype or the strawman I had constructed, leaving me on the losing side of the debate.

Therefore, it is incumbent upon us to navigate our terms and arguments with precision and with an appreciation for the diversity within religious groups and from individual to individual. For example, Rick Warren and Joel Osteen reside under the umbrella of evangelical Christianity yet embody distinct theologies reflecting the plurality of this religious tradition and the individual differences between these two religionists. As an atheist tired of the hypocrisy and avarice of spiritual leaders, I may be tempted to conclude both are just grifters. Perhaps they are, but Warren, who leads Saddleback Church, claims to champion a purpose-driven philosophy that merges individual ambition with a commitment to the Christian service ethic. On the other hand, Osteen, pastor of Lakewood Church, preaches the prosperity gospel, which postulates a correlation between faith, philanthropy, and increased material wealth. Osteen's interpretation claims his god favors devout individuals by providing tangible blessings through success and prosperity. His focus is less on sin and repentance than on personal growth, optimism, and the pursuit of success.

Within the broader context of evangelical Christianity, Warren and Osteen represent disparate paths of interpretation, each reflecting different facets of the evangelical tradition, no matter how much each may fleece their flock. The discourse on religious dogma, then, is complex and treacherous territory. We should exercise caution in attributing specific characteristics to particular religionists, religious sects, or traditions. To do otherwise is a failed strategy that can create a space for religionists to reject criticisms based on the assertion that the beliefs or actions we critique are not emblematic of their "true faith." I hear this mainly from people in more progressive sects, such as the United Church of Christ, Episcopalians, and Unitarians. Stereotyping, in turn, can undermine our argument and be construed as indicative of our lack of knowledge about their religion.

The intensity and fervor of religious movements, particularly those that are heavily invested in acquiring political and social influence like those espousing *Seven Mountains Dominionism*, which seeks Christian domination of all seven aspects of society — family, religion, education, media, entertainment, business, and government — and *Catholic Integralism*, which seeks domination by the Catholic Church of the same, serve as a more germane object of study than an overtly aggressive critique by atheists than chastising individual religionists or sects. These religio-fascist movements not only delineate the landscape of faith since they are the most vocal and aggressive but are often involved in more expansive and destructive societal interactions and, therefore, have an impact that transcends the confines of personal belief and extends into the public sphere. They present themselves as compelling subjects for analysis because of their propensity for imposing their dogmatic beliefs on societal structures in ways that are oppressive and restrictive for atheists and the atheist-adjacent.

Given the all-encompassing societal impact of religious fanaticism and religio-fascist movements, critics should not focus merely on the superficial and overt display of dogma but rather on their underlying motivations, functional mechanisms, modes of propagation, and destructive impact on society. By doing so, we can better understand how such movements acquire, wield, and maintain their influence and how they try to shape societal norms and values.

Moreover, by investigating the interplay between religious extremists and the broader political and social landscape, we can discern how their religious ideologies intertwine with other sociopolitical factors. This recognition can give us a more nuanced understanding of how these movements operate and exert their influence, enabling more effective responses and counteractions.

Our discourse must rise above surface-level stereotypes and seek to comprehend the deeper complexities of politicized religious movements and, perhaps more importantly, their leaders and followers. By doing so, we can generate insights that are not only intellectually robust but also more effective in combating the rise of religious extremism.

Way #11
Understand the Types of People of Faith

Given the fact that most religions share basic values, it is most unfortunate that religious people can be played off against each other so easily. One possible reason for this may be that people do not know enough about other people's beliefs.[72]

Alcee Hastings, U.S. House of Representatives

PEOPLE OF FAITH can be roughly classified into four categories based on their potential threat to atheists: politicized religionists, apolitical religionists, principled religious moderates, and complicit religious moderates. Although often maintaining a faith-based worldview, the nones constitute a category of their own, which I discussed in *Way #5*.

These four categories can be applied to all religious traditions, though here, my examples predominantly focus on Christianity. Note that while some categories are more likely to push a religio-fascist agenda than others, this classification is not an invitation to stereotype all people in one group as oppressive or dangerous. It merely points out the likelihood that they might turn to extreme tactics to oppress atheists or other out-groups if the occasion arises.

It is also worth pointing out that certain religions, such as Islam, do not have a strong concept of separation between the religious and secular realms. Islam exhorts its followers to become deeply involved in politics, to the point where religion and governance are seen as inextricably intertwined. However, even within the *Ummah*, the worldwide community of believers in Islam, some followers practice their religion solely as a matter of personal faith. For instance, my wife's grandparents were devout Shiites, but they were more concerned with being pious, working hard, and donating food and clothing to the poor in Khorramabad, Iran than waging *jihad* and claiming their seventy-two virgins in the afterlife, as some in the West might assume.

Political Religionists

Religionists are conservative believers who adopt a strict, often literalist interpretation of scripture and adhere closely to tradition and authority. This group makes up approximately 70% of American Christians.[73] A subset of these are political religionists. Their percentage of all religionists is unknown, though the rapid politicization of American Christianity and the disproportionate political power wielded in the Republican Party by white Christian nationalists would suggest it is a significant and growing cohort.

Political religionists, specifically those that pose the greatest threat to nonbelievers, are predominantly conservative, white, and lower or middle class without a college education, the core of religio-fascist movements and, not surprisingly, MAGA populism, which has become the *de facto* church for many those who have drifted away from attending church but retained their traditionalist values. They threaten us in our daily lives as they are most likely to strive both personally and at the ballot box to impose their worldview and black-and-white values on every aspect of society. An example of a high-profile politicized Christian religionist is Reverend Greg Locke, founder of Global Vision Baptist Church in Tennessee. Locke has gained notoriety lately on social and Right-wing media for involving himself in controversial culture war topics, denouncing COVID-19 as a fake pandemic, defending the January 6th U.S. Capitol attack while blaming it on Antifa, burning Twilight and Harry Potter books, and smashing a "satanic" Barbie playhouse with a bat wrapped in Bibles.[74] However, the influence of a single unhinged activist like Locke is limited. While he, along with countless other religious zealots, megachurch preachers, and would-be militant prophets, has contributed to injecting culture war issues into the national discussion from the pulpit and shifting the national debate to the right, he does not lead a formal organization that directly steers public policy. He is a bizarre American cultural artifact, little more.

Exceptions include certain billionaires who leverage their immense fortunes and political connections to sculpt the political and social landscape according to their vision. Consider, for instance, the oil tycoon and pastor Tim Dunn from Texas, who embodies the fusion of financial clout and religious zeal. With his substantial wealth, Dunn is endeavoring to transform Texas into a reflection of his Christian theocratic ideals. Through his *Defend Texas Liberty PAC*, he methodically nudges Texas politics and legislation on a distinctly hard-right trajectory, one that surpasses even its conservative populace. This strategic maneuvering involves challenging and defeating Republican politicians who fall short of the radical Christian orthodoxy that his PAC champions.[75]

Small groups of politicized religionists can pose a more personal but still significant danger to atheists, particularly at the local level. For example, an atheist living in a rural city in the Bible Belt where local police and civil authorities may be staunch religionists themselves may have little recourse if their boss, teacher, or local government discriminates against them based on their lack of faith or if a neighbor harasses them. Legal action may be possible, but it can be time-consuming, expensive, and cause waves in a close-knit community. As a side note, the local level can also be a valuable proving ground for atheists who are given to activism, taking inspiration from small numbers of religious activists who have successfully taken over local school boards and governments nationwide.

Larger political religionist organizations pose an even more significant threat to atheists as they often span multiple traditionalist religious traditions and have an incredible amount of political influence through lobbying and pressure groups. *The Family Research Institute* and *Operation Save America* are prime examples, as are conservative political policy groups such as the *Heritage Foundation*.

The most significant political religionist threat, however, comes directly from politicians, police, *Federalist Society* judges, and other legal authorities who might either be religio-fascists themselves or use religio-fascist methods as a cynical political tool to enhance their power or push a political agenda. The efforts of these groups often lead to policies and judgments that disadvantage atheists and limit our freedoms and civil rights.

In contrast to the growing threat posed by white political religionists, the Black church, highly religious and politicized, is a significant exception. While not a monolith, many Black churches do, like their white counterparts, view atheism as a threat to their beliefs and values and see atheists as misguided or immoral purveyors of homosexuality, promiscuity, blasphemy, and the like. However, Black churches, attended by marginalized people, have also historically been at the forefront of fighting for civil rights, social justice, and police reform, three things that white religionists often find anathema and which indirectly insulate atheists from oppression. While Black religionists are political when the need arises to fight for social justice, their goals and political orientation often put them at odds with the predominantly white political religionists most likely to target atheists. White politicized religionists would, therefore, typically form the core of any religio-fascist movement.

So, how do we spot them in the wild? Not all are easily identifiable, especially those in the upper classes. It may seem a little facile, but if they are highly religious and outwardly display allegiance to an aggressive, highly polarized, and politicized group, ostensibly on their bumper stickers, such as the NRA, anti-abortion groups, Blue Lives Matter, QAnon, etc. there is a good chance they are politicized religionists. Otherwise, unless they have a penchant for spouting bible verses or going on political tirades, they look and often sound like anyone else in polite society.

Apolitical Religionists

Apolitical religionists can be as annoyingly pious and self-righteous as those who are political but are more concerned with personal salvation and sometimes missionary work than insinuating themselves into political controversy. Jimmy Carter, a born-again Christian, is the most benign, positive example, having dedicated the remainder of his life after his presidency to building homes for the poor and advocating for peace.

Although adept at virtue signaling through public displays and discussions of their faith, former football quarterback Tim Tebow and actor Chris Pratt would also fall into this category since they tend not to share or promote their political opinions. On a non-celebrity level, Bible study groups and prayer circles may likewise be devout but apolitical, though perhaps less so in the past ten years as pulpits have become increasingly politicized.

While such people and groups may not drive political activism themselves, they often vote with and support the agenda of politicized religionists at the ballot box and would potentially be complicit with any move toward a religio-fascist regime. In the United States, 81% of evangelicals of all stripes, according to Gallup polling, voted for Donald Trump in 2020.[76] Most of these people weren't political activists. However, though dissolute in his personal life, Trump did promise and follow through with pushing an agenda advantageous to religionists, like selecting radical Catholic judges for the Supreme Court and Federalist Society drones to the lower benches guaranteed to overthrow even long-standing legal precedent to push their extremist Christian nationalist agenda.

Principled Religious Moderates

Religious moderates, who take a middle-of-the-road approach to faith, compose about 30% of American Christians. They may or may not affiliate themselves with a specific church, typically a mainline one if they do, and may or may not attend services regularly. They often don't maintain a strict, literal interpretation of scripture or hold religion as the core of their identities and every aspect of their lives.

Principled religious moderates comprise an unknown percentage of the moderate cohort. They include those people of faith who, in addition to maintaining middle-of-the-road religious views, are rock-solid in their commitment to pluralism and defending other faiths' rights as a tenet of their scriptural interpretation. Christians who fall into this category may maintain this commitment based on Biblical commandments to treat the stranger with kindness. Due to their non-judgmental approach to their religion, or at least embrace of tolerance and forgiveness, they represent the one group of the faithful that atheists could potentially rely on as consistent allies in our fight against Religio-fascism.

Complicit Religious Moderates

Complicit religious moderates complicate the moderate picture since they may appear to be identical in every way to principled moderates in their attitudes toward atheists and religious out-groups, at least in times when religious extremism is not a significant political threat and defending religious pluralism doesn't pose a danger to their self-interests. During situations in which politicized religion is on the rise, however, their commitment to the principle of pluralism and secularism may collapse if they feel they and their families are at risk. Unfortunately, differentiating the principled from the complicit can be difficult until we need to rely on them in a crisis, and by then, it is often too late. The adage that "There are no atheists in foxholes," while patently false, should be rewritten, "There are no religious moderates in a crisis." They are either principled allies supporting the notion of equality and religious pluralism or become complicit with religio-fascists. There is no middle ground.

Perhaps the one thing that might suggest someone retains a dangerously flexible ethical framework necessary for complicity may be a willingness to excuse the bad behavior or moral failings of religious or political leaders or claim that they are at heart good men with good intentions, such as Joel Osteen, Jerry Falwell Jr., Newt Gingrich, Donald Trump, and other assorted grifters and moral deviants. Anyone who can overlook behavior that is generally agreed to be unacceptable in a public figure would potentially have few moral convictions that they'd be willing to defend in the face of adversity.

In cybersecurity, where I work, there is a concept of zero trust. It means never trust, always verify before granting access to our computer network and critical data, and only when necessary. We atheists in the real world should follow an analogous rule when it comes to religionists of all types. Never automatically trust anyone based on what one says, what they believe, or who they are, including friends and family. We should grant them access to the depths of our religious skepticism and trust them to protect our lives only if necessary and based on past actions that have proven their trustworthiness.

How can we, as atheists, influence each of these different types of religionists in such a way as to reduce the risk of religious intolerance metastasizing?

1. **Vote and run for office to fend off political religionists:** Political religionists maintain a zealotry and commitment that is nearly impossible to penetrate with logic or education. While we may be unable to convince them to accept or even tolerate atheists, they are, perhaps, the easiest group to address, at least as long as democratic institutions are still robust. Voting is the most straightforward defense, but running for office is the best way to push back the tide of

religious intolerance. The commitment is substantial, but given that school boards and local governments have been targets for religionists like *Moms for Liberty,* who realize that taking over society from the bottom up is more thorough and socially transformative than imposition from the top down, involvement by atheists at the local government level is critical to maintaining religiously pluralistic institutions.

2. **Purposely engage with apolitical religionists and complicit religious moderates to reduce suspicion and misunderstanding:** Apolitical religionists and complicit moderates are often less committed to actively fighting to defend religious tolerance because they have little contact with atheists. As with attitudes toward immigrants and racial and ethnic minorities, positive views of American atheists are inversely proportional to the level of exposure. It's easy to believe propaganda and stereotypes of members of out-groups and dehumanize them when we don't know any, which is why such prejudices are most potent in areas where their numbers are lowest. Periodically, I visit relatives in Montana, which is about 86% white and far from the U.S. Southern border. Yet, as a visitor, I might be led to think "job-stealing immigrants" and "rioting BLM thugs" were rampant there, given the animosity.

Similarly, religious moderates often deem atheists immoral or anti-religious because that is what they hear from the pulpit, conservative media, and

Right-wing politicians, not because they have directly experienced atheists acting immorally. Teaching through example and interacting closely with those afraid of us is the best way to get many people to change their attitudes. A corollary to that is to avoid ostracizing or belittling religionists while in our atheist enclaves. Atheist techies in Silicon Valley or liberal nonbelievers in any blue city in the United States, including myself, have generated a lot of animosity among the religious with our condescension.

3. **Befriend and collaborate with moderate allies:** Principled moderates don't need convincing. What they need is to feel that allyship with atheists is compatible with their in-group and ethical values, as fellowship is what draws many people to religion. As an atheist, I'm a bit of a lone wolf and recluse, a trait typical of many atheists but perhaps extreme in my case due to my neurodivergence. Unfortunately, this reclusiveness can contribute to the view of atheists as anti-social misanthropes and outsiders with alien values, a bias that we need to overcome.

    The best way to strengthen ties with principled moderates and ensure they will remain allies is not through trying to adopt or change their beliefs but by actively working with them and showing that we share the same ethics through right action. Finding common ground in solving community and social issues helps solidify a sense of interdependence. The key is to be tolerant of their views, even if they are sometimes uncomfortable for us, as we, in due course, will want the same from them.

Way #12

Know if Your Antagonists Are Orthodox or Orthoprax

Jesus clearly taught orthopraxy (right behavior) much more than orthodoxy (right ideas).[77]

John Feister

SINCE THE STUDY of medieval European history began in the early nineteenth century, and even after medieval studies became a formal discipline in the late nineteenth and early twentieth centuries, it has been one of the most resistant to progress, retaining echoes of reactionary thinking until relatively recently. It long served as a conduit for national and racist myths and was instrumental in the emergence of theories of white supremacy before WWII.

The study of the Crusades, for instance, was developed during the eighteenth and nineteenth centuries partially to rationalize European colonial enterprises and the westward expansion across North America by propagating the spurious notion that the Crusaders were nobly combating the expansionist threat of Islam. Historians depicted them as analogous to the colonialists of the time, who saw themselves as fighting against paganism and barbarism while disseminating the light of Christianity and civilization throughout the non-Western world.

Race science was similarly employed to advance the notion of romantic nationalism, the falsehood that European nations were forged by a homogeneous people, linked by blood and culture through a shared history stretching back into a misty past: a narrative that marginalized Jewish communities, the Roma, and others.

Most of these archaic academic dogmas have been debunked by post-WWII scholars, though a traditionalist bent remains. I say this despite being a proud medievalist. Since the 1980s, when I entered the field, medieval studies have become responsive to critical theory and cultural studies. At the time, before being drawn by the siren song of high tech, I wanted to be part of the revitalization of this field of study.

However, the original nationalist and racist myths born of the study of the Middle Ages persist in their most noxious forms in the murky corners of the internet and among the political fringes. The political and religious right, for example, has appropriated medieval iconography, such as knights bearing crusader crosses on their armor, Viking runes, and Wagnerian imagery at white nationalist events such as the 2017 *Unite the Right* rally in Charlottesville, Virginia, with their anti-Semitic chant "Jews will not replace us!"[78] and the January 6th U.S. Capitol attack.[79] We need to look no further than the *QAnon Shaman* or neo-Nazi symbolism to see how far history has been bastardized and co-opted.[80] Medieval history is relevant to understanding the forces at work among religionists in general and religio-fascists in particular, who admire the period for the dominance of religious authority over secular ones and the ubiquity of authoritarian rule.

After my first year in the medieval history program at UCLA, the interplay between Christian and Jewish communities at the time became the field of inquiry I deemed most overdue for reassessment. As one of the few cradle atheists in my program, however, I found this topic to be among the most confounding and one that left me feeling unprepared to address. Delving into medieval theology or Canon Law was one thing, but exploring interfaith relations, especially two faiths that were foreign to me personally, was an entirely different matter.

Given that the animosity that permeated this relationship between Jewish and Christian communities at the time was grounded in an abiding hostility, I felt I lacked the requisite religious perspective to comprehend it in any meaningful way. Of course, I could appreciate the historical import of medieval blood libels, expulsions, and massacres, but it remained largely theoretical. Many of my professors and fellow students were either deeply religious Catholics, ex-Catholics, or Jewish, which at least allowed them to fathom their own religion's narrative and the extent to which faith can animate people and nations.

Of course, my Christian professors were occasionally prone to a certain myopia, often glossing over the antisemitism and violence perpetrated by the medieval Church and Christian community. Jewish professors, meanwhile, were usually inwardly focused. In this regard, I saw the potential for a compelling dissertation topic that was, as much as possible, a neutral assessment or comparison of the Christian and Jewish points of view.

In my youthful idealism, I fancied that my impartiality might position me to offer novel insights if anyone can be considered impartial. First, however, I had to attain as much knowledge as an outsider possibly could about Jewish culture and mindset, which was far less familiar to me than Christianity. I surmised that the most effective means of overcoming my ignorance was to immerse myself in the culture by studying and living in Israel.

I took a year-long hiatus from UCLA to explore Jewish history, culture, and the Hebrew language at the Hebrew University in Jerusalem. From my naive viewpoint, the *Haredi* (ultra-orthodox) neighborhoods seemed to maintain echoes of the insularity of medieval Jewish communities, so I sought to understand them and their traditionalist interpretation of the religion through living in the religious neighborhood of Nachlaot for one, and by inquiring about the conversion process for another.

Regarding the first, I found it quite beautiful, if highly rigid and restrictive, how the religious families in my neighborhood went about their daily lives so consciously, following every halachic commandment, 613 in all, laid out in the

Mishneh Torah and *Shulchan Aruch*. These commands were omnipresent in everything they did, even if a god wasn't. A prayer accompanied every bite of food or sip of liquid, every prohibition on activity, such as working on Sundays or praying three times a day, followed to the letter.

As for the second, I eventually approached a Hasidic rabbi, telling him I was contemplating conversion, as I felt it would be the best way to encourage him to talk to me openly. Black-suited with a patchy beard and side locks, he ushered me into his office. He listened intently to me for several minutes, expounding on my experiences with the culture and Jewish religion in Israel so far before asking, very kindly, "So why do you want to become Jewish? It is a long and arduous process."

I thought about what I had learned about the culture since arriving in Israel and had a sudden flash of insight. I said, "I look at it like this by way of an allegory. Imagine three groups of men, one Christian, one Jewish, and one non-religious, approaching a rushing river they must traverse. They find three boats moored off a pier. The Christians jump in the first boat and begin paddling furiously against the current, praying to their god to deliver them, only to find themselves standing almost still in the middle of the river no matter how hard they paddled against nature or prayed. The non-religious men (it is here that I played the poor, directionless atheist) then jump in the second boat and don't deploy their oars, figuring they'd go where the current and fate naturally take them, only to be quickly dashed against the rocks. The Jewish men finally jump into the third boat and begin paddling downstream, steering the boat consciously and deftly around all the obstacles and rapids until they reach their destination safely." Ultimately, I concluded, "I want to be able to steer my way successfully through life."

The rabbi nodded and smiled. "I haven't spent much time with Christians or the non-religious, but that was quite insightful regarding Judaism. It's as much about consciously connecting everything we do with God's will, to live and act with purpose." He went on about the conversion process, the challenges of being Jewish, and perspectives on converts in the Jewish community. It was pretty enlightening, especially his glaring omission of any discussion of a deity. I continued these talks with several other members of various Jewish traditions, receiving similar, deity-free responses.

I realized then that how religions mold people, their worldview, and how they approach life depends, of course, on the type of religion. Some, like the Protestant branch of Christianity, are predominantly *orthodox*, meaning that adherence to a specific set of core beliefs is critical to membership in the faith and conducting one's life. Technically, simply accepting "Jesus Christ as your personal Lord and Savior" and believing that one can only obtain salvation through him is enough for club entry. Thoughts and prayers, as naive as they may sound to us atheists, actually hold power for them. For an atheist who is an ex-Protestant, loss of fellowship within a like-minded community, not to mention the fear of excruciating punishments promised in the afterlife for rejecting their god and Jesus, can be the most challenging aspect of the religious identity to leave behind.

Other religions, such as Islam and Judaism, are primarily *orthoprax* in that adherence to certain behaviors and rituals broadly defines the group. Following the dictates of *kashrut,* praying three times a day, wearing a *kippah,* and keeping the sabbath are all core to being an observant Jew and successfully navigating life according to their god's will.

Similarly, keeping *halal,* ritually washing, praying five times a day facing the *Kaaba* in Mecca, and wearing some variant of the *hijab* or other restrictive covering for women is essential to being an observant Muslim. Losing connection to these rituals and customs, often beautiful in form and rich in tradition and artistic expression, if also frequently misogynistic, insular, and onerous, can result in a terrible loss of a sense of identity and communal connection for Jewish people and Muslims who leave the faith. In a practical sense, though, it can theoretically be easier for an ex-Muslim or ex-member of the Jewish faith to reject a belief in their god than a Christian if they are willing to maintain their traditions and rituals. They can avoid physical separation from the community or, in the case of Muslims, dangerous accusations of apostasy.

Of course, all religions combine, to one degree or another, both orthodoxy and orthopraxy. Catholicism is a prime example that strongly exhibits both, where the faithful can achieve salvation by good works in addition to faith rather than by faith alone. Belief in the tenets of Christianity and the divinity of Jesus are essential, but so are the acts of taking communion, confession, and observing Lent.

For an atheist, the type of risks faced under a religiously extremist movement or regime depend on whether an orthodox or orthoprax religious tradition drives it. Religio-fascists of the orthodox variety will typically suppress unorthodox ideas and thoughts or perceived immoral behaviors that run contrary to their doctrine. In the pre-modern era, this ranged from the bloody, including witch burnings and Jewish pogroms by Catholic and Protestant authorities, to heresy trials of scientists like Copernicus, Galileo, and Giordano Bruno. More recently and immediately, we are faced in the United States with thought policing by conservative Christians through book banning and laws denying fundamental rights based on religion, such as a woman's right to bodily autonomy.

In devout Muslim and Jewish communities and countries, religio-fascist behavior is expressed less by enforcing proper thought than by enforcing obedience to rituals and tradition. If you pray five times a day, avoid gay sex, and abstain from non-*halal* foods and alcohol (and, as a female, cover your hair and body and obey men), your inner beliefs are somewhat secondary beyond your original declaration of faith by reciting the *Shahada*. Rejecting the faith by converting to another religion or adopting an atheist stance is considered apostasy and subject to the death penalty. Still, no one would know unless you gave up observing the rituals and declared your lack of faith.

In Israel, under Netanyahu's far-right government formed at the end of 2022, the religious parties in the coalition have been pushing to enforce halachic adherence even among Israel's non-religious population. Modifications to the Law of Return, limitations on electricity production on the Sabbath, and the expansion of gender-segregated beaches are all on the legislative agenda for Haredi politicians. Nowhere is policing thought a part of their agenda.

Some considerations for atheists:

1. **Orthodox religio-fascist movements want to control what we think and believe in addition to monitoring our moral behavior:** Orthodox authoritarian governments, especially Christian ones, place a high level of importance on proper thought and adherence to religious doctrine and moral dictates, especially those related to sex and gender, and view atheistic thought as a threat to the spiritual order. At the extreme, we may face significant persecution and discrimination for blasphemy or pushing back on morality codes. The government may also promote religious education and propaganda that supports the superiority of the dominant religion and the dangers of other religions, atheism, and science. By brainwashing the population, such governments can be difficult to dislodge. Compounding this, they also can look to police morality and deny equal rights to women, minorities, and the LGBTQ+ community.

   Overall, atheists can mitigate the risk under an orthodox authoritarian government by keeping quiet about one's atheism, with minor modifications in lifestyle unless overtly libertine. However, it might require overt declarations of faith and exposure to religious brainwashing.

2. **Orthoprax religio-fascists control ritual and morality more than thought:** Orthoprax religio-fascists, especially in Muslim and Haredi Jewish communities, place a greater emphasis on culture, ritual, and practice, including policing morality, than on strict adherence to religious doctrine. In this type of government, atheists may find it easier to hide their lack of faith, as the focus is less on doctrinal purity and more on outward appearance. An atheist who performs the rituals follows moral directives and, above all, avoids discussing their atheism can often appear to be devout while flying under the radar.

Way #13

Be Wary of the Zeal of the Convert

For the person who converts, it is a matter of fierce conviction and defiance. Our belief is based on a combination of faith and logic because we need a powerful reason to abandon the traditions of our families and community to embrace beliefs foreign to both. Conversion is a risky business because it can result in losing family, friends and community support.[81]

Kareem Abdul-Jabbar

YOU MAY HAVE heard or even used the expression "zeal of the convert," typically viewed as a derogatory term in popular culture, to describe individuals transitioning from one faith or state of nonbelief to another. Perceived to have a greater propensity for public displays of faith and mounting a vigorous defense of religious doctrine, their tiresome virtue signaling and aggressive attempts to convert others are incredibly irritating to the nonbeliever. We have all met or been accosted by them at some point, as we atheists seem to be magnets for zealots. Such converts are often driven by adherence to orthodox and fundamentalist versions of their new faith, believing them to be the purest expressions and the most likely to help them prove their devotion and piety.

Yet, a 2009 report by Pew Research, "*The 'Zeal of the Convert': Is It the Real Deal?*" suggests that while individuals who have switched faiths or joined a religion after being raised without affiliation exhibit greater religiosity than lifelong adherents to their new faith, it is often only moderately so. 82% of converts express absolute certainty in their belief in a god, as opposed to 77% of non-converts.

In addition, 29% report discussing their views on their god with others at least once a week, whereas only 20% of non-converts do so. Most notably, 27% of converts assert that their new religion is the one true faith, while 22% of non-converts hold the same belief.[82]

What accounts for this discrepancy between our lived experience with converts and the statistics? Of course, the most aggressive and zealous are the ones we remember, while the quiet ones slip into their new faiths inconspicuously. But more importantly, the Pew report covers a broad spectrum of different types of converts, including many who may have switched religions for more practical, mundane reasons such as appeasing religious spouses and in-laws or fitting into a spiritual community, so their conviction may be, if not less than wholly heartfelt, at least less vociferous. If nothing else, the Pew report suggests a broad diversity in religious fervor among converts.

It is still worth remaining vigilant against the segment of converts, buried in the statistics, who are much more radical and perhaps insecure in their new faith. The stereotype does contain a kernel of truth. I've found individuals who have overcome addiction or seek to redeem their public image and self-esteem after living a dissolute lifestyle often exhibit greater zeal and commitment as if to wash themselves of their past sins. Likewise, those who have converted from one radicalized religion to another may bring their previous zealotry with them. It is these converts who pose the most risk for atheists, as outing us might be perceived as a way to demonstrate proof of their commitment.

Lest we be disingenuous, "deconverts" to atheism can often be similarly overzealous, which is how we can perhaps identify and understand the radicalism of this segment of religious converts when we see it. Many of us have experience with fellow ex-theists who had been fed a heavy dose of religion before rejecting it and who often need to aggressively deprogram themselves, just as newly minted religionists need to brainwash themselves to dispel any doubts they may have about their new faith. What raging against the historical atrocities perpetrated by Christians and scoffing at religionists who reject science and reason is to some newly minted atheists, aggressive door knocking, proselytizing, and accosting women outside of abortion clinics is to the Christian convert.

But how can zealous converts be so dangerous? The need to prove their faith or take advantage of the political power and authority vested in them by their new religion plays a big part. Paul the Apostle, who transitioned from a Pharisee to a leading figure in the early Christian movement, is perhaps the most prominent early example of such fervent conversion. Despite having never met Jesus personally, he played a pivotal role in shaping and spreading Christianity's dogma. Indeed, out of the twenty-seven books in the New Testament, thirteen are attributed to him or his followers writing in his name. He was also partly responsible for contorting the pacific and tolerant message of Jesus and his early followers into the misogynistic, aggressive, judgmental, and not to mention fantastical religion that has driven many former Christians into the arms of nonbelief.

Others may look to wield their newfound religion as a political or rhetorical cudgel. Ross Douthat, a Right-wing Christian commentator often published in the *New York Times* to no doubt boost ad revenue by way of raising the blood pressure of its liberal readers, exemplifies this type of convert. I single him out only because I find him insufferably parochial, with a knack for turning a clever if ill-informed phrase. Having converted to a particularly revanchist version of Catholicism after jagging between various flavors of Protestantism, Douthat extensively discusses in his articles the virtues of his adopted faith and delivers a perpetual finger-wagging condemnation of what he sees as societal decay resulting from the loss of his god in the public sphere. As he states in his book *Bad Religion: How We Became a Nation of Heretics,* "America's problem isn't too much religion or too little of it. It's bad religion: the slow-motion collapse of traditional Christianity and the rise of a variety of destructive pseudo-Christianities in its place."[83] Of course, after years grazing at the junk food-laden buffet that is American Protestantism, it is his newly discovered, though thoroughly retrogressive, radical Right-wing Catholicism that embodies for him the "right" kind of Christianity. It is one he believes can defeat liberals and the godless in the culture wars and once again bring society under the control of a paternalistic Catholic Church, or at least leaders and institutions guided by traditional Christian values.

Other faiths have also seen high-profile converts. For instance, in Islam, converts like the late Muhammed Ali and Cat Stevens (now Yusuf Islam) have notably embraced the faith wholeheartedly, transforming their lives and becoming advocates for the religion. In Judaism, high-profile converts like Marilyn Monroe and Ivanka Trump have drawn attention to the faith, although modern Judaism does not encourage conversion. However, their commitment to their consciously chosen faiths becomes a core part of their identity, much more so than many delivered from the womb into those traditions. Each of these instances underscores the intense dedication and vigor often displayed by converts to their faith, which can push them to extremes to prove themselves worthy. Historically, religious communities have always viewed converts with suspicion, perceiving the depth of their sincerity and knowledge of their adopted dogma as wanting.

Cognitive dissonance, the mental discomfort from holding conflicting beliefs, can fuel fervent religious dedication and politicization among the newly faithful. Converts, hoping to silence their doubts and align their old and new beliefs, may intensify their commitment to their new faith. This drive for mental consistency can turn a new believer into a zealot who fervently backs and advances the goals of politicized religious movements and regimes. The convert's desire for inner harmony merges with the regime's demand for ideological conformity.

Historical accounts and research highlight the dangers posed by zealous converts. The Second Great Awakening in 18th-century America, which drew moderate or lapsed religionists and mainline churches *en masse* into more fervent, evangelical expressions of the faith, is a poignant example. The movement was a stark departure from the Enlightenment ideals that had shaped the foundation of the United States. Its followers rejected rationalism and deism and embraced a god who actively engaged with individuals and society. The core of nineteenth-century evangelicalism was the experience of conversion.[84] This wave of religious fervor left an indelible mark on American culture, fueling a passionate commitment to a more personal and interventionist divine presence and the intolerance that it bred. While Protestants continued to become more tolerant of different sects, anti-Catholic[85] and anti-Mormon[86] sentiments ran hot among them.

We can easily extrapolate from history that some converts during a Third Great Awakening or religio-fascist convulsion would be among the first to draw their religion close around them like protective armor, shielding themselves from any doubts about the unfolding acts of Christian chauvinism as well as from the eye of suspicion cast by their co-religionists.

When dealing with converts, there are a few recommendations for treading carefully:

1. **Avoid demeaning or criticizing their religion, especially in public:** Nothing will trigger a zealous or insecure convert's compulsion to virtue signal, especially in front of their peers, than to mock their new faith as they are often still grappling with lingering doubts about their decision. Even polite criticism can spark an unwanted heated debate if we question their identity, which may still be gestating.
2. **Neither hide nor flaunt atheism:** Do as Dad said, don't talk about sex, religion, politics, or money among strangers, particularly converts, as a matter of etiquette. For Gen Zers who never listen to Dad, hop on TikTok. I'm sure there are twenty-second videos of your favorite influencers saying the same thing.
3. **Determine the type of convert they are:** Yes, they aren't all the same; some are innocently ebullient about their newfound faith and are mostly just obnoxiously optimistic as the sun shines on their spotless minds. Then there are the more dangerous ones who, if not politicized, have embraced righteous outrage as a proper response to every perceived moral failure, progressive notion, and defiance of authority they see in secular society. The Iranians call them "Morality Police." I call those in the United States Christian Karens.
4. **Consider the religious tradition they've embraced:** Muslim, Protestant, Catholic, and Jewish converts differ in their religious expression. Many conservative Christians and Muslims are becoming highly politicized and militant, with Muslims joining Christians in

their culture wars and quixotic tilting at woke windmills. Their converts may be especially sensitive to political discussions. Jewish people, as members of a non-proselytizing religion and one given to intellectual discourse, tend to be less aggressive unless they are ultra-Orthodox, many of whom have embraced the Right-wing war against gays, feminism, and modern views on sex and morality. In either case, as members of a small religious out-group, they are less of a threat than Christians or Muslims, at least in the United States.

Way #14

Identify Your Future Oppressors Next Door

Love your neighbor, but don't pull down your hedge.

Benjamin Franklin

WHO ARE THOSE who might, on a day-to-day basis, pose an existential threat to us as atheists, either today or when religiously extremist governance is on the rise? Look to the quiet, unassuming neighbor who lives in the well-kept house to the left. Now look toward the sweet older couple that lives to the right. Even if we are in a religiously pluralistic country, state, or city, chances are that at least one, if not both, would be likely to accept an extremist religious regime, if only for self-preservation. Unfortunately, few of them brazenly run a Christian flag up the flagpole on their porch or hang a biblical quote on their front door for easy identification.

I live a stone's throw away from the heart of Silicon Valley, a supposed bastion of unabashed atheism and "wokism," at least if we were to listen to Right-wingnut talking heads and social media pundits complaining about the liberal, anti-Christian bias of tech and social media.[87] If I had never met or spoken with them, I might have thought all of my closest neighbors were politically and socially similar to us. They drive similar cars, live in similar houses, and are of similar income and race. They're also quite pleasant and ready to help when dealing with them daily.

Yet, most have turned out to be MAGA supporters, Blue Lives Matter defenders, Second Amendment absolutists, and, of course, conservative Christians. Most are thoughtful neighbors, but we avoid political or religious discussions after a few unfortunate run-ins.

We rightly tend to accuse this country's corrupt and mendacious spiritual leadership, from megachurch demagogue to prosperity gospel grifter, and their religio-fascist political allies, of instigating and leading both the state-sanctioned and unsanctioned religious intolerance we are seeing today. Yet, it's our often pleasant, though politically and religiously extremist neighbors, coworkers, and family members who are the ones that enable such leaders to come to power. They are the ones who coerce their pastors to become more political rather than vice versa. They vote. They take over school boards and ban books, and they have been shockingly successful. More problematic is that they are also often the ones that would, in all likelihood, end up enforcing the brand of morality and obedience now being hocked by religious extremists at the local and neighborhood level if empowered or sanctioned to do so. Not a few Americans would relish the power of brandishing their many weapons and activating their militia organizations in defense of their religion and traditional way of life.

Iran provides some insight. Since the Iranian revolution, a volunteer militia known as the *Basij* has been tasked by the government with, among other responsibilities, enforcing public morals, such as ensuring women correctly wear the hijab and preventing unrelated men and women from consorting in public.[88] Even my elderly Iranian mother-in-law, who lives in the United States, has been accosted by them during visits to Iran and threatened with arrest for allowing hair to show in public or having her headscarf accidentally slip back on her head. These *basijis* are puritanical and violent appointed arbiters of morality with little oversight, and there is no shortage of them, given that corruption makes their positions quite lucrative. This arrangement lends itself to abuse and the carrying out of personal grudges, as they are also friends, neighbors, and family members.

Today, armed militias in the United States like the *Proud Boys*, *Three Percenters,* and *Oath Keepers* (the last lousy with ex and current military and law enforcement who have dishonored or are still dishonoring their uniforms) already work as crowd control and personal protection for Right-wing politicians and celebrities.[89] It would be easy to see them stepping up in an official or unofficial capacity as self-appointed arbiters of morality and political purity like the Iranian *Basij*.

We are also already getting a taste of religio-fascist vigilante justice in Texas today, where civilians are legislatively empowered by *Senate Bill 8* to enforce Christian morality enshrined in the law by turning in, for a bounty, those suspected of illegally aiding and abetting women seeking an abortion.[90] The Supreme Court, in turn, is packed with Catholic extremists who, pushing the equivalent of *common good constitutionalism*, turned away all challenges to this law, stating it cannot prohibit such civilian law enforcement. The mechanisms that would underpin sanctioned vigilante justice are already in place.[91]

Of course, an American *Basij* is the most extreme and hopefully unlikely scenario. Still, today, in many of the more religious parts of the United States, atheists can be abused by their neighbors and community with few repercussions. One atheist living in the Bible Belt recounted how all of his neighbors in his ex-neighborhood would get together at a home prayer group and ask their god to "strike down" his family. He received threatening letters signed by his neighbors, and they poisoned and killed his family pets. Neighbors terrorized him and finally forced his family to move as local authorities would do nothing, and the terrorism never made the news. Again, this is an extreme example, but it shows that harassment does happen in American communities and online.

Such anecdotes are all interesting, but how widespread is such harassment? An insightful quote often misattributed to German cinematographer Werner Herzog but authored by satirist and historian William Pannapacker states, "You are waking up, as Germany once did, to the awareness that one-third of your people would kill another one-third, while one-third watches." Though meant to be a grimly humorous take on America's flirtation with populist authoritarianism at the time, it can be considered a truism. The depth of religious conviction and belief in their righteousness that motivate the one-third or so of the U.S. population that is highly religious makes a religio-fascist outcome possible.

Another misquote, in this case, mis-attributed to Sinclair Lewis, though paraphrasing many of his comments, holds, "When Fascism comes to America, it will be wrapped in the flag and carrying a cross." Despite its murky origins, this quote captures the fact that among democratic nations, the United States has historically been the most stubbornly religious, even as belief has rapidly declined in the rest of the Western world. It has, at the same time, shown highly undemocratic tendencies justified through that same religiosity, such as slavery and systemic racism toward non-white citizens and the disenfranchisement of women.

These quotes, though misattributed, bear a kernel of truth. According to a 2021 Gallup poll, 76% of Americans identify as religious, 69% as Christian, and 7% as non-Christian. A further 23% are religiously unaffiliated, including atheists.[92] In addition, 50% of Americans said religion was "very important" in their lives. These numbers, taken together, suggest one-third of Americans are highly religious Christians, one-third are marginally so, and one-third are either non-Christian or nonbelievers.

Being highly religious doesn't necessarily translate into political extremism. Yet, 81% of white evangelicals voted in 2018 for Donald Trump for President, as did 70% of all white Americans who regularly attend Church, according to a 2021 Pew Study. Further, 70% of Republicans, evangelicals included, believed the Big Lie and a considerable portion supported the insurrection on January 6th, 2021.[93] There is a high correlation between religious fervor and a tendency toward political authoritarianism.

We can easily see the potential for a significant plurality of Americans becoming radicalized by religious extremism who could, in turn, coerce the one-third who are Christian moderates into accepting the persecution of the one-third who are non-Christian believers and nonbelievers. If this roughly equal balance between the three groups places the United States at high risk of Religio-fascism if pluralistic democratic institutions break down, then countries that have a higher percentage of citizens identifying as religious would naturally tend to be more so, especially as democracy and pluralism tend to be much weaker to begin with in such societies. The degree of religiosity varies across the Middle East, for instance, from urban moderates to conservative Wahhabists in Saudi Arabia to the downright medieval Taliban. It is also by no means a monolith, with Sunnis, Shias, and other sects in an uneasy state of coexistence. Yet, for the most part, the citizenry in Middle Eastern countries as a whole is more than 93% Muslim as of 2010, according to Pew Research.[94]

Unlike other contemporary religions, Islam is inherently political in the sense that it makes no distinction between secular and religious authority. It encourages its adherents to take and hold power and, once they do, to impose the often draconian laws of Islam, known as Sharia (*Sharīʿa*), on its citizenry. In the Middle East and North Africa, eighteen of the twenty countries (90%) in the region have laws criminalizing blasphemy, and thirteen of them (65%) outlaw apostasy. In some countries, such as Afghanistan, Brunei, Iran, Mauritania, Nigeria, Pakistan, and Saudi Arabia, violations of blasphemy laws can carry the possibility of the death penalty, as per Pew Research.[95]

Building a relationship with hostile religious neighbors can be challenging but is extremely helpful in minimizing any potential abuse, given the extent of the problem. The following are some steps we can take to defuse the hostility of religious neighbors:

1. **Befriend (most) neighbors:** With most people, regardless of ideological differences, it is challenging for them to bear animosity toward us if they can see us as ordinary people and if we can find a degree of common ground. Of course, there are exceptions — some people are fundamentally disagreeable, and it is a challenge to befriend someone with repellent views. This insight may seem obvious, but it is common to exacerbate tensions with annoying neighbors. We've all done it. Initiating even simple interactions or exchanging pleasantries can make a tremendous difference in humanizing ourselves with religious neighbors who might otherwise view us with hatred and suspicion.
2. **Make an effort to understand their perspective:** Try to see things from our neighbor's point of view. Are they feeling threatened or vulnerable? Maybe we

denigrate religion when talking with friends in our backyards or fly gay pride flags from our porches. We shouldn't hide our beliefs but be aware of the potential repercussions. By understanding their perspective, we may find ways to mitigate their hostility.

3. **Be non-confrontational:** When interacting with our religious neighbors, we should avoid reacting to their hostility with more hostility, which can escalate the situation. Instead, we should stay calm and understanding, even if we disagree with their behavior or viewpoints.
4. **Remain vigilant:** In some cases, it might be prudent to install security cameras and alarms or change our routines to avoid interacting with neighbors as much as possible if the relationship is toxic. At a minimum, this will make them think twice about harassment.
5. **Document harassment:** We should keep a record of any threatening behavior we experience. This documentation can include notes on the incident's date, time, details, and witnesses who may have observed the behavior. This documentation can be helpful if we need to escalate the situation or seek help from authorities, who may be reluctant to side with us without ironclad proof, given the authoritarian bent of many police officers and politicians.
6. **Look for opportunities to build trust:** I've forged a bond with one of my neighbors by offering to keep an eye on their house while they are away and another by paying for mending a jointly owned fence and

greeting them warmly when I see them — typical neighborly day-to-day acts that show there is no animosity and that we are as pleasant and trustworthy as any religionist.

7. **Find common interests:** One way to build a relationship with our neighbors is to find activities we can enjoy and do together. These could be something as simple as starting a joint garden, chatting about a shared interest in rescuing animals, or finding a hobby that would be an excellent excuse to have them over and build a friendship.

Way #15

Avoid the Enemy of Our Enemy

Fake friends like the weaker, poor, suffering, sad and useless version of you. Once they see that you are stronger, richer, doing well, happier and useful, they feel threatened.

De philosopher DJ Kyos

A FEW DAYS after the Supreme Court officially handed down its ruling on *Dobbs v. Jackson Women's Health Organization*, I sat highly dejected at my work desk. Overturning fifty years of precedent that had guaranteed a constitutional right for a woman to control her reproductive health outcomes, it was clear the extremist Conservative Catholic majority was only beginning to flex its muscle. Of course, many Americans legitimately hold different opinions on this particular topic, including some atheists. Yet, given the comments by Justices Thomas and Alito, the ruling portends additional cases seeking to roll back other rights that offend delicate Christian sensibilities, like protections for trans people, gay marriage, and contraception. Any atheist or non-Christian should, regardless of political persuasion, be highly concerned that the rights of atheists and religionists who are in the minority could eventually end up in their sights.

With this in mind, I found myself on a *Zoom* call commiserating with a colleague about how the Christian Right-wing was eroding our longstanding religious rights, including freedom from religion. I assumed she would be like-minded since she is Jewish and lives on the East Coast. I was very wrong. My colleague didn't miss a beat and said, "Let me stop you there. I think this is a first step in the right direction to get us back to morality and traditional values."

I was floored. I thought for sure that we would be of like mind until I remembered she had refused the COVID-19 vaccination because of conspiracy theories that it negatively affects fertility. Radical Christians and the Jewish Orthodox in alliance — Martin Niemöller is undoubtedly spinning in his grave.

Barbara Kingsolver, Pulitzer Prize-winning novelist, essayist, and poet, has noted a similar convergence in the thinking of Right-wing Christians and Muslims on wokism, namely the issue of LGBTQ+ rights. She points out that Republicans have, over the last twenty years, sought to portray Muslims as antithetical to Western values, echoing the sentiment of many European Right-wing populists. However, a shift in sympathies now appears to be manifesting, where Republicans are now extending an olive branch to Muslim voters, promising solidarity in their anti-LGBTQ+ agenda. This startling new alliance signifies a revival of a Right-wing initiative that saw a temporary pause due to the 9/11 attacks, one that had once sought to unite traditionalists across the globe against secular modernity.

Muslims are falling for it. Asra Nomani, a Georgetown professor and former foreign correspondent, is a prime example per Kingsolver. She had been a self-described liberal and a Muslim critic of Islamic fundamentalism who voted for Trump in 2016 only as a blow against Muslim terrorism. Yet she recently joined a protest by Muslim parents who wanted to opt their children out of courses that contradicted their professed values, like LGBTQ+ rights. While Asra had previously been critical of Islamic extremism, she has drunk the Kool-Aid of those who have perverted the concept of "woke" to be an existential danger to society greater than radical Islam, especially to children.[96]

The point is that while religionists who are typically at odds can align on specific issues where their interests intersect, the maxim "the enemy of my enemy is my friend" doesn't apply to atheists. Religious leaders, especially extremists, see themselves, among other things, as god-ordained power brokers for their tribe. They and their in-group, in turn, see other religions and sects as competitors for that power in the form of followers and money. Yes, they may malign and kill their competitors as Christians did Jewish communities with blood libels, *pogroms,* and exclusionary business practices since the Middle Ages, or slaughter them as infidels as the Muslims and Christians did to each other during the Crusades. In the modern world, however, religionists also see each other as legitimate rivals in a pluralistic society with whom they must compete and deal roughly as peers. They may even form temporary inter-tribal alliances as long as their interests align, like Christians and Muslims against LGBTQ+ rights.[97]

We have also seen, over the last forty years, radical U.S. Catholics and Protestants, historically at odds since the Protestant Reformation, allied with each other over divisive gender, racial, and sexual issues. Protestants who didn't give much consideration to abortion in the 1970s have since then submitted to Catholic views on the subject to forge a powerful political alliance. They have captured the Supreme Court, much of the U.S. judicial system, the House of Representatives, and most state governments. However, if and when a full-blown radical religionist government takes over, in all probability, one that is evangelical Protestant in nature, the alliance between the two may very likely rupture. Until that happens, they are uncomfortable bedfellows.

Atheists stand alone. We are not competitors or power brokers in any sense. We hold no governments in thrall like religionists, nor do we have powerful monied interests, lobbyists, or longstanding organizations backing us. Though religionists may stereotype us as being all of the same mind, methodically orchestrating the downfall of civilization, we are, at most, a loose assemblage of somewhat like-minded individuals without an organized tribe or discernable locus of political or economic power. Our only distinguishing feature is the fact that our nonbelief notionally threatens every faith-based worldview, so we are just a minor threat to be crushed, not a rival group with which to negotiate.

Further, we are seen across conservative religious groups

and societies, contrary to all evidence, as immoral heathens more prone to violence and unethical acts than religionists, even more than members of rival religious groups who are, after all, seen as being bound by a divine moral code.[98] There are few avowed atheists in political positions. Despite our nation's history of Islamophobia, homophobia, misogyny, and racism, more Americans say when polled that they would vote for someone who was Muslim, gay, female, or Black before they'd vote for an atheist. Only socialists fare worse.[99]

We may be tempted to point to the Iranian Revolution in the late 1970s, where Ayatollah Khomeini and his theocratic cohort aligned themselves with secular socialists to form a united front to overthrow the autocratic monarchy of Mohammed Reza Pahlavi. But secular doesn't automatically translate to atheist. In Islamic cultures especially, the notion of atheism is, for the most part, an alien concept. Those born into a Muslim family are by default Muslim and any that stray are apostates. The current Iranian regime legally regards a Muslim as always Muslim. An Iranian socialist was still a fellow religionist, if only an unobservant one that dared to embrace secularism and pluralism. In any case, the fact that Khomeini perceived the socialists as a legitimate power locus made them allies of convenience only until he accomplished his objective of overthrowing the Shah and then summarily excluded socialists from the new government.

So, as atheists, we can't expect, if one radical sect or another takes over politically, that we can align ourselves with a rival faction or cozy up to the new regime. Even at a local level, we cannot expect to seek sanctuary among other persecuted minorities like Muslims (or among Christians in a Muslim-majority country), especially if they are under threat of persecution. In addition, it is not hyperbolic to say that, outside of a handful of nations and communities, we are universal pariahs and outcasts in a world where every facet of it, from its political and economic forms to its social conventions, is wrapped up in a religious fiction ruled by those who consciously or subconsciously want non-conformists banished from it, or at least ground down under its jack-booted heel for the sake of the common good.

All of this being said, we should not treat out-group religionists as enemies or, in any case, violate their fundamental human rights. That would only invite opprobrium from them in addition to followers of the dominant religion. While we may never be in alliance with them or be able to look to them for assistance, we can leverage them against the prevailing religio-fascist regime. For instance, by supporting the Jewish community against antisemitism and hate crimes or Muslims against Islamophobia, we can help these communities to survive and, hopefully, remain a bulwark against Christian fanaticism. Building goodwill for self-preservation may be a highly cynical strategy, but it will hopefully create a sense of mutual respect over time.

To recap, atheists cannot readily turn to out-group religionists for support under a religiously intolerant regime because:

1. **We lack formal organization:** Atheism is not a belief system or a group to which one can belong. It simply refers to the absence of a belief in a god

or gods. As such, it is not a cohesive movement or a cause with any form of leadership that can negotiate with another religious-out group on our behalf. If we hope to grow our numbers beyond 3.1% of the U.S. population as of 2017, we must build effective, inclusive organizations and leadership structures to draw people in.[100] Conservatives and religionists have together built influential lobbyist and political donor pools, as well as think tanks and public policy pressure groups like the *Heritage Foundation* and *Federalist Society*. We need to do the same. Strangely, for a group that, from a philosophical standpoint, is as materialistically focused as atheists, our efforts to date have been much more academic than practical.

2. **We are perceived as having fundamentally incompatible beliefs with all religionists:** To religionists, our beliefs and values differ from theirs, often markedly so, even though it is typically the source of those values that diverge rather than the values themselves. We reject gods, not morality, except maybe the strict sexual and gender role segregation on which religionists fixate. Aligning with them simply because we share a common threat would pose a complex challenge because it would force religionists to see value in us, which would be difficult since they might share many of the same religious biases as the religio-fascists in power.
3. **Religionists, including their future religionist victims, tend to form temporary alliances:** In the early stages of a religio-fascist regime, Muslim or

Orthodox Jewish communities, for instance, may align with Christian religio-fascists on a host of social issues, such as the need to constrain or even punish us deviants who support or promote the LGBTQ+ community, women's rights, or religious pluralism for practical reasons. The desire to control these powerful social forces is consistent whether we are talking about Haredi politicians in Israel, Christian Nationalists in the United States, or Wahabbist Muslims in Saudi Arabia. Indeed, religionists are forming alliances even now. Orthodox Jewish and white evangelical Christian communities vote Republican at similar rates, for instance, and for many of the same socially conservative reasons.[101] Although they would likely face persecution alongside atheists, they may not be amenable to aligning with atheists in the short run since we threaten their belief systems as well. As atheists, we must learn to be comfortable being lone wolves among other lone wolves to survive. If we can pick up allies along the way, all the better, but we cannot assume that we can rely on anyone but ourselves.

4. **Betrayal of atheists is no vice:** Any group as fundamentally different, or perceived as fundamentally different, from people of faith as atheists would have little goodwill established. Even if the *Freedom From Religion Foundation* or the *ACLU* were powerful enough to negotiate an agreement with a religio-fascist regime to protect atheists' rights, doesn't it seem reasonable that breaking any agreement with a

morally inferior group would be acceptable to a diehard religionist? Just ask any Native American how sacrosanct treaties are to a Christian-dominated U.S. government that has historically viewed them as inferior and regularly found political or economic benefit in violating their rights.

WAY #16

REMOVE THE FAMILY TIES THAT DON'T BIND

A family is a tyranny ruled over by its weakest member.[102]

GEORGE BERNARD SHAW

WITHIN THE ANNALS of our family's history, a long-estranged half-uncle carries the weight of George Bernard Shaw's words about the weakest among us. This half-uncle, "Jack," strong in religiosity but weak in spirit, violated a deep familial understanding: that every one of us has the inviolable right to choose our religious path or the path of irreligiosity without malice or prejudice.

Yet, during a pivotal event etched in my memory, he shattered that familial bond. With one act of weakness when the Bible trumped blood, he defied that shared understanding, covertly attempting to impose his own beliefs on me behind the backs of my parents. The fallout was profound. The tight-knit kinship offered him and his family was forever altered, leaving fragments of broken trust and continued estrangement. As the dust settled, I was left grappling with the truth that fractures can emerge even within the closest familial circles.

I was fifteen, and my license to drive was still what seemed eons away, so I relied on a few upper-level students whose parents were also military or my parents themselves to transport me to and from campus, our home being too distant for the school bus. One rainy day early on in the school year, my mother found herself stuck at work and unable to pick me up after classes, and my student rides all had after-school plans. She then asked Jack if he would take me to his home. She would come and pick me up after dinner. He all too readily agreed.

My mother had only recently reconnected with her half-brother after a lifetime apart, having been raised separately. Uncle Jack and his wife "Pam" were decent people, if a bit religiously overzealous. Yet, they never actively tried to convert any of us and operated somewhat at the periphery of our daily lives. Plus, I, for one, was excited to have nearby relatives, having always lived half a continent or half a globe away from all my grandparents, uncles, aunts, and cousins.

At most, they seasoned our dinnertime conversations at our home with a tang of faith, and occasionally, they made odd, somewhat uncomfortable comments about occult societal influences. I recall with some humor my aunt Pam's pride in recounting her reluctance even to touch a bank receipt totaling $6.66 with her fingertips, lest they spontaneously burst into flame. They were evangelicals, of course, as it has been my lot to have to deal with their nonsense more frequently than those of other denominations. Still, they were dissimilar to our pushy neighbors in Colorado and relatively harmless, or so I thought.

Their religiosity had all been tolerable until my uncle pulled into his driveway where, from the passenger seat, I saw a tall, skinny man cradling a dog-eared Bible, standing just inside the doorway next to my aunt Pam to greet me. At first, I hoped for exorcism, which would have been a hoot, but I quickly recognized it as some sort of intervention. The pastor must have been in his late twenties or early thirties but looked no more than a few years older than I, fidgeting in his horn-rimmed glasses and Mr. Rogers sweater vest.

I greeted him with a perfunctory shake and tight-lipped smile. He smiled back awkwardly and proffered a warm greeting, introducing himself as "Pastor Steve." I drew some strength from the knowledge that my uncle would catch holy hell from my parents for attempting this stunt.

Mercifully, Pastor Steve mainly kept to pleasantries throughout dinner but grew bolder when he picked up his Bible and sat beside me before the fireplace after we had adjourned to the living room. I can't recall all the details of the protracted conversation other than his gripping the Bible like a security blanket, which he flipped through nervously while he talked. Nevertheless, snippets of animated discussions of Pascal's Wager and circular arguments about Biblical truth still rattle around in the back of my fifty-six-year-old mind. I do remember standing up at one point and asking something to the effect that if I, as a poor, misguided atheist with no smarts or religious training, were plopped down at a table with the Koran, Bible, Bhagavad Gita, and other religious texts in front of me, how would I choose? They were all just moldy dry books full of equally nonsensical stories to me, each claiming to be the sole repository of truth and threatening punishment of the nonbeliever, though none stood out to me as such.

At some point, Pastor Steve finally grew exasperated and gave up, except to reiterate at the end that my soul was in danger of eternal damnation if I didn't reconsider. Mercifully, soon after arriving, my mother hustled me out, leaving her admonishment of Uncle Jack for another day.

Fortunately, my parents had raised me in an environment where the rest of my immediate family members knew I was not a religionist, which perhaps enabled me to stand my ground at my uncle's house. There was no coming out, so to speak, to parents and other family members. Yet, as with many atheists, my extended family is a mix of religionists, from devout Catholic cousins and Protestant aunts and uncles to a few Gen Z nones. They, in turn, run the political gamut from ultra-conservative to liberal.

The one question that still bothers me to this day is, would that same uncle, as weak yet as zealous as he was, betray me or my family if pushed to do so in a religiously extremist environment? Maybe one day, he feels wrongly estranged from us or belittled for his religiosity. It only takes one weak link to bring the entire family down.

Before coming out to family members, we may want

to think first about whether any of the following applies to our situation:

1. **Potential for familial estrangement:** The notion of "love the sinner, not the sin" is a pretty Christian maxim, but it is often expressed much differently by different sects, traditions, and individuals from what the phrase means on its face. Those religious hardliners who don't outright shun the sinner, as they frequently do, often believe that they are acting out of love by attempting to "steer" them away from what they perceive as hellbound behavior. This "steering" can be expressed as a judgmental and condemning attitude toward those they perceive as sinners, resulting in mistreatment or discrimination. When atheists say, "There is no hate like Christian love," it is this attitude to which we are referring.

   It is worth pondering whether any of our family members hold this definition. As with homosexuality, extramarital sex, and interracial dating, it may prompt them to disassociate from or confront us, driven by a sense of moral duty to protect themselves, their children, and the family at large from the corrupting influence of our atheism. Alternatively, their actions may stem from a resentful desire to retaliate against those who are perceived as scorning or mocking, even indirectly, their religious convictions — a zealot's urge to claim victory over their adversaries. Without fully understanding the intricate dynamics within our families, it may be wise to reconsider sharing our atheism with anyone we can't trust to keep our confidence. We may be in non-religious households but have, as we all do, religious zealots in our family tree, many of whom may be beloved but for whom faith trumps family.

Therefore, before deciding to disclose our atheism, we should carefully consider the multifaceted nature of our family dynamics and its potential repercussions on our relationships.

2. **Fear of social backlash:** Our religious family members may love us very much and may even make peace with our atheism even if they have strong religious beliefs, but only if they are deciding on their own. That's rarely the case. If they are devout, then they most likely have a tight-knit, intrusive, and often politicized religious community to which they belong. In the current climate of political polarization, where religion and conservative politics frequently intertwine, it is vital to acknowledge the potential convergence of these two forces. It would not be unexpected for a relative to ostracize us to maintain favor within their political or religious in-group.
3. **Sense of betrayal:** A relative may feel a sense of betrayal or disappointment if our nonbelief contradicts their values or expectations for the family and decides to ostracize us out of a sense of hurt, anger, or wounded family pride. We must ask ourselves: do we understand how much loyalty and honor mean

to our parents and other family members? In strictly religious households and many traditional cultures, obedience to parents can be sacrosanct. Violating that expectation can call into question their role as good parents and their competence in raising a child to have the same beliefs they hold. The shame can be enough for them to shun us.

4. **Emotional trauma:** Were our parents or other family members abusive, neglectful, or violent to the point that they traumatized us during our childhood? If so, they know they wronged us as much as they may avoid discussing it now. Their guilt may be overwhelming, and announcing our atheism may cause them to see our nonbelief as a rejection of them and a further reminder of their bad behavior. Conversely, they may use our declaration to justify their past abusiveness, spurring additional mistreatment.
5. **Communication breakdown:** A lack of communication or understanding between family members can contribute to shunning or turning on us over religious differences. Suppose we are unwilling or unable to understand and empathize with our relatives' beliefs or actions. In that case, they may feel frustrated and push us away, weakening their bonds with us.

Our best route is to avoid being angry or accusatory. Instead, we should listen to their concerns and slowly educate them on our nonbelief. We should also emphasize that we are good people with strong morals who do this out of conviction, not hatred toward them. The less attacked they feel, the more likely they will make peace with our choice.

WAY #17

BEWARE THE VIRTUE SIGNALING ZEALOTS

"What a noble aim is that of the zealot who tortures himself like a madman in order to desire nothing, love nothing, feel nothing, and who, if he succeeded, would end up a complete monster!"

DENIS DIDEROT

ABOUT TWENTY YEARS ago, my wife and I had a young lady over for dinner at our tiny bungalow near the beach in Santa Cruz, California. Let's call her Paksima ("one with an innocent face" in Farsi). My wife had taken her under her wing because they had many cultural experiences and traditions in common, having immigrated from Iran and Afghanistan, respectively. The big exception was that Paksima was a young devout Muslim who covered everything but her hands and face in expensive silk scarves and long elegant chemises. At the same time, my wife is a pantheist and a bit of a bohemian at heart, dressing like the free spirit she is.

Paksima's religiosity was unusual since she had immigrated from Afghanistan as an infant, and the rest of her family was secular, if not entirely progressive. Having fled Iran to escape the forced imposition of conservative Islam, my wife has always found it hard to fathom why a young woman would voluntarily choose to cover and subordinate themselves to men when they were in the United States and had a choice. Since we've always been open to different cultures and figured young people are still trying to find themselves, we never pressed her on her choice.

That evening began uneventfully, with my wife and Paksima sitting on our couch chatting and drinking tea in the living room while I was in the attached kitchen making dinner. Despite our friendship and hospitality, the discussion degenerated quickly. For nearly an hour, Paksima periodically needled my wife for not being a good Muslim spouse. She insisted it was a wife's duty to cook and wait on her husband even after I popped my head through the kitchen door and insisted that I prefer to cook, which I do. But she kept insisting. Now, understand that my wife is a strong-willed and passionate Middle Easterner, so it took quite a bit of self-restraint to avoid verbally eviscerating Paksima.

Everything eventually calmed down until, shortly before I served dinner, Paksima abruptly announced it was *time* for Isha, the last prayer of the day. My wife offered her our bedroom to do her ablutions and pray in private, but she insisted on rolling out her prayer rug in the middle of the living room and, after washing up, praying in front of us. We stood patiently, waiting for her to finish her performance before serving dinner.

The act of berating my wife for not being a good Muslim spouse in our own home, even though she was never a practicing Muslim, was brazen but not the kind of thing that many atheists haven't witnessed before. Devout women in Islam, Christianity, and Hinduism are often quick to shame and guilt each other into religious observance or moral behavior, and it is often more successful than if a man were to do it. We usually assume that men are the sole oppressors in religiously conservative societies, but it is often the internalized oppression among women that enforces religious adherence.

The insistence on publicly praying and performing religious rituals or talking loudly about one's faith in public is also not uncommon. Charismatic church services and big tent revivals are spectacles in the Southern United States. At the same time, mass public prayers by Muslim men are a common sight in the markets throughout the Middle East. Such acts are perhaps indicative of the proselytic nature of these religions and their compulsive need to publicly coerce and convert to keep themselves convinced of the righteousness of their faith. From a non-religious person's viewpoint, it's just virtue signaling at its worst.

On the flip side, virtue signaling can have one positive side effect: it can serve as the canary in the coal mine for atheists or anyone who fears religious zealotry. It's always been around, but the need to fly our freak flag publicly in our social media-driven society has exacerbated it. The guy with

Christian bumper stickers festooning his jacked-up truck, often alongside *Molon Labe* and *Three Percenter* decals, is a good example. The impromptu multi-week long "Ashbury Awakening" in February 2023, where thousands traveled to a chapel on the Ashbury University campus to see and be seen dramatically expressing their religion in public and online, is another.[103] Muslims taking to the streets and social media to display exaggerated outrage anytime a publication like *Charlie Hebdo* "insults" their religion is still another. Such people are those most likely to feel compelled to make a point of publicly proving their hatred for enemies of the faith because their virtue signaling has conditioned them to it.

And Paksima? As it turns out, we eventually severed our friendship with her, not because of her ill manners or religiosity, but because we found she wasn't entirely as innocent as her virtue signaling would suggest. She eventually confided in my wife that she had recently become pregnant through an illicit affair with her Imam and had a secret abortion at his insistence. Of course, the cad had professed his love for her as his "spiritual second wife" to get her into his bed, but he disappeared after the procedure. It was religious hypocrisy at its finest. The second factor, though, was her zealous support of terrorist attacks, including 9/11, and her desire to see Israel eradicated. Both are deal breakers for us.

How can we spot these virtue signalers who may also harm us and our rights?

1. **Insecurity combined with religiosity is a red flag:** A relative of mine, "James," once insisted on wearing a massive gold cross around his neck to a Jewish wedding despite never wearing even a tiny crucifix in the past. It is also important to note that James was also one who, despite being "born-again," was not exactly a paragon of church-going virtue. During the celebration, he didn't want to be mistaken as Jewish. The blatant antisemitism aside, James' insecurity about his faith made him more ready to make an aggressive show of it.
2. **Anti-social disregard for others is both rude and concerning:** We've undoubtedly seen posts on *Instagram* by so-called Christians who, after service, go out for Sunday brunch, treat the staff poorly, and then stiff the waiter on his tip. Often, it is a snub to an atheist or someone who deigns to work on Sunday despite making possible the brunch in the first place. They then post a picture of their zero-tip receipts with snotty notes about proudly not tipping non-Christians or leaving fake $20 bills with scripture on the back, just as a brunching Jesus would presumably do.[104] While not indicative of Christians or religionists as a whole, there is a cadre of them that act in anti-social ways publicly toward those not in their in-group.

Conservative religion is as much about maintaining and respecting tradition and institutions as it is about belief. The eternal nature of religious truth demands that it and the institutions it has built never change. A religionist willing to disrespect the rules of etiquette, manners, and custom is also one whose rage against perceived enemies of the faith would have few bounds, including the persecution of atheists.

WAY #18

BE SKEPTICAL OF "LIBERAL" BIG TECH

People I don't follow but are in my newsfeed: @charliekirk11 @RealCandaceO and @ RealJamesWoods. Why Twitter why?[105]

REYNOLDS HUTCHINS, WEB PRODUCER FOR THE WASHINGTON EXAMINER

IF YOU LIVE in the United States, I'm sure you've been unfortunate enough to watch at least news clips of our nearly annual political spectacle. No, I'm not referring to the State of the Union or the Super Bowl. I'm talking about Congressional hearings where tech leaders like Meta CEO Mark Zuckerberg are dragged before the cameras to provide their Rainman-like responses to claims of liberal bias on Social Media platforms. The first in April 2018 had Zuckerberg, trademark bowl cut hovering over his deer-in-the-headlights expression, testifying in a joint hearing of the Senate Judiciary and Commerce Committees on the role of the platform in the 2016 U.S. presidential election in supposedly censoring conservative content.[106]

Republican politicians and media pundits have claimed for years that there is a persistent pro-liberal, anti-Christian bias in social media algorithms and content moderation teams, pointing to the preponderance of liberals, atheists, and those hostile to Christianity in high-tech. I've been in tech for nearly thirty years and can vouch that many of my fellow rank-and-file techies in Silicon Valley are liberals, though a surprising number are libertarian as well. This is perhaps natural since the liberal mindset tends to be more conducive to scientific inquiry, innovation, and technological change than one calibrated to maintain tradition and the status quo.

The reality is that techies don't make the major business decisions. The executives do. As in most industries, tech-bro CEOs skew, if not Republican, at least toward economically *laissez-faire* libertarianism. Peter Thiel and Elon Musk are more the rule than the exception, albeit more high-profile and socially regressive than most. To a man, and I've known a number of these billionaires, they are committed to their tech and the idea of advancing technological progress but are driven first and foremost by the desire for fewer regulations and lower taxes.

In their quest for profit, it is only natural that they, and the AI algorithms on which they depend, cater to those with the greatest numbers and money or at least those most engaged with their platforms and advertising. Surprise, these tend to be conservatives. Conservative conspiratorial outrage and sensationalism, and most of it online is politically

Right-wing and religiously extremist, breeds online engagement. Conspiracists' outlandish claims also compel liberals to respond like a dog to Pavlov's bell. The ensuing melees generate views, clicks, and followers.[107]

Unfortunately, CEOs like Zuckerberg are often so monofocused on building their technology and their brand that they genuinely have very little understanding of the negative social, psychological, and human ramifications of their technologies, leaving them flat-footed when called to testify and try and muster what minimal EQ (Emotional Quotient) they have to respond. The reality is that there is mounting evidence showing that major social media platforms have allowed their algorithms to promote topics and perspectives favored by the MAGA, Right-wing fringe, not the woke crowd. Many platforms do this, not just Musk-owned *X*. Perhaps Bluesky *will be* different, but I'm not holding my breath.[108]

For atheists, we should realize that the internet, for us especially, is not a guaranteed friendly platform for our views, no matter how liberal and open-minded tech employees are. These platforms want to keep nonbelievers engaged and monetize their attention, but the future is far less certain. We have seen many internet providers and web application vendors comply with censorship rules for countries like India and China to maintain a foothold in those markets. In the United States, it may eventually make sense for them to give in to censorship pressure from religio-fascists because the conservative market is too large to ignore. In that case, they will deplatform or deemphasize atheist voices in a hot minute.

While technology has played a significant role in enabling

free speech and expanding access to information, there are several reasons why atheists cannot count on high tech to protect their free speech as religious extremism spreads:

1. **Corporate power and greed:** Social media companies are multinational corporations driven solely by short-term profit and shareholder value. They have significant influence over the public sphere and have the power to shape public discourse in ways that benefit their interests or comply with the censorious policies of authoritarian governments. They may not always be willing to protect free speech for atheist voices if it conflicts with their own business interests or religious or political leanings. As we see today, many companies are backing off their commitments to the environment, the LGBTQ+ community, and DEI (Diversity, Equity, and Inclusion) programs as soon as even a small number of conservative and religious activists threaten their bottom line with boycotts.
2. **Algorithmic biases that favor outrage and controversy:** The algorithms and artificial intelligence systems that drive social media platforms are biased in various ways, favoring conservative perspectives since their outrage drives visitors and ad revenue far more efficiently than progressive ones. These biases can result in the suppression of atheist voices because they challenge the status quo and existing conservative power structures like religion or merely criticize the platform's egoistic and narcissistic owners like Elon Musk.

3. **The numerical dominance of religious groups:** If religio-fascist groups and individuals increasingly use social media to spread religion, their sheer numbers can overwhelm atheist ones. Even though nones are multiplying in the United States and Europe, Christians and minority religions still make up the majority and are typically the loudest. Irate religionists can also create a toxic environment that can result in harassment, doxxing, and other forms of online abuse, given the vindictiveness of far-right, often religious, activists.
4. **Government censorship on behalf of religion:** While the U.S. Constitution guarantees the right to free speech, there are limits to this right, such as in cases of hate speech or incitement to violence. There is no guarantee that religiously conservative politicians, backed by an extremist Supreme Court, might curtail anti-religious speech as a violation of the rights of the religious not to have their religion maligned because it may incite them to violence. We are already seeing governmental attempts to promote religion through so-called "Religious Freedom" legislation, which could set the stage for such free speech curtailment.

Section III
Know When Religio-fascism is Rising

If your government says, "Not only am I your government, but I represent the true religion," if you disagree with it you're not just of another faction. You're evil.[109]

Margaret Atwood

In America today, labels like "fascist" are thrown around quite carelessly, often aimed at those on the right, just as "communist" and "socialist" are misused to target and vilify anyone even slightly left of center. Precision in our definitions becomes crucial to navigating these muddy waters. I prefer the term "Religio-fascism" to describe the fusion of religious zealotry with political authoritarianism, not because it vilifies a movement that I detest but because it neatly encapsulates many traits associated with traditional fascism, albeit with a religious twist.

Fascism manifests uniquely across different historical and cultural contexts. The brand of fascism that surged through Hitler's Germany, fueled by a toxic amalgamation of antisemitism and fervent nationalism, presents a stark contrast to the incarnation seen in Franco's Spain. Franco's regime was initially rooted in traditionalism, nationalism, stringent social control, and vehement anti-communism with solid ties to the Catholic Church. Today, the fascistic visions of Marie LePen for France and Geert Wilders for the Netherlands, more subtle in expression than their antecedents and focused on immigration, in turn, differ significantly from those of both Hitler and Franco.

Though not every authoritarian or nationalist regime fits the mold of classic fascism, common threads weave through these movements. They often share a penchant for Right-wing populism and ultra-nationalism, coupled with a staunch authoritarian streak. These regimes also typically exhibit a deep-seated aversion to liberal democracy, usually interlaced with racial prejudices and xenophobic sentiments. In situations where these movements intertwine with radicalized religious beliefs, a unique form of fascism emerges. Here, the imposition of religious doctrines becomes paramount, either as a sincere expression of the desire for faith to dictate politics and the law or a cynical attempt to use it for political gain, leading to encroachments on the rights and freedoms of LGBTQ+ communities, the imposition of restrictive roles and controls over women's bodies and sexuality, and the marginalization of minority religions and the non-religious.

Populist leaders can use religion to provide legitimacy for authoritarian actions and racist ideologies and even to claim a divine mandate for their rule. Many U.S. politicians, such as Donald Trump,[110] Florida Governor Ron DeSantis,[111] and House Majority Leader Mike Johnson,[112] have all made such claims. This blend of political and religious fervor creates a particularly potent form of governance, where the lines between spiritual belief and political ideology blur, reinforcing the authority of often cult-like leaders and justifying their actions in the eyes of their followers.

Today, we find those essential elements of fascism finding resonance in the surging political and religious movements. Just as the fascist regimes mentioned above sought to extend their control over all facets of society, from the economy to the media, education, and culture, so too do the proponents of the *Seven Mountain Mandate* within the *Protestant dominionist* and the *Catholic integralist* movements aim to ascend and dominate seven societal pillars: family, religion, education, etc.

Finally, fascist regimes exhibit strong centralization and authoritarian tendencies, concentrating power within the hands of a single, often populist leader or a privileged elite. They suppress personal liberties and democratic principles, as liberal democracy threatens the state's iron grip. The current MAGA movement, deeply entwined with Trump worship and white Christian nationalism, similarly eyes the centralization of power under the next Republican administration through the unitary executive theory (see *Project 2025* at the *Mandate for Leadership* devised by the *Heritage Foundation*) and could potentially use this newfound power to bypass legislative and judicial controls to advance a radical Christian agenda.[113] The MAGA movement is, in a word, proto-religio-fascist, as are the Hindutva movement in India, the Haredi parties in Israel, and Radical Islamists throughout the Middle East. It is possibly only a matter of time until some of these movements in the West transform into full-blown religio-fascist regimes.

Religio-fascism in the United States has gained a foothold through "Religious Freedom" legislation that purports to protect religious expression. However, it *de facto* privileges Christian chauvinism over the civil rights and freedoms of other religions, the non-religious, and those that run afoul of Christian moral sensibilities. In a full-blown religio-fascist legal system or regime, such legislation may extend to government-endorsed denial of services and employment to non-Christians or other limits that disadvantage them.

Even without official sanction, the Right-wing media, churches, and politicians in the United States already take the government's partiality to religion and religionists' right to discriminate as a license to perpetuate the idea that atheists are immoral, untrustworthy, and often unworthy of full citizenship rights. This narrative significantly marginalizes us, frequently excluding us from public discourse and making it difficult to gain and hold political office.[114]

Should the idea of the United States descending into Religio-fascism appear improbable, consider my connection to an extended family member who is related to John Ashcroft, the former Attorney General known for his extreme religious views. "Laura" is a Christian charismatic who nonchalantly and without apparent malice at dinner one night told my in-laws and their entire family, which included a mix of Muslims, mainstream Christians, and atheists, that all non-Christians should be stripped of citizenship and thrown out of the country. Of course, to a person, everyone was too polite to correct Laura. Such venom from someone whom the family had whole-heartedly embraced despite her religious eccentricity (yes, speaking in tongues is eccentric by any measure) was shocking. Unfortunately, such politeness and often undue deference to the religious beliefs of others enables politicized religionists to propagate their poison with impunity. Yet this is what Laura's church leaders had taught her, and it's much deeper than 'love it or leave it' rhetoric, but a deep-seated belief that the United States was founded by and for Christians in a way that nullifies family and friendship bonds. Many atheists I've met have had similar and often more disturbing stories.

Since mild forms of Religio-fascism and religious chauvinism often don't spark a backlash from the majority, even when they stray into socially repressive legislation, they can and frequently do persist for long periods within democratic societies. A sudden, critical shock, a burning of the Reichstag moment like the one that helped vault the Nazi party to power in Germany, can precipitate the most extreme religio-fascist outcomes. For atheists, it is vital to be aware of and brace for such impending shocks, especially those for which we may be deemed culpable.

Nations have historically descended into authoritarianism during actual or perceived economic and social instability or national decline. People with authoritarian personalities, in particular, as mentioned previously, about 40% of the U.S. population, then gravitate to a demagogue or strongman to establish order and guide them through the chaos. The political weakness of the Weimar Republic in the 1920s and 30s, German humiliation in the face of defeat after WWI, and hyperinflation caused by punitive wartime reparations and economic depression, for example, opened a path for the rise of National Socialism. Naziism had previously been relegated to the political margins. A demoralized, economically deprived nation was ultimately willing to embrace the deranged ideas of Hitler and the Nazi party that vilified traditional scapegoats such as Jewish communities, socialists, and other undesirables, the implementation of eugenics programs, and the promotion of an expansionist vision for the German people as an antidote to their nation's ills.

Beyond the well-trodden history of Nazism, which I don't need to belabor here, it is crucial to focus on its religious elements. It is inaccurate, as many religionists have claimed, that the Nazis were atheistic, especially given that they suppressed atheist societies and organizations. For the most part, the Nazi regime recognized the influence and deep roots of Christianity among the German population. The Catholic and Protestant churches were competing centers of power, and the Nazis tried to co-opt them. The people's faith was acknowledged and embraced, though redirected toward glorifying the state and the German people. State expressions of religion came as a hybrid of Nordic paganism, Christianity, and Indo-Aryan symbolism. Embracing pagan artistic motifs like the swastika and the myth of a white Aryan Jesus were all part of a broader attempt to cast an aura of German ethnic and national superiority with the Nazi party as its defender, not to elevate religious authorities to a position where they might steer governmental policy. It was as much a religio-fascist regime as any divine right monarchy, though inverted with the Church subservient to the state yet nonetheless intertwined.

For a religio-fascist regime to emerge in the United States or elsewhere, all of the same authoritarian, ultra-traditionalist attributes associated with a secular autocracy must be in place. However, it must also have at its core not only a desire to resuscitate political and social greatness and exert iron-fisted control over society but also exhibit a will to drive a religious agenda, particularly one motivated by the myth of some golden past where Christians alone built the nation on Christian values and governed it by and for Christians. In Western European nations and other secular countries, this component is mostly lacking, at least overtly, given the advanced secularization of their societies. Without some massive catastrophe that might drive the desperate and fearful back to religion (or political and social convulsions due to surging radical Islam within their borders), Europe may perhaps avoid such a fate.

However, the path to religious dominion is much more apparent in the United States and other relatively religious societies. Despite the lip service we give to the "separation of church and state," our politics and religion have too often been comfortable bedfellows. Blue laws, anti-sodomy regulations, and abortion and contraception bans, not to mention religious justifications for slavery, have no rationale outside of a religious context yet have pockmarked our history until relatively recently and in virtually every corner of our nation.

Just a few years ago, for instance, my wife and I drove through Idaho, only to find the town we stopped in still had blue laws that forbade the sale of alcohol on Sundays, to my great disappointment after a long day's drive. Religion has been so infused and normalized throughout American society that most of us are often only passingly aware of instances like this or shrug them off as regional oddities, but they are widespread. Placing voting and COVID-19 inoculation centers in houses of worship, granting religious businesses the right to discriminate in terms of who they employ and to whom they provide service, and allowing religious schools to discriminate against LGBTQ+ and minority teachers and students are but a few examples. Yet it is a common thread throughout every aspect of society that can be artfully pulled by religio-fascists to call the 60% of Americans who identify as Christian to arms if they can sufficiently amplify fears of losing their privileges and right to exclude and look down on out-groups.

Religio-fascism is not a *fait accompli* in the United States or anywhere else religion holds undue political sway and where religious extremism is on the rise. It may burn out quickly or accelerate due to some economic or geo-political shock. Having a clear understanding of the dynamics that drive society in a religio-fascist direction is critical for those of us who are atheists.

Way #19

Know How to Spot Religio-fascism

The Christian Right and radical Islamists, although locked in a holy war, increasingly mirror each other. They share the same obsessions. They do not tolerate other forms of belief or disbelief. They are at war with artistic and cultural expression. They seek to silence the media. They call for the subjugation of women. They promote severe sexual repression, and they seek to express themselves through violence.[115]

Chris Hedges

BIBLE-THUMPING AND GUN-TOTING religious zealots are often dismissed as extremists and crackpots: the guy with the lifted truck in the Walmart parking lot festooned with anti-abortion stickers, Bible verses, and a silhouette of a soldier kneeling before a cross; the enraged Karen in the school board meeting demanding to take godless books promoting a hidden "homosexual groomer agenda" out of the library; the pastor who thunders from the pulpit that the followers of Christ need to "take back" the nation from drag queen story hours and sex ed classes, with their Second Amendment rights if necessary. Yet, dismissing this fringe minority out of hand underestimates the real danger it poses. Religiously extremist regimes don't just arise as top-down movements strategically orchestrated by populist leaders or manipulative elites but simultaneously take root and grow from the bottom up as religionists who feel alienated and disenfranchised begin to seek solidarity with like-minded people. Today, with its expansive online communities, the internet acts as a catalyst in this process, significantly amplifying the reach and resonance of religious messages. It becomes a virtual congregation space where ideas can find a massive audience, gain traction, and evolve into movements, no matter how extreme or unorthodox. In the past, such crackpots would have had difficulty gaining a platform, even in the opinion section of their local newspaper.

Radical beliefs gain explosive momentum when a populist political figure emerges who resonates with the group's frustrations and aspirations and possesses the charisma and cunning to harness and direct their energy. We can observe a pertinent example of this dynamic among the American political right wing, where Donald Trump has adeptly parlayed the prevailing discontent into the formidable MAGA populist movement. While Trump himself may not be a fervent religious ideologue, his trajectory has been increasingly influenced by advisors and supporters advocating a shift toward the religious right.

For us atheists, the increasing likelihood of today's Right-wing movements metastasizing into religiously radical regimes calls for a heightened sense of vigilance and a proactive stance. It is imperative to not only identify and speak out against acts of religious bigotry when they occur in isolation but also to understand their potential to evolve into more pervasive forms of oppression. The early recognition and reporting of these incidents are crucial in preventing their growth into more entrenched and systematic discrimination. In doing so, we contribute to a broader effort to safeguard against the insidious spread of extremism, ensuring that the seeds of bigotry and intolerance do not find fertile ground to flourish and expand.

We must consider various factors when assessing the potential for religious extremism in a particular community or nation. One is the degree to which religion is intertwined with the culture. In some societies, the open religiosity of a significant segment of the population may lead to the overt use of religious symbolism in political movements and legislation that blatantly privileges one religious group over others. In Florida and many red states across America, for example, public proclamations of faith are often a badge of pride, and anti-gay and anti-trans legislation are openly justified through religion and championed from the pulpit and political lectern alike. In some areas, police departments emblazon "In God We Trust" on their vehicles, and courthouses post the Ten Commandments. Many Right-wing government officials across the United States are open about their willingness to join this movement for political gain.

Conversely, in societies where a majority of citizens may be outwardly apathetic toward religion, such as Western Europe, the underlying currents of religion-infused fears and Right-wing fever dreams can still be remarkably resilient but must be hidden in a secular wrapper before they can be fed to the public. Far-right leaders, astutely perceptive of these undercurrents, often exploit them to consolidate power. They tap into deep-seated, religion-based apprehensions about foreigners, LGBTQ+ communities, and feminists, framing these groups as threats to the very fabric of Western civilization. These European far-right leaders don't always deploy overtly religious rhetoric. Instead, they cloak it in the secular language of nationalism. It is a clever ruse where the rhetoric of national identity and cultural preservation is employed to give a socially acceptable veneer to what are essentially religiously motivated fears and biases. The narrative is artfully constructed: national traditions and heritage are under siege by these "other" groups, necessitating a draconian response.

Another critical factor is whether a nation has stronger democratic or authoritarian tendencies. Determining this can be difficult, as we have seen with seemingly strong secular democracies like Israel, where radical religious forces have nevertheless gained ground. In 2022, Israeli Prime Minister Netanyahu, consistently secularly conservative, agreed to promote religiously-driven laws that many Israelis oppose to win over the ultra-religious *United Torah Judaism* party, which represents a growing ultra-religious community, to his fragile coalition government. These laws have included as yet unsuccessful attempts to eliminate the eligibility of non-Jewish grandchildren of Jews to immigrate to Israel, preventing the non-Orthodox from worshiping at the Western Wall, and allowing businesses to discriminate against customers based on religion. Moshe Gafni in the Ministerial Committee for Legislation is also seeking to expand rabbinical courts' powers to decide on a wide range of civil matters.[116] In addition to Netanyahu's plans to curtail the power of the judiciary and claim additional power for politicians, this poses a challenge to liberal democratic institutions and the ability of the high court to provide checks and balances on the Knesset, the Israeli parliament.[117] As someone who has lived, traveled, and worked extensively in Israel and has a great fondness for its people, culture, and values, which in many ways mirror our own, this shift toward Religio-fascism is particularly distressing to observe. Fortunately, the one benefit of the military action in Gaza is that it has momentarily distracted the Israeli government and forestalled many of the religiously radical legislative proposals.

Additionally, when investigating the origins of Religio-fascism, it is imperative to consider any potential social disruptors that could trigger a widespread movement toward religious-based despotism. Sudden economic or political shocks and ensuing instability can create an environment in which people become disillusioned with ossified, slow-moving democratic and secular institutions and are more receptive to extremist ideologies promising quick, radical change or simple, religiously sanctioned solutions to complex problems. For example, in Egypt, during the devastating 1992 Cairo earthquake, the government left a huge vacuum when it failed to provide adequate humanitarian relief, a gap eagerly filled by radical Muslim groups that stepped in offering food and aid, which won over supporters.

Finally, we must assess the level of political power held by the rural segment of society, which is typically bound by religion and tradition and resistant to change, as this can significantly impact the potential for Religio-fascism to take hold. This is true whether we are talking about rural red-state America, which punches above its weight relative to the heavily populated urban areas, or rural Turkey, Iran, and Hungary, where traditionalist and religious peasants represent a majority or large plurality. By examining these factors, we can better understand the forms of religious extremism in our communities, allowing us to take appropriate measures to combat it.

When we seek to identify archetypes of religio-fascist regimes that could be superimposed on Western nations, it is tempting for us to look to modern theocracies like Saudi Arabia and Iran. On its face, this seems reasonable since they give the fullest expression to theocratic despotism in the ruthless brutality and suppression of opposition movements deployed by their religious-political leadership. They are both horrifyingly conformist and socially stifling countries where it is not unreasonable to fear being targeted and murdered like Mahsa Amini in Iran,[118] who was arrested by the morality police for something as innocuous as wearing a headscarf incorrectly or butchered like dissident journalist Jamal Khashoggi in the Saudi Arabian Consulate in Istanbul, Turkey.[119] While these nations represent the pinnacle of religio-fascist tyranny, we must acknowledge that their histories are unique and not analogous to more democratically advanced Western countries.

In many ways, Saudi Arabia is a throwback to the age of divine right monarchy. Its founder, Muhammed Bin Saud, rose to power in the 17th Century with the help of Muḥammad ibn ʿAbd al-Wahhāb, a religious scholar whose strict interpretation of Islamic jurisprudence, known as Wahhābism, has been a defining feature of the Saudi state ever since. Today's Kingdom of Saudi Arabia, established in 1932, is still ruled by the Saud family, and they maintain control through a combination of the monarchy's role as guardian of the two holiest cities of Islam, Mecca and Medina, and the country's vast oil reserves. Without these factors, the regime could not exert the same degree of social, political, and spiritual dominance over its citizens.

During my wife's childhood in Tehran before the revolution, Iran had little history of democracy or modern political forms before succumbing to a theocratic regime. Religious and non-religious citizens alike viewed Shah Mohammad Reza Pahlavi as a puppet of British and U.S. colonial powers, which had overthrown democratically elected prime minister Mohammed Mosadegh with assistance from the CIA in 1953 and reinstated the monarchy. Mosadegh had attempted to modernize the country through widespread reforms but had run afoul of British oil interests when he nationalized the Iranian oil industry. Upon regaining the throne, Pahlavi continued to appease foreign powers while suppressing dissent and resisting democratic reforms, leading to growing resentment among secular Iranians. Since secularists didn't provide a large or powerful enough force to overthrow the Shah, they had to join forces with religionists.

Religious Iranians, conversely, resented the push toward modernization and secularization promoted by Pahlavi. The religious authorities, led by Ayatollah Khomeini, only tolerated support by secularists until they could seize control. The theocratic Islamic Republic that emerged from the revolution in 1978-1979 established a system where religious authorities maintained ultimate control over all aspects of government and society, leaving secularists out in the cold. The secular National Front was subsequently outlawed in 1981, further consolidating the theocratic regime's power.

In Saudi Arabia and Iran, the peculiar ideological structure of Islam, both Sunni and Shia, in which there is no concept of a wall between religion and state but encourages the enmeshment of the two, facilitated the establishment of religio-fascist regimes unabashed in their overt religiosity and puritanical moral codes. Indeed, throughout the Middle East, most nations, whether nominally democratic or monarchical, are deeply enmeshed with Sharia and Islamic authorities and, therefore, offer poor blueprints for would-be Western religio-fascist regimes. Margaret Atwood's *The Handmaid's Tale,* which envisions a Christian variant of this, makes for excellent reading but has a low likelihood of coming to fruition despite the recent attacks on women's bodily autonomy and the rise of violent, hyper-misogynist incels like Eliot Roger[120] and toxic masculinists like Andrew Tate, both of whom have drawn an almost cultic following.[121]

We should seek more applicable models elsewhere if we are looking to predict the form that Religio-fascism might take in the West. Some current religio-fascist regimes, for instance, have arisen in previously pluralistic, relatively secular nations such as India and Turkey, both of which made religiously rightward turns relatively recently under Indian Prime Minister Narendra Modi's Hindu nationalist BJP party and Turkish president Recep Erdogan's Justice and Development Party (AKP).

When I first backpacked across India in 1991, the relationship between Muslim Pakistan and Hindu-majority India was as tense as it's always been, and disagreements over the disputed Kashmir region were palpable. In the states outside of the disputed areas, however, even those on the India-Pakistan border, I could discern little, if any, inclination to violence between Hindus and Muslims. The situation in India today is much more volatile, mainly due to the exploitation of the political ideology known as Hindutva. This dangerous doctrine, formulated by Vinayak Damodar Savarkar in 1923, is marked by ethnic absolutism and Right-wing political extremism. India has always been a massive and complex democracy, trying to address the needs of a diverse people spanning 122 primary languages and nine major religions. In addition, India has four main castes: *Brahmins* (i.e., priests and teachers); *Kshatriyas* (i.e., warriors and rulers); *Vaishyas* (i.e., farmers, traders, merchants); and *Shudras* (i.e., menial laborers), and then *Dalits*, or "outcasts" (i.e., street sweepers and latrine cleaners). The main castes are further divided into thousands of sub-castes, each based on their specific occupation.[122] This tremendous diversity, much like that in the United States, has at once ossified the country's social order while also contributing to its chaotic and dysfunctional politics.

Narendra Modi has provided hope and inspiration to the predominantly rural masses and impoverished citizens who feel left behind in a country with a volatile economy and high youth unemployment. He speaks their language, shares their background, and promises to build a modern, powerful national identity based on Hinduism and Hindu culture. This populism, however, has come at a steep cost. Many Hindus feel that their values and traditions have not received as much respect as those of other groups, particularly the significant Indian Muslim minority. By stoking anti-Muslim resentment, Modi and his BJP Party have been able to establish a Hindu nationalist government while maintaining India's pluralistic and democratic institutions in name only. The parallels to the populist movements in the United States, where rural populations have gravitated toward backward-looking politicians like Trump and his MAGA Republicans, are striking.

The transformation of Turkey into a soft religio-fascist state is also a cautionary tale for Western democracies, even if its population is predominantly Muslim. In the Republic's early years, Mustafa Kemal Ataturk established a secularist, nationalist military rule and embraced progressive reforms and modernization. However, decades of such policies culminated in a traditionalist backlash that brought Recep Tayyip Erdoğan to power in a populist electoral wave. Erdogan's AKP party exploited existing democratic institutions to gain control, much like how Americans elected Donald Trump.

Once in power, the AKP purged the government of secularist military leaders and modernists who espoused closer ties to the EU and Western values. Erdogan also silenced critical media voices and used the media to promote his government's agenda, creating a zombie democracy devoid of serious opposition. This mirrors Donald Trump's plans for his second term in office if reelected. The result for Turkey has been a chauvinistic Islamist agenda that limits free speech and fosters religiosity.

The changes in Turkey have been swift and stark. When I first traveled to the country in 2008, few women wore headscarves, public prayer and expressions of religiosity were rare in cities, and the Hagia Sophia was a museum. However, in subsequent visits, women were often pressured to wear head coverings, bazaar vendors were praying *en masse* in the streets, and the Hagia Sophia is now a mosque. Erdogan is trying to wipe away the vestiges of Ataturk's secular society and resurrect Turkey's Ottoman past. This soft religio-fascist state serves as a warning for Western democracies to remain vigilant in protecting their democratic institutions and values, where Religio-fascism can ride in on a mythical past of Teutonic heroism, Gallic conquest, or American God, guts, and guns Christian nationalism depending on the country.

To understand further how Religio-fascism might manifest in the United States and Western Europe, we can look to Eastern European nations such as Russia, Hungary, and Poland. When they cast off the secular autocracy of the USSR, they reverted to their historical submission to corrupt kleptocratic oligarchs and autocrats whose rule is intertwined with the Catholic and Orthodox Churches. Russia, for instance, maintains a form of church-state symbiosis where the government and the Russian Orthodox Church often collaborate on social and cultural issues. The government supports the church through various means, including financial aid and the construction of churches, while the Russian government looks to the church for moral guidance and legitimacy.

In these Eastern European nations, religion is used as an instrument to legitimize zombie democracies and stoke fear of traditional out-groups such as immigrants, Muslims, gays, and feminists. Recent amendments to the Hungarian Constitution, for example, impose a "Christian cultural identity" on the country and promote a legal definition of "the family" that excludes same-sex couples and transgender individuals. Such policies have earned praise from Christian nationalists in the United States, with Viktor Orban speaking to great fanfare at the Conservative Political Action Conference in Texas in 2022.[123] He is now trying to foment a populist uprising in the EU against what he considers the immoral urban elites.

These nations illustrate how strongmen can manipulate religious sentiments to maintain power while suppressing opposition and dissent. While they lack the democratic traditions of Western democracies, their experience provides insight into how Religio-fascism might play out in Western democracies where conservative Christian sentiment and ethnonationalism are on the rise, especially in the US where

MAGA radicalism and anti-immigrant sentiment have fused with a uniquely American "muscular Christianity" that completely ignores Sermon on the Mount 'wokeness' in favor of Old Testament vengeance and brutality.

With its ambiguous language, the U.S. Constitution has invited creative and revanchist legal interpretations that favor religion. The current Supreme Court, dominated by ultra-conservative Catholics selected by the *Federalist Society,* has shown a distinct lack of respect for religious pluralism. Recent decisions like *Dobbs v. Jackson Women's Health Organization*, which overturned 50 years of precedent set by *Roe v. Wade*, were motivated not by solid legal reasoning but by the religious faith and anti-choice sentiments of the conservative Catholic justices and conservative lobbyists who pressured them. Justice Clarence Thomas has indicated his willingness to revisit other precedents based on the 14th Amendment protections of the right to privacy, but only those that he deems contrary to his faith, such as *Obergefell v. Hodges* that granted the right to same-sex marriage in 2015, *Lawrence v. Texas* that struck down sodomy laws in 2003, and *Griswold v. Connecticut*, which in 1965 granted the right to married couples to buy and use contraceptives without government restriction.

If the right to privacy is in jeopardy, extrapolated as it has been from the 14th Amendment, the separation of church and state, inferred from the anti-establishment clause of the First Amendment and various correspondence from the Founding Fathers that protect atheists from religious intrusion, may not be far behind.

Conservatives have manipulated the U.S. electoral system to amplify the power of rural, often more religiously traditionalist, voters who were already wielding disproportionate power due to the anti-majoritarian Electoral College and the disproportionate representation of the Senate that favors smaller states. The rightward tilt of the legislative and judicial branches of government results from the *Heritage Foundation's* grip over Republican federal and state legislative priorities. They virtually guarantee a steady stream of extreme pro-Christian legal cases, which run counter to the values of the majority of the U.S. public, wend their way through the court system. Together, these factors are slowly eroding the wall of separation between church and state.

Despite many Western Europeans claiming their societies are secular today and pointing to polls to support their claim, the truth is that religious bigotries have only been sublimated over time, lurking just beneath the surface, ready to be exploited by authoritarian zealots seeking political power. The abiding anti-Indian, anti-Pakistani, and anti-Eastern European sentiment in Britain, the relegation of Muslim and African immigrants to second-class citizenship on the continent, and the barely contained antisemitism across Europe are all vestiges of ancient, deep-seated religious hostilities. Crypto-Christianity, disguised as ultra-Right-wing secularism, would, in all probability, reign supreme in much of Western Europe if neo-fascists have their way.

Indeed, Crypto-religious movements are rising in bastions of secularism like France, where neo-fascist parties like Marine Le Pen's National Rally party have gained strength.

Though such parties claim to uphold secularism, they espouse many of the same prejudices against non-white, non-Catholic immigrants, particularly Muslims, favored by religiously extremist regimes. This bias is concealed within the guise of safeguarding French national identity and customs, which are closely intertwined with religion. While these parties have tried to distance themselves from their anti-Semitic and anti-LGBTQ+ roots, they can easily backslide into religious chauvinism during crises, as they have since the October 7th, 2023, terrorist attacks in Israel by Hamas.

In Western authoritarian political movements, whether driven by overtly religious or Crypto-religious platforms, fear of cultural change, economic inequality, and loss of social and ethnic privilege often motivate their supporters. These fears are on the rise in the West as secular governments struggle to address pressing issues like climate change and social and economic dislocation caused by globalism while giving voice to historically marginalized groups. These seismic shifts instill fear and resentment among privileged in-group members, particularly white Christians, and may ultimately lead to a government dominated by religious authoritarians under the right conditions.

We atheists must remain vigilant against the political exploitation of religion, whether as the primary driving force in political decision-making or as a tool for anti-democratic tendencies. Religio-fascism does not always appear overtly religious, as it can also be disguised in secular clothing, with religious prejudices repackaged for modern audiences.

There are many signs that religious extremism is on the rise of which atheists need to be aware:

1. **Escalating religious intolerance:** Extremist religionists often reject any form of compromise with moderate believers and nonbelievers alike. They view recent progressive changes and societal pluralism as threats driven by secular, anti-religious forces posing a dire threat to the nation and their way of life. A deep-seated nostalgia for an idealized past and vilification of their secular enemies makes compromise nearly impossible.
2. **The politicization of religion:** A clear indicator is when religious leaders, who are traditionally neutral, begin to participate in politics actively. This includes priests and ministers endorsing political candidates and legislation from the pulpit and serving as advisors to Right-wing politicians. This politicization often occurs not out of their own volition but in response to the radicalization within their congregations. As a result, politicians adopt religious symbols to enhance their appeal to them. This leads to the widespread rise of religious nationalism, where religion becomes deeply entangled with national identity and citizenship, giving rise to movements like Christian nationalism, Radical Islam, Hindutva, and Ultra Zionism.

3. **The emergence of populist demagogues:** The rise of demagogues, who often use religious and nationalistic language and symbols and push religious agendas that stoke the culture wars, signifies growing intolerance. These figures claim to represent the "godly" people, giving them a sense of representation, albeit often without any real power. The demagogues consolidate power for themselves while appearing as champions of religion and traditional values.
4. **Manipulation of critical institutions:** Religious, primarily Right-wing politicians and their supporters actively seek to dominate or manipulate crucial societal institutions. They focus on those that can place a religious lens on public opinion and perception, such as the media (including social media), education, the arts, local politics, and business sectors. Their goal is to cultivate future generations of obedient and religious citizens and reshape society's beliefs and values, circumventing parents to target impressionable children who are future voters, assuming some vestiges of democracy remain.
5. **Suppression of dissent:** Religio-fascist regimes resort to censorship, media control, intimidation, and even violence to silence opposing secular voices. These voices include members of minority religions, nonbelievers, political opponents, and protesters, effectively stifling any form of dissent.

6. **Erosion of civil liberties:** One of the hallmarks of a religio-fascist rise is the curtailment of fundamental civil liberties. This includes freedom of expression, religion, assembly, and association, which are essential to provide a voice to those otherwise politically disenfranchised, like atheists.
7. **The undermining of the independent media and civil society:** By obstructing the free flow of information and impeding citizens' ability to hold leaders accountable, religio-fascists can control the media narrative and manipulate democratic processes. Obstruction can include tampering with elections and other democratic institutions while maintaining an outward appearance of support for democratic norms.

Way #20

Understand the Psychology Behind Religio-fascism

Collective fear stimulates herd instinct, and tends to produce ferocity toward those who are not regarded as members of the herd.[124]

Bertrand Russell

TO ESTABLISH RELIGIOUSLY oppressive political movements effectively, psychological drivers that attract and retain a critical mass of true believers must accompany the political dynamics. Even the most oppressive regime cannot maintain dominance without the tacit approval and emotional buy-in of the governed, or at least those who wield enough economic and social clout to keep the rest in check. Unfortunately, groups with tight in-group/out-group orientations and those open to authoritarian social controls are often the most fervent supporters and defenders of religio-fascist regimes.

These supporters include many CEOs and small business owners, consumers of highly polarized social media and news, and conservative social groups such as the NRA, each of which has a vested economic or political interest in maintaining law and order and the status quo or is emotionally and intellectually hard-wired for authoritarianism. Moreover, it often includes law enforcement and military personnel who lean right and whose support is vital in seizing and maintaining authoritarian control under both autocratic secular and religious regimes. Although these groups are not the majority, they command disproportionate economic, legal, and coercive power in society relative to their numbers. Sadly, they also possess and garner uncritical social respect and unearned political influence. Given their worldviews, job roles, and values, they exhibit more authoritarian tendencies than the general population. As a result, they often become the foundation of any totalitarian regime, especially its leadership. Their strict adherence to rules and obedience to the chain of command frequently translates into following an autocrat's lead in oppressing immigrants, minorities, and religious, political, and sexual dissidents, including atheists, if they are framed as a threat to the nation and social stability. Their obedience often results in the "I was just following orders" defense.

Matthew C. MacWilliams, author of *On Fascism: 12 Lessons from American History,* conducted a national survey in 2016 on authoritarianism in the United States. He found that 18% of Americans were highly disposed to authoritarianism, while an additional 23% were somewhat disposed, resulting in about 40% of Americans who favor obedience and conformity over freedom and diversity. They don't necessarily outright prefer an autocracy over democracy, although some studies have exposed a growing disenchantment with democracy and an openness to alternatives, even among a startling percentage of younger Americans. Given the right circumstances, these people can be triggered by the charisma of a populist who validates their angst and prejudices or by an intolerable degree of social instability brought on by political, economic, climatic, or other shocks. It makes sense to understand what mental framework guides both hardcore authoritarians and those who might consent to it in times of emergency.

To explain the motivators of authoritarian-oriented people, I often like to use the analogy of teenagers. For those of you who have had them, you know what I'm talking about: teens on their own typically lack the rational judgment one would expect from mature adults. Their minds and emotions are unpredictable and volatile as their brains are still developing. Assuming halfway competent parents raise them, however, they are by and large striving to be ethically upstanding and defer, if grudgingly, to their parents; otherwise, most wouldn't mature as they typically do into law-abiding and productive citizens, both necessary prerequisites for successful interpersonal relationships and a functioning society.

The trouble starts when teenagers roam the streets unsupervised, seeking belonging and guidance and exhibiting what sociologists term in-group/out-group tendencies or, more colloquially, a herd mentality. Those within the group abide by whatever arbitrary rules they or a self-proclaimed leader set to define the group, which then becomes the collective authority that guides them. The in-group can define itself as jocks, popular kids, goths, or whatnot, depending on the image they are trying to project. These identities are then vigorously enforced through the collective authority manifested as peer pressure, and more often than not, members direct their anger toward those outside of the tribe.

For instance, an average teenager on their own would most likely never think to commit an assault or seriously break the law. Groups of average teenagers, however, can and often are compelled to do so. To see this group dynamic in action, we need only look at illegal auto sideshow events in the city of San Jose near where I live, where average teens illegally block streets and freeways and congregate *en masse* to watch others race and perform stunts in their cars. Many participants exhibit group-driven anti-social behavior that they wouldn't otherwise do on their own, placing pedestrians in danger of being run over, drinking illegally, or even shooting or assaulting bystanders.

You can probably see where I'm going with this. Authoritarian and religiously extremist organizations and regimes, like teen cliques, take advantage of the natural human propensity toward in-group/out-group behavior, especially among authoritarian-oriented individuals and organizations that value conformity, to make otherwise sensible individuals complicit in their extremism. When movements gain critical mass, many of those not given to authoritarianism yet want to be part of the in-group and fear ostracization will frequently go along for the ride.

This tendency is magnified tenfold with the introduction

of religion, given the emotional and intellectual sway religious ideologies maintain over their believers. To one degree or another, whether Iranian mullahs, white Christian nationalist leaders, or Hindu nationalist politicians, they seek to impose their peculiar vision for the nation on nominal co-religionists and those oriented toward authoritarianism through guilt, fear, and intimidation or by offering them positions of power in the new regime. With moderates co-opted, they can, as a group, freely persecute and oppress those in the minority, like atheists.

While the beliefs of moderate religionists typically maintain a legitimate foundation in universal ethical principles shared by atheists, such as reciprocity or the golden rule (at least when dealing with members of their in-group), they, much like teens, also include arbitrary, often nonsensical rules to define their in-group identity and to test members' fealty to religious authorities. This demarcation for believers, in general, may consist of "virtue signaling" by way of refraining from consuming pork, circumcising boys, or enforcing the hijab, depending on the specific tradition.

The difference for religio-fascists is that while, at most, moderate religious leaders may wield the threat of eternal damnation in the afterlife, social shaming, or even shunning to enforce conformity among their tribe, politicized religious movements go many steps further using everything from their control of the courts and law enforcement to the threat of extra-judicial action by vigilantes to enforce compliance and punish enemies.

Unfortunately, the degree to which even members of

the in-group must conform in a religio-fascist-run society to avoid ostracization must grow increasingly extreme over time for it to perpetuate itself. As we've seen with the political right in the United States, leaders and followers constantly strive for ever more extreme positions and greater ideological purity to ensure that they maintain outrage and fear at the highest level. Another example is the Iranian regime, which has grown increasingly more draconian since its inception in 1978, not less, in its often violent punishment of women for not wearing the *hijab* as well as other perceived immoral behavior. The regime under its current president, Ebrahim Raisi, deems the enforcement of the hijab as the lynchpin for maintaining the entire theocratic order when it was not a pressing issue at the beginning of the regime.

Eventually, to question even the most nonsensical of a religiously authoritarian government's dictates would be to admit that the anointed religion that undergirds it is not the only source of divine truth. Refusing to impose these beliefs on others, either peaceably through the power of law or violently at the muzzle of a gun, would be a virtual act of apostasy and treason. It is a self-reinforcing cycle of increasing extremism. For atheists or any religious out-group, that means that they may tolerate us at first but will typically ensure our rights erode over time with growing fanaticism and more stringent purity tests.

Throughout history, believers, including moderates, have been guilted into these fanatical movements and even subsequently whipped into a mob-like frenzy through often manufactured fear of out-groups by leaders thirsting for power. The results are all too familiar: Crusades, *pogroms*, inquisitions, and the Holocaust. The upshot today is that as atheists, we should remain vigilant against politicized religion but should also refrain from the otherization of believers lest we fall into the same in-group/out-group dynamic. To do otherwise would be the height of hypocrisy. We must increase our awareness of the dysfunctional group dynamics of the religio-fascists emerging around us and identify the scapegoats and out-group enemy ideologies that may become targets for disenfranchisement or persecution. As atheists, we aren't alone and should continuously defend the rights of other religious and social dissidents since their fight is our fight.

Identifying groups and individuals who are in the throes of or are susceptible to religio-fascist groupthink rather than making decisions based on a careful evaluation of the facts or alternative viewpoints is critical for atheists to be able to predict who may be likely to pose a threat. Several factors can contribute to such groupthink, which we can use to identify friends, family, and acquaintances who may be susceptible to it:

1. **They prefer conformity:** In human societies, the tendency to groupthink has deep evolutionary roots to protect them from unknown and external threats. Today, this conformity is pronounced in groups exhibiting high cohesion and cultural similarity and among individuals with a strong desire to belong. Consider, for instance, the segments of white America that nostalgically yearn for a bygone era marked by racial homogeneity in their neighborhoods,

schools, and workplaces, a time of little religious and ideological diversity. Their discontent with today's multicultural society echoes a broader human story of resistance to change and unfamiliarity.

Similarly, religious fundamentalists, including radical Islamists and members of insular sects, demonstrate a solid commitment to uniformity and rigorous observance of their beliefs and practices. This strict adherence acts as a tool for strengthening group unity, clearly distinguishing members from those outside the group. For instance, in Islam, unity is fostered through practices such as obligatory prayer five times a day, the growing of beards, and the wearing of veils by women. Meanwhile, Orthodox Judaism emphasizes the wearing of kippahs and tallits and the use of tefillin during prayer. These practices not only embody their spiritual convictions but also serve to mark a clear boundary between followers and non-followers, thus reinforcing a sense of community identity.

In the United States and Europe, Muslims and Jewish people, alongside atheists, often find themselves marginalized. This shared experience of otherness somewhat mitigates their potential threat. For atheists, notably, the perceived threat from minority religious groups correlates with the latter's proximity to societal power structures and dominant cultural norms.

Many secular groups, including militias, sports

fanatics, conspiracy theorists, and political parties, also exhibit similar patterns of strong internal cohesion and a clear separation from outsiders. With a mix of shared beliefs and activities, these groups demonstrate unwavering allegiance to their in-group, though typically to a lesser degree than religious ones.

2. **They are intolerant of dissent:** This dynamic is not exclusive to religious groups but is particularly pronounced where expressing divergent views risks backlash or punitive measures. Of course, not all religious groups, even those of a conservative or traditionalist bent, are inherently resistant to dissent. Take, for instance, the Catholic Church, with its rich history of theological debate. Despite a framework that resists doctrinal contradictions, there is a latitude for diverse perspectives within certain boundaries. Intriguingly, even core Catholic doctrines, like those concerning abortion, homosexuality, and contraception, are not uniformly adhered to by a significant portion of Catholics.

The allure of secret group knowledge is not confined to the religious sphere. It also finds resonance in secular groups drawn to esoteric "truths" known only to them. This allure can be seen in various groups across the political spectrum. On the far right, there are QAnon adherents, election denialists, and school shooting conspiracy theorists; on the far left, those who believe in chemtrails; and across both sides, the anti-vaccination movement. These groups are tightly bound by a shared belief in irrational narratives that brook no dissent.

3. **They may share a common distrust of institutions and rejection of the status quo:** In political science, the *Horseshoe Theory* suggests a surprising similarity between the far ends of the political spectrum. Beyond their propensity for irrational conspiracy theories, both extremes share a deep-seated distrust of the established order. This distrust can potentially make individuals from both the far-right and far-left susceptible to the promises of a religio-fascist regime that offers a departure from the current status quo and an alternative one that conforms to their ideals. This inclination highlights a broader human tendency: the search for change and the allure of narratives that promise a radical break from an intolerable present, irrespective of their alignment with traditional political ideologies.
4. **They show undue deference to authority figures:** Groupthink often emerges in environments dominated by authoritarians. Wielding considerable influence, they usually become the primary decision-makers, inadvertently stifling dissent and critical thinking in their wake. This dynamic is mainly observable in religion, where leaders of charismatic sects, media-savvy mega-churches, and various white evangelical groups captivate their congregations with their teachings and the compelling force of their personalities.

Contrastingly, other religious traditions like Catholicism, Eastern Orthodox Christianity, and Orthodox Judaism lean on the pillars of tradition, ritual, and intellectual heritage to assert their authority. The charisma of individual leaders, with some exceptions, plays a less central role here. Yet, these religious systems can inadvertently prime their followers for receptivity to authoritarian political systems.

5. **They are willing to use stereotypes:** Groupthink strengthens when members rely more on stereotypes and preconceptions about "others" rather than considering the nuanced perspectives and unique experiences of those outside their circle. This tendency is not limited to religious and secular communities but is a pervasive aspect of human social behavior. Individuals, whether part of a defined group or not, often fall into the trap of stereotyping, thus opening vast segments of society to the dangers of vilifying those deemed outsiders.

   The tendency to negatively stereotype out-groups is deeply embedded in our collective consciousness. This propensity is not merely a contemporary phenomenon but a historical constant that those in power have often manipulated. Authoritarians have exploited these prejudices for centuries to establish common enemies and unite followers under shared disdain. In doing so, they simplify complex social realities into binary us-versus-them narratives, which are more accessible for the masses to digest and rally behind.

This process of othering not only serves as a powerful tool for solidifying group identity but also paves the way for justifying acts of exclusion, discrimination, and even violence. By casting certain groups as fundamentally different or threatening, authoritarians find an opportunity to justify their actions against out-groups. The scapegoated communities become not just outsiders but also targets, bearing the brunt of societal fears and frustrations.

WAY #21
ALWAYS BE SKEPTICAL OF RIGHT-WING POLITICS

I'm a Christian, a conservative, and a Republican, in that order.

MIKE PENCE

ONE OF MY wife's friends, a native Hispanic Texan, is one of the most religious and traditional Catholics I've ever met. Almost always formally dressed, with a gold crucifix around her neck, "Camila" goes to mass several times during the work week and attends with her family every Sunday. Her daughter sings in the choir and attends a local private Christian school. The entire family strictly observes Lent, eats fish on Fridays, and bears sooty gray crosses on their foreheads during Ash Wednesday. Their lives outside of the Church are as traditional as they are inside. Her husband, "Miguel," has spent his entire career in law enforcement. By any measure, they would be ideal Republicans, MAGA activists even, yet they exhibit a high degree of religious, social, and political tolerance.

The reality is that there are many highly religious people on all points of the political spectrum. In the cases where religion has played a vital political role on the left, it has typically fulfilled social and economic justice goals, not tried to promote a socially regressive agenda or an authoritarian candidate or government. People of deep faith also serve as left-leaning politicians at all levels of government. Pelosi, Biden, and the entire Congress are far more religious than the American population as a whole.[125] Despite the perception of the party being hostile to religion, the reverse is the case. Instead of the Old Testament punishments and prosperity gospel that inform the right, the left's religiosity often drives their support for enhancing the social safety net for the poor, socialized medicine, or worker safety legislation based on biblical exhortations to help people experiencing poverty and the disempowered. They don't privilege one religion over another. That is typically the province of Right-wing movements and regimes.

That is not to say that there is a shortage of brutal authoritarian left-wing movements that eschew religion. But the difference between most Right-wing regimes and left-wing ones is that the right embraces religion to oppress and brutalize its citizens more effectively. In contrast, left-wing governments don't want religion competing with them for the right to exploit their citizens. From Cuba to China to the USSR, we have seen our fair share of leftist governments that have made the lives of their people miserable, believer and nonbeliever alike. Leftist authoritarians, like their Right-wing counterparts, are typically motivated by a will to power, but while the extreme left tends to be enamored of rigid, materialistic ideologies like Marxism, the radical right invariably gravitates toward the rigidity of religion. They do so because they typically share similar values with religious institutions, such as a reverence for tradition, hierarchy, and strict maintenance of social control.

For religio-fascists, the ultimate goal is to either claim the government rules with the religious sanction of submissive religious authorities, as in Russia today, or entirely place the government and other institutions under the direct control of politicians who are true believers, such as those in the United States who would usher in Dominionist rule. In either case, by claiming an unchanging patriarchal hierarchy of obedience with a deity at the top followed by religious authorities, down through the government, oligarchs, men, their wives, and finally children, religio-fascists seek to grip all aspects of society tightly in their clenched fists.

Both Right-wing religio-fascist and left-wing authoritarian regimes are arguably unethical, destructive, and antithetical to human rights relative to pluralistic democratic societies. Yet, while left-wing authoritarianism is currently in relative decline, save perhaps for China (Though its current economic weakness and population decline may eventually change that), Religio-fascism is in ascendance on virtually every continent.[126]

As atheists, regardless of whether we are conservative

or liberal, several issues should be considered when deciding who to vote for in an election, especially as liberalism and progressivism are connected in the minds of religionists with irreligiosity:

1. **Work to keep church and state separate:** Separating church and state is a cornerstone of modern governance and vital for preserving individual rights and freedoms. While seemingly self-evident, this principle requires constant vigilance and active reinforcement. When voting, we must identify and only support candidates who are staunch advocates of this separation, ensuring that religious beliefs do not infiltrate government decisions and policies. The rising tide of religio-fascist politicians underscores the importance of this separation.

   The emergence of figures like Colorado Representative Lauren Boebert and Georgia Representative Marjorie Taylor Greene, alongside justices Samuel Alito and Clarence Thomas, signals a movement to erode the boundary that keeps religion in its lane. Their actions and rhetoric often reflect an agenda that seeks to integrate religious dogma into the fabric of governance. This trend should serve as a clarion call not only to liberal atheists but also to conservatives.

   This development is not merely a political maneuver but a fundamental shift in governance approach with far-reaching implications. When religious ideology begins to dictate state policies, it often leads to the marginalization of minority beliefs, the erosion of scientific reasoning in policy-making, and the imposition of a singular moral framework on a diverse populace. This encroachment of religion into the state's affairs risks transforming inclusive democracies into exclusive religio-fascist regimes, which suppress secular voices and curtail individual liberties.

The intertwining of religious dogma with state power has been a recurring theme historically, often leading to periods of intolerance, intellectual stagnation, and social unrest. The call to action is clear: those who cherish these values must remain vigilant and proactive in supporting leaders and policies that uphold secularism.

2. **Fight "religious freedom" legislation in all its forms:** Supporting candidates committed to protecting the rights of all religious groups is a critical aspect of fostering a pluralistic and inclusive society. However, this support should not extend to so-called "religious freedom" laws in the United States, which often serve to camouflage legislation that, in practice, privileges certain religious viewpoints, predominantly Christian, at the expense of other beliefs and the non-religious. This nuanced understanding of religious freedom versus privilege is vital in navigating contemporary social and political issues.

   These "religious freedom" laws frequently allow for the enactment of policies under which individuals and businesses can refuse services or deny rights based on their religious beliefs. At the heart of this issue is a conflict between the right to religious expression and the right to equal treatment under the law. More broadly, the challenge lies in balancing these rights in a way that does not infringe upon the freedoms and well-being of others. In a pluralistic society, the government should safeguard the individual's right to practice religion, but this right reaches its limits when it begins to impede on the rights of others, including us atheists.

3. **Remain vigilant against all types of discrimination:** Fighting discrimination is not just a moral imperative but a pragmatic strategy to preserve our rights as atheists. Discrimination, in its myriad forms, often precedes a rise in religious bias and intolerance. This phenomenon is not isolated; it reflects deeper undercurrents in the collective human psyche and societal dynamics.

   Candidates' positions on issues related to religion, race, gender, sexual orientation, or other criteria serve as a sign of their ability to either perpetuate or break down existing biases and inequalities. We should support candidates dedicated to eliminating discrimination and promoting equality for everyone, atheists included. It's an essential truth that any system built to limit the rights of one group inherently has the potential to harm any other group, even those who might believe they are unaffected.

4. **Education is the best defense against extreme religiosity:** Look for candidates who support science-based education and freedom of expression and will work to keep religious beliefs out of the classroom. Given recent attempts by religious conservatives like the recently disgraced *Moms for Liberty* and other activists to take over school boards at the K-12 level, as well as states such as Florida, which have placed limits on intellectual inquiry (Anti-Woke laws, etc.), this is critical since the educational system is where children are either taught the value of unfettered inquiry or indoctrinated into oppressive ideologies by authoritarians from high-profile politicians to grass-roots movements.
5. **Remain open-minded on social issues:** The opposition to freedoms related to reproductive rights, gender equality, and sexual orientation intersects with religious doctrine. When transformed into law and public policy, such opposition does not merely affect those directly involved but has a cascading effect on the broader society. It sets precedents that religious authoritarians can leverage to impose similar restrictions on other groups, including atheists and secularists, under the guise of upholding moral and spiritual standards. This phenomenon is not just about regulating personal choices; it's about the imposition of a specific worldview on the diverse tapestry of human society.

    The issue transcends individual rights; it touches

upon what it means to be a free-thinking and autonomous being in a complex, interconnected world. Allowing laws that curtail women's rights over their bodies or restrict who one can love and marry is not merely a legislative action; it is an act that further entrenches a religiously informed mindset into our social fabric and collective psyche that ultimately oppresses our rights as atheists.

Way #22

Be Aware That Modernity Can Inflame Religiosity

Modernity is not necessarily secularizing; it is necessarily pluralizing. Modernity creates a new situation for belief; it creates a market situation for religion. Thus, the believer may find himself or herself competing with other religious offerings in the marketplace.[127]

Peter L. Berger, Sociologist

AS I EMBARKED on my journey through graduate school, I harbored lofty ambitions of mastering a significant swath of the vast corpus of historical knowledge and acquiring linguistic fluency in multiple languages. After delving deeper into my studies for a couple of years, a humbling realization dawned on me. Rather than a sudden flash of enlightenment or a breakthrough in understanding, I discovered the daunting scope of my ignorance and the vast expanses of knowledge that lay beyond my reach and would always remain so. The universe and our understanding of it constantly evolve, and no matter how much we learn, there will always be more to explore and uncover. Yet, far from being a source of despair, this insight fills me with awe and wonder at the infinite possibilities that await us. As an atheist and a seeker of knowledge, I find solace in the understanding that the world is a dynamic and ever-changing place ripe for perpetual exploration and discovery.

Such a revelation can be highly discomfiting for traditionalists less at home with the rapid pace of social and scientific change or the prospect of facing the great unknown without a divine guiding hand. The rise of reactionary politics and a yearning to return to a fictional past where people felt their world was eminently understandable has been the result. The global economy is becoming increasingly technology-dependent and requires a high degree of skill and flexibility to navigate successfully, characteristics most people don't possess. Skilled and semi-skilled laborers in fields such as agriculture, energy, mineral extraction, and manufacturing now find themselves relegated to the low-paying, low-prestige service jobs that are their last refuge as many of the jobs they were trained for get automated out of existence. For those raised on the American Dream that promised the average family a middle-class lifestyle even with minimal education and a modicum of effort, they now often find themselves disillusioned, humiliated, and angry. While many atheists have been left behind as well, much of the blame has been laid at our feet and those of liberals in general, whom the left-behind condemn for pushing change too far too fast. We are perceived, rightly or wrongly, to be substituting scientific advancement, secularism, and technology for good old-fashioned hard work, family, and faith.

Though still lagging in terms of pay and positions of authority, women, minorities, and immigrants have made inroads into conventional white male roles, fueling much of the disillusionment in the traditional patriarchy that had white men at the top of the pecking order but is now crumbling beneath them. Again, godless technocrats are the villains in the fevered minds of religionists, challenging traditional values and the natural order. The mere fact that women or minorities are moving into specific jobs and industries, as well as entering universities at a higher rate than white males, is seen to be devaluing those endeavors and institutions, which, in turn, white males perceive as devaluing them if they also hold those jobs or educational credentials.

The pace of cultural change has been nothing short of breathtaking for many. Just a decade ago, *Don't Ask, Don't Tell* was still in effect in the military, and gay marriage was considered a political taboo even among liberals like Barack Obama. Yet, in 2015, three short years after the landmark *Lawrence v. Texas* case that finally overturned state anti-sodomy laws, the U.S. Supreme Court legalized same-sex marriage in *Obergefell v. Hodges*. This chain of events marks a remarkable reversal for a nation with such a recent history of legally codified intolerance toward the LGBTQ+ community.

The battle, sadly, is far from over. Transgender rights, in particular, remain a contentious issue. Despite most Americans' support for protections for transgender individuals, many still cling to the traditional gender binary and feel uneasy with the rapid pace of change on this issue. This discomfort has manifested itself in a wave of bathroom bills, attempts to ban drag queen shows, and even bans in schools on books that dare acknowledge the reality of gender fluidity. These regressive measures are a backlash against progress, and we must continue to fight against a rollback of the transgender laws and rights we have won so far, or else they will target gay marriage, civil rights, women's rights, and freedom from religion next.

Is it any wonder that some Americans have experienced whiplash with the rapid pace of change and have been driven into the arms of MAGA radicals and white evangelical megachurches seeking to reverse their fortunes and join the warm embrace of a familiar white Christian community seeking to reclaim the past? Even Gen Z is at a tipping point that could either continue to see them become increasingly secularized and tolerant or snap back into a Third Great Christian Awakening to revive our historical over-religiosity if we aren't careful. The fulcrum is not traditional social structures but society's ability to provide the sense of community and belonging that we naturally crave as humans, but which has become less effective since Gen Z was born. That 50,000 young people descended on a small chapel on the Kentucky campus of Ashbury University for an impromptu two-week Christian revival is an ominous sign for atheists and shouldn't be taken as a one-off.[128] Social alienation resulting from numerous factors such as social media, which has reduced friendships from in-person engagements to remote Zoom meetings and text messages, is driving some lonely young people into the arms of religion, often the most charismatic or extremist sects that offer the emotional depth and passion missing from their online relationships.

Religionists are also trying to take over university boards and influence curriculums outright, such as Governor Ron DeSantis, who successfully took over and transformed New College in Florida from a center for alternative learning into a conservative educational flagship. Such traditionalist, Christian takeovers could spread to other campuses, including non-religious ones.[129] If we don't become more vigilant, student religious radicals and religious politicians may together quickly transform universities from centers of learning to Christian indoctrination centers that put atheists and secular education out into the cold.

Sexual relationships, too, have been depersonalized through a pick-up culture driven by *Tinder* and *Grindr*, as well as the ready access to porn through *Pornhub* and *Youporn*. Even an atheist like me, who may not consider such sexual outlets as inherently immoral, would be obtuse to deny the social alienation that these platforms have brought about for some.

Further, the under-thirty cohort has seen their share of trauma, including school shootings, economic uncertainty after the great recession, the rising costs of college loans, and the disruption of their life plans due to COVID-19 lockdowns. Political authorities have provided few solutions. To stave off losing yet another generation to enthrallment by religion, we as atheists need to do the following:

1. **Feed the need for meaning, purpose, and belonging:** In an increasingly secular and materialistic world, many people are turning to religion, especially more radicalized and extreme forms, as a source of meaning and purpose. Religious traditions often provide a framework for understanding the world and our place in it and offer a sense of community and belonging, perhaps one of the few positive aspects of religion. Religion is not required to build a sense of belonging; however, historically, the two have been intertwined. Coercion and guilt can be powerful forces that drive people to church. As atheists, we need to build a community not dependent on in-group/out-group divisions or coercion and guilt, perhaps organized instead around providing a guiding hand through social dislocation and religious extremism.

   Some have already begun to do this online and in real life. Among the groups springing up, *Sunday Assembly* is a non-religious gathering founded in January 2013 in London, England, and has built forty-eight chapters in the United States and Europe. The gathering is mostly for non-religious people who want a communal experience similar to that of a religious church, though religious people are also welcome. *The Oasis Network* similarly provides Sunday meetings to discuss real-world principles supported by evidence and free thought.

2. **Reframe social and political change as a net positive:** Reframing social and political change as a positive force is a significant but necessary endeavor. It requires a nuanced understanding of the historical, psychological, and technological dimensions that shape human civilizations. We atheists, or anyone advocating progress and rationality, face the challenge of compellingly and empathetically presenting the benefits of technological and social evolution to those apprehensive about these changes or suffering their adverse effects.

   The resistance to change, often exhibited by traditionalist groups, is rooted in a complex web of psychological, cultural, and existential anxieties. This resistance is not merely a rejection of new technologies or social norms but a more profound expression of fear about losing one's identity and place in a rapidly transforming world. It becomes even more deeply entrenched if they are also losing jobs or experiencing increased crime or incivility in their communities. Herein lies the critical task for advocates of progress: to articulate a vision of the future that acknowledges their fears while simultaneously demonstrating the tangible benefits of embracing change.

   In this context, technological and social advancements should be presented not as forces that undermine traditional values but as opportunities to enhance human well-being and societal cohesion. This narrative needs to be interwoven with a strategy that aids traditionalists in navigating the transition to a more advanced and inclusive society. It involves empathetic engagement and a deep understanding of the concerns and values that define these communities. Failure to constructively engage with these groups could result in their further alienation and push them towards religio-fascist ideologies, which exploit their fears and offer simplistic, albeit destructive, solutions.

Way #23

Know How Perceived Decline Triggers Religio-fascism

Reality doesn't bite, rather our perception of reality bites.[130]

Anthony J. D'Angelo

SINCE THE DAWN of human societies, we have lamented the decline of civilization. Ancient Greeks and Romans perceived a decline from the Golden Age of heroes and virtue to their time of diminished valor. During the medieval period, people perceived society as being deeply corrupted, leading them to anticipate eagerly the second coming of Jesus. My parents occasionally romanticize the 1950s as the epitome of morality and good manners. I'm sure twenty years from now, my generation will look back to the days of *Depeche Mode*, *Members Only* jackets, and unadulterated *Ecstasy* as the peak of human civilization.

Societal decline can take many forms. It can manifest as economic stagnation, increased crime, and violence, or a loss of cultural and moral values. A sudden shock like war, economic depression, or natural catastrophe can also precipitate it. Whether slow-moving or sudden, such decline can lead people to turn to a strongman leader and traditional religious organizations that often promise to restore order and security.

But what happens when people only perceive a decline in society, even if it isn't rooted in objective reality? That is the state in which we currently find ourselves, where social media and 24/7 sensationalist news thrive on magnifying our every fear for ratings and that politicized religion then exploits. The United States and much of the developing world are far better off than thirty years ago. Violent crime, while on an uptick between 2020 and 2021, is now dropping and is far below the crime rates of the drug and gang-ridden early nineties. According to the Federal Bureau of Investigation's (FBI) Uniform Crime Reports, the overall violent crime rate in the United States dropped by 50% between 1990 and 2021.[131]

Health has also improved in the United States. Advances in medical technology have led to better treatments and more effective medications. According to the CDC, death rates from cancer dropped 27% between 2001 and 2020.[132] Additionally, the rate of uninsured Americans has dropped significantly, thanks to the Affordable Care Act (ACA), implemented in 2010, which enables us to ensure better health outcomes.

While income inequality has increased, there has been steady GDP growth, with only a few short-lived recessions in recent memory and an unfortunate bout of inflation just after the COVID-19 pandemic subsided. This growth has led to more jobs, higher wages, and increased prosperity for many Americans. The unemployment rate has also improved, having been on a downward trend, reaching a 54-year low of 3.4% in 2023.[133] More Americans have been able to find work and provide for their families than ever before.

The end of the Cold War in the early 1990s marked a significant decrease in large-scale conflicts between major world powers. Of course, the number of smaller-scale disputes and acts of terrorism have continued in recent years, particularly in the Ukraine, the Middle East, and Africa. But at the moment, the United States and Western Europe are not engaged in any significant hostilities where the lives of their troops or civilians are at stake.

Though we can point to other measures of concern, such as the recent rise in health, food, fuel, and education costs, etc., all of which stick in people's minds more persistently than long-term advancements, we have been in historically stable, prosperous times for a generation. Why, then, are so many people, especially on the right, perceiving us to be in decline to the degree that they would storm the capitol or believe that secession, civil war, or an extremist religious takeover are the only options?

Perceived societal decline, as we are seeing now, is often rooted in feelings of insecurity and uncertainty about the future and perpetuated by politicians and power brokers eager to exploit them. When people feel that their dominance and privilege are threatened or the social order has shifted against them, they naturally look for someone or something to blame. The most disaffected groups today tend to be the older, less educated, and rural Americans who resent what they perceive as an attack on their wholesome, Christian values by minorities, immigrants, elites, and those who hold sexual and cultural values they perceive to be un-American and anti-Christian. Ensuring these groups get fair access to the social safety net and economic opportunities is not seen as the realization of our Enlightenment ideals of liberty, equality, and equal rights but as a bestowal of special rights and privileges on the undeserving.

Across much of the Western world, this same dynamic is playing out, with those who feel their place in society slipping turning to a strong leader who can restore not only order and security but traditional hierarchies and values as well. Authoritarian leaders like Donald Trump, Viktor Orban, Recep Erdoğan, and Vladimir Putin present themselves as the solution to fictional societal and moral decline and promise to restore the prosperity and safety of their mythical Golden Era. Putin seeks to resurrect the glory of the USSR, if not its sclerotic economic structure, Erdoğan wants to revive Ottoman greatness, and Trump seeks to Make America Great Again. This appeal to feelings of nostalgia is a powerful narcotic.

In times of perceived societal decline, like now, people are more willing to accept authoritarian policies and practices, including restrictive religious ones that they wouldn't otherwise condone. Unpopular laws monitoring schoolgirls' periods in Florida or cutting off abortion and contraceptive access in many states are examples that get passed by a determined minority with disproportionate control over the levers of political power.

Fearful people may be willing to give up personal freedoms and civil liberties in exchange for a sense of security and stability that they are not getting from a politically deadlocked democratically elected government. Authoritarian leaders use this to their advantage, passing laws and policies restricting civil liberties and increasing government control. Laws curbing gay and trans rights, despite same-sex activity and marriage being legal, are emerging in response to hysterical fears for child safety and lack of parental control ginned up by political opportunists and cultural warriors in the Right-wing media. Red states have been at the vanguard of this, with the Parental Rights in Education (*Don't Say Gay*) bill in Florida, bills banning books in classrooms and schools in thirty-two states as of 2022,[134] and bans pending in numerous states curtailing drag shows.[135] With solutions in search of a cause, they settle for manufactured ones.

Extremist legislation and movements may also gain traction when the mainstream political parties (such as Republicans and Democrats in the United States) prove too sclerotic and fractious to address people's real or imagined concerns. Extremist politicians who are willing to buck the system and try unorthodox and often illegal measures such as flying immigrants from Texas and Florida to Democrat-run cities, running razor wire along the border in defiance of the Constitution, and placing bounties on those who may assist a woman leaving the state for an abortion can quickly gain a following. Such antics are never the solution to societal decline but can cause tremendous damage, often going to Reign of Terror extremes before receding. It can lead to an almost unrecoverable erosion of civil liberties and human rights, ultimately making perceived societal decline a reality.

Religion, especially Christianity, is public and performative, given to end-of-the-world doomsaying. If it weren't, it wouldn't be so successful in dominating societies and governments, so expecting it to be otherwise is desirable but unrealistic. To fight inaccurate perceptions of decline:

1. **Don't play into the doom-and-gloom hysteria:** Denying problems in society when they occur would be naive and damage our credibility, but buying into the hyperbole that society as a whole is in decline only feeds into the unwarranted negativity fueling current Right-wing rage and dissatisfaction that threatens the rights of atheists and others deemed to be the source of the decline.
2. **Promote historical awareness:** Promote awareness of the actual state of national and social affairs and historical events. Share accurate data, statistics, and historical context, especially regarding the brutality of religionists in the past, demonstrating progress or improvement in various areas, such as economy, healthcare, social justice, and religious tolerance. Given so many, including politicians, are trying to sweep historical racism, slavery, and religious bigotry under the rug to demonstrate that the good old days were superior, pointing out the fact that past histori-

cal periods were largely brutish, unequal, and short can help break such fever dreams.

3. **Check facts, use critical thinking, and encourage it in others:** Encourage people to verify the information they receive and think critically about the sources of that information. Fact-checking websites and organizations can be valuable in helping people determine the accuracy of claims made in the media and by public figures. Of course, the current unfortunate trend toward disbelieving experts and turning to influencers and other sources of misinformation on *YouTube* and *TikTok* is a significant challenge. It can only be confronted and reversed by reiterating verifiable facts.
4. **Emphasize positive news stories of progress without being a Pollyanna:** Share stories of scientific progress, social advancement, and tolerance. Highlight communities' resilience and strength and focus on solutions rather than problems. This will help shift the narrative and inspire hope for the future.

SECTION IV
PREPARE FOR THE COMING STORM

The only thing necessary for the triumph of evil is for good men to do nothing.

MISATTRIBUTED TO EDMUND BURKE

THE APTLY RIDICULOUS acronym conjured by the U.S. Army for a survivor of a cataclysmic, civilization-ending disaster, the LaMOE, or Last Man on Earth, amuses me no end. Let's take a moment to consider the life and obsession of such an individual, one whose every waking moment is imbued with the spirit of survivalism, preparing for the remote chance of a world-altering calamity.

This hypothetical *LaMOE* squanders his fortune on guns and freeze-dried meatloaf, forsaking modern comforts for the rugged solitude of the countryside, where he painstakingly erects a shelter, poops in a bucket, and acquires the skills needed to scrape by surviving off the land. The price of this obsession is steep, including the alienation of the very family he seeks to protect, who regard his behavior as certifiably nuts. Should the anticipated disaster eventually strike, reducing civilization to ashes, what is the reward for our survivor's exhaustive preparations? What new Eden does this *LaMOE* emerge into from the safety of his underground bunker? The spoils of his 'victory' will most likely be a smoldering ruin of a world, potentially teeming with lethal pathogens, a ravaged environment, irradiated debris, or a swarm of destructive AI-directed nanobots.

A love for life propels such drastic measures, but they strike me as perverse expressions of it. Who in their right mind would wish to inherit such a dystopian world, with its scorched earth and broken monuments to civilization? The idea brings into sharp relief the fundamental futility and the breathtaking lameness of such an existence. So much for the glory of being the "Last Man on Earth."

I am not immune to indulging in end-of-the-world fantasies as I play *Fallout 4* on my PS4 and watch the swarming zombie hordes in the movie *Train to Busan*; these appear to be typical modern obsessions. However, as one committed to rationalism, a characteristic I find is commonly shared by fellow atheists, I place considerable stock in weighing these potential outcomes against their corresponding odds and preparing for each in a manner commensurate with its level of risk. For the record, I have neither a fallout shelter nor zombie-hunting paraphernalia. The question of Religio-fascism is no different in this respect; as with all matters of complexity and import, time will be the ultimate judge of outcomes.

Considering both the trends propelling Religio-fascism, namely, the pervading religiosity and conservatism that define much of the American psyche, and the opposing forces that challenge its rise, such as the enduring spirit of libertarianism and the remaining unmolested parts of our Constitution, I find it reasonable to wager that a form of quasi-democracy, on the brink of total descent into authoritarianism akin to the situations in Hungary or Turkey, is entirely possible.

Substantial diplomatic engagement would be the appropriate course of action if this is the case. We must tirelessly work to dispel the widely held but profoundly misguided notion that atheism is synonymous with misanthropy and reclusiveness, painting us as outsiders in our society and, most importantly, a threat to religious foundations that undergird it. Furthermore, forming alliances with other marginalized groups, those who, like us, find themselves on the fringes of the mainstream, becomes a vital strategy. By presenting a united front, we can offer a robust defense against further encroachments upon our liberties and guard against the advent of even more extreme outcomes. Ultimately, we may hope to weather the gathering storm of Religio-fascism through such strategies.

Way #24

Gray Rock Extremist Believers

The best way to deal with a sociopath is to avoid him or her, to refuse any kind of contact or communication. The only completely effective way to protect yourself is to disallow him or her from your life altogether. Sociopaths live wholly outside of the social contract, and, violent or not, they are always destructive.[136]

Martha Stout

WHEN I WAS in my mid-twenties, I had a close female friend "Julia" who bore the curse of an emotionally abusive sister. Her sister "Kelly," was an utterly charming, charismatic extrovert who was outwardly the fun-loving and confident life of every party and belle of every ball. But she also harbored a darkly manipulative side; she was completely self-absorbed and mendacious, bordering on the sociopathic. She would subtly use condescension, criticism, gaslighting, and humiliation on a routine basis to keep her victims continually off balance and questioning themselves. She would fly into an accusatory rage to distract people from her acts of deceit when someone caught her in a lie. Coming from an upbringing where such outbursts were foreign to me, I could only watch stupefied as she deftly wielded her anger and fear as tactical weapons in her games of psychological warfare.

Like many of her toxic type that I've met throughout my social and work life since, Kelly relied on the fact that most people are too polite and conflict-avoidant to call her on her bad behavior and lies, which in turn only served to feed her growing sense that she possessed a superior intellect and ability to bend people to her will. Everyone saw through her game but said nothing for fear of reprisal. Even I just sat back and watched as the sister flattered and manipulated nice, unwitting boyfriends, men to whom she had no intention of committing, into buying her expensive cars, gifts, and vacations, only to wring them dry and cast them aside.

Julia was the one person who could keep her balance in this chaos. As one might expect, she did not achieve this by standing up to and confronting Kelly. On the contrary, that approach would only have triggered explosive bouts of rage and emotional blackmail that would have escalated the situation. Plus, she was a quiet, introverted type who, albeit very strong, avoided confrontation like the plague.

No, she unwittingly stumbled on a psychological technique now known as *gray rocking*.[137] Simply, gray rocking is a means to fend off a toxic person's behavior by both minimizing interaction to only what's necessary and acting as emotionless and unresponsive as possible when confronted by the manipulator's abusive behavior. This technique allowed Julia to limit the disruption to her life and defuse potentially volatile situations without becoming emotionally exhausted.

The result? Kelly could never gain a psychological foothold in Julia's psyche. She was undoubtedly frustrated by her inability to push Julia around, but this stalemate never triggered a backlash for lack of psychological oxygen and fuel.

Most of us have been unfortunate enough, usually more than once in our lives, to have had a toxic co-worker or boss, usurious friend, or abusive family member who made our life a living hell. Constant gaslighting, passive aggression, and emotional blackmail, the typical stock in trade of malicious narcissists and sociopathic personalities, can devastate entire families and even put careers and lives in jeopardy. Typically, in situations where I've had to confront such individuals, no amount of logic or reasoning could stave off the constant lies, fits of anger, and twisted logic, and no amount of clear-headed confrontation could coax the perpetrator into a productive dialog. After trying every civilized method to deal with the situation, from attempting a reasoned heart-to-heart discussion to the extreme of counseling or mediation as a last resort, it would seem most prudent to terminate the toxic relationship altogether.

Unfortunately, we cannot always outright cut off or even avoid our coworkers, neighbors, or the obnoxious MAGA guy with the *Let's Go Brandon* stickers on his toolbox, who is the only one available to come to fix our broken furnace. We often don't have the luxury of switching jobs, moving households, or selecting alternate contractors. Cutting toxic people entirely out of our lives may be easy online, but it's much more challenging in real life. Though it takes a high degree of emotional discipline, resorting to minimal, emotionless interactions that reduce the potential for conflict can be most effective.

Aggressive and extremist religionists often exhibit, sometimes as an integral part of their faith, many of the same traits and manipulative techniques used by my friend's sister. Evangelism and missionary work themselves entail an abusive disregard for boundaries and an aggressive insistence on engagement that opens up opportunities for emotional abuse.

Unfortunately for them, obnoxious behavior from those trying to convert or control us is catnip to many of us atheists who, often reveling in intellectual combat, can quickly get drawn into discussions with door-to-door missionaries, neighbors, and others who may not have our best interests at heart. Under normal circumstances today, this can be a misstep that ends, at worst, in a mind-numbing barrage of nonsensical religious arguments that end in neither side convincing the other of the logic of their position, and we end up with an armful of *Watchtower* literature. When in a hostile environment, such as a community of intrusive religious neighbors in the deep South of the United States, when confronted with those wielding legal or political authority, the results can be considerably less benign.

At its most basic, gray-rocking religionists or their enablers means avoiding reacting to inquiries about one's religious beliefs as well as to more objectionable, even highly offensive, religious comments and attacks. A Christian coworker claims atheists are un-American and the government should deport them. Don't take the bait. Fighting bigotry through one-on-one rhetorical battles won't bring about change. We can't persuade our coworkers, but they may hold the power to damage our reputations or our careers if they take offense. It is better to leave our resistance to group action where there is some safety in numbers.

The pros of gray rocking when dealing with religionists include:

1. **Camouflage from hostile religionists** can prevent the exposure of our nonbelief in situations where we could experience negative repercussions, such as job termination. Being wholly open or combative about our nonbelief is a luxury best saved for at least moderately safe environments and situations.
2. **De-escalation of conflict when one arises:** It can help to de-escalate a situation and prevent a hostile religionist from provoking a reaction that can escalate into violence and serve as justification for reporting us to our bosses, hostile neighbors, or authorities dominated by religionists.
3. **Avoidance of annoying proselytizers:** It can make the religionist discontinue their attempt to convert us. Many religionists thrive on feelings of persecution, and evangelism is more about reinforcing their faith than converting us. By avoiding engagement, they get bored and leave.

4. **Emotional protection from being drawn into combat:** It can prevent us from becoming emotionally invested in the manipulation. As much as we may enjoy intellectual battles, they are an emotional drain that draws negativity, stress, and anger into our lives, damaging our health and well-being more than those with whom we argue.

Cons of gray rocking a religionist include:

1. **Potential failure in a group environment:** It may not work when more than one religionist is involved. As noted, people generally act irrationally in a group, and when emotions become amplified, beliefs get reinforced. Surrounded by religionists, our silence may be interpreted as disagreement and mark us as members of the out-group. At that point, groupthink alone can encourage an escalation in hostilities that wouldn't occur in a one-on-one situation.
2. **Escalation when tempers run hot:** Grey-rocking is not recommended in situations that have progressed to physical and overt verbal abuse or where lives may be in danger because it can cause an angry person to become more irate and enhance the violence. In these cases, the best long-term response is to contact authorities such as the police, one's manager, or HR to take action.

WAY #25

CAREFULLY CONSIDER WHERE YOU TRAVEL

People of different religions and cultures live side by side in almost every part of the world, and most of us have overlapping identities which unite us with very different groups. We can love what we are, without hating what – and who – we are not. We can thrive in our own tradition, even as we learn from others, and come to respect their teachings.

—*KOFI ANNAN, FORMER SECRETARY-GENERAL OF THE UNITED NATIONS*

DURING THE JIM Crow Era, a unique artifact emerged as a beacon of guidance for African American travelers: *The Green Book*. From its inception in 1936 and continuing publication until 1967, this travel guide meticulously cataloged an array of establishments that included everything from diners and hotels to beauty salons and drugstores. It was designed to ensure the comfort and safety of African Americans navigating the perilous roads of a nation yet to embrace the equality promised by the Civil Rights Act of 1964. The author, Victor Hugo Green, was a Black postman in Harlem, New York City, whose creation was not merely an intelligent list of Black-owned and color-blind businesses but a testament to the resilience and resourcefulness of America's growing black middle class who now had the disposable income to travel across the country, but not always a safe route.[138]

Members of other oppressed groups have emulated Green's success, such as Bob Damron, whose *Address Books* became valuable resources for gay travelers seeking friends, fun, and safety from 1964 to 2021, and the guide's spirit lives on in *Mapping the Gay Guides* online exhibition.[139] No one, however, has attempted to publish something similar for atheists. Today, such a guide would be less about providing safety than guidance for avoiding the wasteland of local religious radio programming as we drive across the country. Or perhaps it would offer recommendations to thirsty atheist travelers navigating the dry spells cast by Blue Laws like the one that caught my wife and me off-guard in Idaho, parched and pondering the weird quirks of rural legislation.

In an America where the clouds increasingly darken with peril for atheists and our kindred spirits, grasping the constant shifts in the cultural and political winds from one state or even town to the next becomes more than an exercise in geography — it's a necessary weather check to ensure we remain free of the brewing storms of bias and oppression.

The dangers loom large, especially for those of us who are either forced to move or travel for work or who dream of a life unbound, wandering beyond the familiar sanctuaries of coastal cities and urban retreats into a heartland that pulses unpredictably, especially as MAGA Christian Nationalists threaten a major national infarction.

Amid the pandemic, caught up in our digital nomad dreams, my wife and I toyed with the idea of staking our claim in some more affordable corner of the country. It was a notion, it turns out, more whimsical than our *Zillow*-fueled fantasies, where the grass seemed infinitely greener and the living cheaper than in the Bay Area's cramped and astronomically-priced confines. The strategy seemed straightforward enough at the outset — steer clear of the deep red zones, the heart of political darkness on the map, and we'd soon be luxuriating in a hot tub under a clear mountain sky, a stone's throw from the conveniences of civilization. Yet, as we delved more deeply, the simplicity of our plan unraveled into a complex web of decisions, each illustrating a more nuanced picture of America's vast and varied religious and political landscape.

The US is a complex patchwork of varying degrees and dimensions of religious tolerance that have implications, especially for people with complex identities as atheists. For example, if we were to look at a map showing voting patterns, would we be safe in diverse urban areas that voted blue? At first glance, yes. But if you overlaid that map with ones showing where anti-LGBT+ or anti-choice legislation has been passed at the state level, blue cities that look like a safe bet often become much less so. Many have had their progressive local laws superseded by the anti-democratic and draconian ones of their gerrymandered Republican-controlled state governments. For a gay atheist who eschews the closet or a woman of child-bearing age who values her right to control her reproductive future, this would not be an ideal fit, to put it lightly. Further, overlaying the voting and legislative maps with one showing church density and attendance, we see very few places in the country, including nominally blue states like California and New York, that are entirely safe. If Congress passes a national fetal personhood law or enforces the Comstock Law to make abortions all but impossible, as the Republican Project 2025 envisions, nowhere will provide sanctuary.

Our identities comprise the other dimension to consider when looking to move, travel, or hunker down and prepare for the worst. Just as there are minority atheists in their prime who need to plan carefully, there are those atheists who are white, hetero, apolitical, and beyond their childbearing years who could live relatively freely virtually anywhere, including dark red rural areas. If I weren't such an outspoken atheist and liberal, and my wife weren't so Persian, we could survive virtually anywhere, if not blend in. Another elderly atheist couple that does check all of the outwardly conformist boxes might consider moving to so-called enemy territory to work towards pluralism and diversity.

Some considerations when seeking safe harbor as atheists or when evaluating the status of our current hometowns:

1. **Employment Environment:** Local employers who respect diversity, including religious beliefs and the lack thereof, and have inclusive policies can create a more comfortable overall environment for atheists. Even anti-DEI legislation cannot easily cast a chill over a work environment where employees naturally respect each other.
2. **Access to Secular Services:** Look into the availability of secular services, including therapists, social groups, progressive bookstores, non-religious wedding officiants, and funeral services. Areas with a broader range of religiously neutral service options provide a *de facto* support network in case religious intolerance grows, as this indicates that the local area has a critical mass of like-minded people.
3. **Political Representation:** Having secular-minded representatives, school boards, and city councils can influence local policies and the overall social climate in a way that respects and somewhat protects the rights of atheists, even if state or federal laws try to supersede them. Even a national *panopticon* can only partially keep an eye on or stamp out all resistance at the local level.
4. **Public Symbols and Monuments:** Are there lots of billboards for churches, conversion therapy, or "Crisis Pregnancy Centers" everywhere you look? Do giant crosses, flags, or Confederate monuments dot the landscape? While not direct indicators of intolerance, the prevalence of religious symbols in

public spaces can sometimes reflect the community's negative attitudes towards secularism and diversity of belief. A higher number of churches relative to the local population can also be a significant indicator.

5. **Education Systems:** In districts where the school curriculum is shaped by religious beliefs, certain books and topics are prohibited, teachers are armed, and comprehensive, science-based education is lacking, your child's educational experience may be significantly compromised. These characteristics can also signal strong local religious influences, as schools are governed at the local level. It's essential to thoroughly research these aspects before moving to a new area.
6. **Cultural and Recreational Opportunities:** Cities and towns that offer diverse cultural amenities and activities, including boutique art theaters, unique bookstores and cafes, pride events, arts festivals, and non-religious community events, can enrich the lives of atheists by offering leisure and social opportunities that align with secular values. Such amenities can also indicate a broader intellectual openness within the community, creating a more inclusive environment for those who do not adhere to religious beliefs.

WAY #26

EXTEND A HAND TO PERSECUTED MINORITIES

He who wishes to secure the good of others,
has already secured his own.[140]

CONFUCIUS

AS AN UNWAVERING critic of religious dogma, I find myself deeply unsettled by any action that might facilitate the dissemination of its toxic influence or fortify someone's religious convictions. Beyond the apparent wars, Inquisitions, and pogroms conducted in the name of various deities, destroying countless communities and lives, I am horrified by the less conspicuous yet equally detrimental consequences of deliberate ignorance fueled by devoutness. Pernicious beliefs about the nature of disease, mental health, and science have led to the intense suffering and intellectual subjugation of billions.

My viewpoint is not singular; many atheists would argue that religion has impeded human advancement, smothering scientific curiosity and endorsing erroneous assertions about the cosmos and natural laws. Throughout history, religious authorities have muzzled some of the brightest intellects, and their insidious influence persists across various disciplines, from philosophy to history to science. One can only speculate how much humanity could have progressed if Galileo had been spared persecution and imprisonment by the Inquisition or if medieval theologians had devoted more of their formidable minds to scientific exploration and improving society than theological ruminations.

Despite my steadfast opposition to religion, I am not devoid of empathy and compassion, as so many prosperity gospel swindlers,[141] abusive Catholic priests,[142] and callous everyday believers often appear to be.[143] Should I have surplus clothing or food to give away, I will deliver them to people experiencing homelessness directly. The added benefit is that I, and I suspect most atheists, do so without attempting to convert them to atheism.

While we may not be able to reliably depend on moderate believers, members of minority religions, or even atheist quislings to protect us or our interests in extreme circumstances, that doesn't mean that we shouldn't always strive to be "Good Samaritans" and reach out to defend them and anyone else who will likely suffer at the hands of religious extremism every bit as much as we will. Protecting human life and dignity and showing empathy should always be the atheist's trademark, even when under threat. If not for our all-too-short lives and the high value we place on humanity, what else do we, as atheists, have of greater value to protect?

Even persecuted religious groups such as the Orthodox Jewish community in the United States, Shiites and Christians in the Sunni parts of the Middle East, and Muslims in India, may recoil from atheists like those of the majority religion or sect, not remembering, ironically, that they are often categorized as degenerate and evil by the dominant religionists, every bit as much as those of us who are atheists. Preventing religious sects that are in the minority from making common cause through divide and conquer tactics is a crucial chapter in any authoritarian's playbook. We cannot let them succeed.

Suppose we are ever to emerge from any potential dark age of religious chauvinism. In that case, we need to build goodwill with minority religionists through our actions to win over other ostracized groups to our common cause. That cause is not atheism but a return to pluralism and tolerance. Not to mention, it's the logical and moral thing to do.

In addition to proffering an open hand to religious minorities, we need to do the same for those who are systematically disadvantaged based on ethnic, racial, gender, and other characteristics. Intersectionality has been much maligned of late by conservatives, especially in the United States, who are intent on delegitimizing any field of inquiry that challenges their traditionalist views. It can, however, be a critical learning tool since it is a framework for understanding how different forms of discrimination intersect and exacerbate each other, creating complex overlapping experiences of oppression for those who belong to multiple marginalized groups, as many are atheists. For example, an atheist who is also Black may experience discrimination and marginalization based on both their lack of belief in a deity and the color of their skin. Their experience cannot be reduced to simply being one or the other, as both aspects of their identity interact and influence one another, as well as the means and degree to which they experience oppression. A white male atheist may experience harassment and ostracization for his beliefs, but a Black female nonbeliever may be assaulted, arrested, or killed by whites for her race, oppressed as a female, or maligned for her disbelief within both the white and Black communities. Her experience is potentially magnitudes more complex and dangerous than the white male atheist's.

The value of intersectionality for atheists is twofold. One is that white men have unfortunately dominated atheism, and that needs to change if we want to grow our numbers and have the atheist perspective be relevant and resonant to a diverse population, not to mention enabling us to be able to push back more effectively on Religio-fascism, where religionist have far greater numbers. Second, for white men insulated in progressive urban areas, the full magnitude of the potential threat of religious oppression may not be readily apparent as their privilege, relative wealth, and location may have insulated them from experiencing the full effect of hostility religionists are capable of mustering when they control the levers of power. Understanding and studying intersectionality concerning religion and atheism can help educate them on the many possible outcomes.

There are multiple reasons for atheism's monotone. A high degree of religiosity and respect for religion among some minority ethnic groups and social norms that tie female value to their religious observance play a part in propelling those groups away from openly embracing atheism, but so too does the false perception that atheism is a white boys club. This perception isn't necessarily rooted in explicit antagonism or exclusion but rather stems from a limited comprehension of experiences divergent from those of white males. This lack of diverse understanding has hindered the ability to construct and convey atheist narratives that challenge this dominant perception, thus shaping the face of atheism in contemporary society. By engaging with those outside of our echo chamber, listening to their stories, and dispelling their negative perceptions of atheists, we can begin to heal the divide and convey the message that atheism is welcoming to everyone. If something as historically exclusive as skiing and tennis can become more diverse, surely so can atheism if we are as clever and accepting as we think.

Secondly, there is much to be learned about the dynamics of oppression from those who have experienced it in its ugliest, most virulent forms. A white atheist can learn a lot about what to expect when oppressed and how to navigate it from a Black or female atheist. Of course, it is not the responsibility of a member of a minority group to educate white people. That's not what I'm implying. I'm suggesting that as a group, we atheists can compound our understanding and means of defense against oppression by pooling the combined knowledge of multiple, overlapping out-groups. By doing so, we can build safe spaces for marginalized groups within the atheist community, actively addressing and dismantling all forms of discrimination and oppression and centering the voices and experiences of those who are often overlooked or ignored.

There are several ways we can help build a bulwark against the rise of religious intolerance and build a reputation as an ally of other marginalized groups:

1. **Become educated about the issues oppressed groups face:** All oppression is linked. Race, class, gender, etc., create overlapping systems of discrimination. From this, we, as atheists, can learn how to understand and navigate persecution from these groups. Learning about the history of discrimination and oppression and understanding these groups' current challenges can often provide insights into the possible mechanisms used to oppress atheists. Additionally, it's essential to know how our privilege may contribute to the problem and actively work to counteract this to avoid being unwittingly complicit with those who oppress us.
2. **Speak out against discrimination and inequality:** This can be as simple as identifying racist or bigoted language or behavior when it is encountered or taking a public stance against discrimination and inequality. It enables us to fight for pluralism and equality and dismantle systems of oppression without drawing undue attention to our atheism.

3. **Support organizations that work toward equality:** Donating money or time to organizations that advocate for the rights of marginalized groups, such as the *Anti-Defamation League*, *NAACP*, etc., or supporting businesses and organizations owned and operated by members of other outgroups helps strengthen their political and economic clout. Given that atheists have no organizational power base of our own, this provides an alternative where we can indirectly build a bulwark against religious oppression.

Way #27

Realize Your Fate Has Already Been Written

What happens in Vegas stays in Vegas; what happens on Twitter stays on Google forever![144]

Jure Klepic

PUSHING THEIR EIGHTIES, it's not as if my parents don't want or need the maximum convenience of online banking and purchasing. Yet, they are inordinately concerned about having their information stolen or hacked, and outside of a few trusted websites like *Amazon*, they rarely avail themselves of online stores or fully explore the less well-traveled corners of the internet. For those like me who have been online since *AOL* hissed and gargled its way through our phone lines and even met our spouses online as my wife and I did, this sometimes seems perplexing. Many of us are well aware of the dangers online and know hackers and online services have spread our personal information here to Beijing, but we have often weighed the danger and convenience and chosen to embrace the latter. Better the convenient Amazon we know than the devil store in the mall with its rude employee minions and inflated prices that we don't.

However, as someone in cybersecurity, I must admit my parents are right. From our buying habits to search history, any savvy algorithm can extrapolate from them not only our buying habits but our political views, whether or not we are in ill health or pregnant, or even potentially our atheism.[145] With the growth of the surveillance state, we should assume that virtually every online comment or purchase we make and every action we perform in a public space can and will, if not already, be uncovered and recorded. Combined with the sheer will to power that has infected religion-powered Right-wing politics over the last decade, we never know when we may find ourselves suddenly and unexpectedly trapped in a religio-fascist *panopticon* facing the repercussions of every past thought and action as they sift through our digital paper trail and monitor our every move, no matter how free and democratic our circumstances may be today.

It is tempting to believe that remaining silent today would be solid self-preservation advice to stave off suspicion and persecution if and when the veil of religious zealotry descends — and we would be correct, but only to a degree. With the internet, the prevalence of security cameras and facial recognition, and even the persistence of human memory, the words we have already uttered or written will live on well into whatever dystopian future may await. We may have been cautious to avoid doing or saying anything that would impact our future career or attract social opprobrium, like posing naked or wearing blackface to a party. Wise decisions.

But have we also been cautious about the negative things we've said regarding religion, religious zealots in government, or hot-button social topics held dear by the religious right? In my case, definitely not. Defending gay rights, freedom of choice, and civil rights, while the right thing to do, can also mark us as godless, even if we've never explicitly declared our atheism. Increasingly, criticism of Right-wing politics, as inextricably intertwined as it has become with religion in the United States, could be construed as anti-religious. Everywhere, religious speech is becoming political speech. If we have not been cautious, and most of us haven't, our fate under a future religionist dystopia may be in the process of being sealed as we speak.

We may not be able to take back all our incriminating comments to date, but we shouldn't despair. We can still minimize our online footprint; hopefully, its blackmail potential will fade. We must always fight back, but we might consider going underground with our resistance. We should avoid commenting online if not necessary, erase unnecessarily inflammatory social posts and *TikTok* videos, and delete any unused social accounts.

The criticism that some may make is that to withdraw from public view would be ceding the public sphere to religious conservatives. We should realize, however, that social and media outlets are already being withdrawn from us. Wealthy, conservative owners of *Fox News* and even the

Wall Street Journal have aligned themselves with the pretenders to religio-fascist leadership. They are becoming tools for religious, Right-wing propaganda, while *X* and *Facebook* frequently suppress critical comments regarding religion.

Weaning ourselves off extraneous use of the internet and erasing as much of our digital footprint as possible would be a wise move sooner rather than later. It may not prevent a future surveillance state from poring through our data that is stored on anonymous servers somewhere and exposing us as atheists. Still, we don't need to make it overly easy for them either by leaving breadcrumbs for them to follow. Plus, in a world of internet hackers and scam artists, reducing our digital footprint makes practical sense regardless of whether or not Religio-fascism comes for us.

As someone who works in the cybersecurity space, I can recommend several steps anyone can take to minimize our digital imprint in a religio-fascist surveillance state, which is still wise to do even if it never materializes:

1. **Be selective about personal information online:** Avoid sharing unnecessary personal details on social media or other websites, no matter how seemingly trivial. These details include pet names, birthdays, recent locations, and political and atheistic affiliations.
2. **Turn off the microphone and camera:** To prevent unauthorized eavesdropping, turn off the microphone for specific apps and digital assistants like Snes. Likewise, cover cameras on phones and other devices. Even

using just a sliver of opaque tape over the lens to prevent surveillance.

3. **Encrypt online communications:** Encrypting messaging and email apps and hard drives can protect personal information from being intercepted or stolen.
4. **Use a VPN to access the internet:** Virtual private networks (VPN) encrypt internet connections and hide IP addresses, making it more difficult to track online activity.
5. **Use privacy-friendly search engines and incognito browser windows:** Some search engines, like *DuckDuckGo*, *Startpage*, and *Qwant*, do not track user data or personalize search results. Switching to *Incognito mode* on common browsers like *Chrome* can also anonymize search activity.
6. **Use privacy-friendly apps and operating systems:** Look for open-source apps and operating systems with built-in privacy features. These features make verifying that the software is not collecting or sharing personal data easier.
7. **Be aware of the apps downloaded:** Be careful about which apps you download to devices. Many apps, especially those developed in Russia, China, and other nations known for collecting and sharing personal data.

8. **Choose complex passwords and rotate them periodically:** Don't use the same simple password on all devices, one based on personal information, or anything easy to guess. Use a password vault that stores randomly generated complex passwords and changes them every month or two.
9. **Use two-factor authentication:** In addition to a password, enable a second authentication method using biometrics (i.e., facial recognition), authenticator codes, challenge questions, etc.
10. **Regularly reduce unnecessary data exposure:** Keep track of all data shared online and delete or edit any information that is no longer needed or shouldn't be publicly available.
11. **Be aware of your physical surroundings:** In the physical world, be mindful of who might be listening or watching when discussing sensitive information in person or on the phone. Assume that public spaces have multiple surveillance cameras. While most don't retain video imagery for more than a short time, they could be made to do so in the wrong hands.

Way #28

Build Your Resistance Library

Books are good company, in sad times and happy times, for books are people — people who have managed to stay alive by hiding between the covers of a book.[146]

E.B. White

WHEN I WAS fourteen, I regularly rode my bike to the local library, several miles from my insular neighborhood. It was no ordinary library, at least not to me; it was my secret sanctuary where the latest books, magazines, and periodicals lived, from *The Economist* to *Foreign Affairs,* publications I couldn't afford or even find in the few small bookstores downtown. It was also a personal retreat that emotionally centered me when I returned to the United States after two years in the UK since I was struggling to readjust to an American culture that shocked me almost as much as moving to the UK originally had. The library, its aging books exuding a distinct aroma that seemed to tell a story of its own, grounded me and became my haven. The deep faux leather reading chairs, nestled in a secluded corner where no one ever ventured, were like thrones in a kingdom I had claimed as my own. Something about the artificial lights and the climate-controlled environment seemed to cocoon me in a world far removed from the one outside. Those lights didn't just illuminate pages; they lit up my passion for the secular, the rational, and often the unconventional and profane, as well as my understanding of the depth of my secularism.

As years passed and the constraints of youth began to loosen, I collected old books, from linguistics and history to sci-fi and classical literature, curating my little library at home over the next twenty years until the digital revolution. In this era, everything I ever wanted to read, every scrap of knowledge I yearned to uncover, was suddenly accessible with a few clicks. The transition was electrifying, akin to a million-volt jolt to my brain. With its vast ocean of nonstop information, the digital age transformed my relationship with knowledge. It was a new world, a different kind of paradise, where the wisdom of the ages was not bound in leather but floated freely in the ever-shifting ones and zeroes of the internet. Eventually, even my career in cyber security would be driven by my desire to protect that world of endless digital knowledge just as the brick-and-mortar library had saved me.

This evolution, while magical in its accessibility, also carried a bittersweet tinge. The tactile joy of flipping through pages and the smell of old books, these sensory experiences were now rare luxuries. Yet, the essence of my journey remained the same. The tools had changed, but the quest was as enduring as the stories and ideas that had first beckoned me to that library years ago.

Physical books still have a special allure and mystique to me. My desire to collect and read them in their physical form hasn't waned, but when it comes to the sheer amphetamine-like charge one gets from immediate access to any topic or obscure publication, with every question answered almost immediately, the internet is my drug of choice. I spend far too much idle time scanning the news, and now, I use AI tools like *ChatGPT* to perform sophisticated research as if I had an academic intern. Of course, being constantly bombarded with sensationalized news of global tragedy can be incredibly stressful and anxiety-inducing as it comes in a flood of far more information and emotion than we humans have evolved to handle. Taken as a whole, however, my life as an atheist is far more manageable when I have unlimited access to knowledge without the government or church filtering everything I see and hear through their prism.

Of course, the internet is littered with inaccuracies, lies, and outright conspiracies, including those surrounding atheists, but where else can a nonbeliever living in a Muslim country with death penalties for apostasy or in any rural, heavily white evangelical part of the United States find fellowship with other atheists or books that would be deemed heretical or scandalous by the religionists around us? Further, for many of us who may have had substandard educations or parents who were not intellectually inclined, *YouTube* and *TikTok* provide access to enough legitimate news, knowledge, and how-to information to satisfy even the most savvy and committed autodidact.

And yet, we have come full circle today, where the importance of physical books is only increasing. When authoritarian governments take over, especially religiously-oriented ones, the first thing to be restricted is internet access. Sure, television and radio are also ready targets — stifled as they are today by China, Iran, and North Korea, but their influence is waning. When populations protest or riot, the internet is immediately shut down to prevent protesters and government opposition from communicating with each other and publicizing the government's atrocities worldwide. It is a global library of living information that can go dark instantly.

Even when populations remain pacified, any dissenting view or website is typically blocked or censored. For secular regimes, the focus is on political and intellectual dissent. In religio-fascist societies, we also have to contend with censorship of materials considered blasphemous, anti-religious, or immoral. We see this in many Muslim societies, including those not seen as specifically theocratic, such as Pakistan, which nevertheless have harsh penalties for blasphemy, including imprisonment and the death penalty. These Pakistani laws extend to the internet, for instance, where atheist bloggers have been targeted for imprisonment, kidnapping, and lynching since the government cracked down on atheism in 2017.

Lest we think that the United States is immune, until the 1930s, the First Amendment did not prevent states from establishing anti-blasphemy laws. Numerous states, such as

Massachusetts, Maryland, and Maine, had such laws since the nation's founding, and some are still on the books, though currently invalidated as unconstitutional. However, U.S. Supreme Court Justice Clarence Thomas has questioned whether the First Amendment applies to the establishment of religion by the states, which has been settled law since the Fourteenth Amendment established that most of the provisions of the Bill of Rights should be incorporated against (applied to) the states. If, in a rare scenario, a case arose in the Supreme Court that affirmed Thomas's interpretation, anti-blasphemy laws affecting atheist speech could likewise be reintroduced through judicial fiat.

The second order of business of any authoritarian regime, especially a religio-fascist one, is to ban or destroy subversive literature and other sources of immoral art, music, film, and knowledge. Anything that isn't either purely utilitarian or explicitly religious, and more specifically in alignment with the regime's orthodoxy, typically becomes suspect and a target. It is here when the value of traditional paper books becomes invaluable in maintaining our connection to the past and knowledge untainted by censorious religious authorities, and they are far easier to conceal and protect than internet access.

Today, there has been a growing number of symbolic book burnings in the United States by radicals like high-profile Rev. Greg Locke and campaigns to ban certain books in school libraries and classrooms that offend religionists' delicate sensibilities. Is it far-fetched to believe that as a religiously oriented Right-wing political movement achieves nationwide dominance, they wouldn't normalize such acts? Of course not.

With our current cohort of religionists and their politicians who believe that science and education impede communing with their god, *Fahrenheit 451* could become not just a novel but a plausible look into our future.

The Iranian government has censored books to exclude the female form, even from classical art books, and has erased any meaningful historical or societal contributions of women. And, of course, in all Muslim countries, any book, article, or work of art that is deemed an insult to Islam or Mohammed is forbidden and subject to a *fatwa* or extrajudicial attack against the author, artist, or other detractors. Even thirty years after writing the novel *Satanic Verses* and being virtually exiled from his home country of India, atheist Salman Rushdie was attacked and lost an eye and use of his arm, though thankfully not his life, at the hands of a Muslim extremist.[147]

In the future, then, is it not unreasonable to expect that Christian Dominionists in the United States who espouse the Seven Mountains Doctrine, which includes Christian control over all aspects of society, including education, the media, and arts and entertainment, wouldn't attempt a degree of censorship similar to what exists in Iran and the Middle East? Potentially, but accurately guessing what information may or may not be acceptable under a future religiously extremist regime would be impossible at this point. The best preparation would be to ensure access now to physical books, art, films, and music that we find valuable, and would be especially important in ensuring that our children will never be deprived of a well-rounded education. We shouldn't worry about preserving knowledge for posterity's sake. Unless religious extremism engulfs the entire globe, someone or some organization will seek to preserve human knowledge.

The media we do collect doesn't have to be overtly atheist-themed. Our tastes and interests aren't that narrow or consistent, so examples would be pointless here. Some may be religious if our tastes run to that. A Buddhist text on meditation, a guide to Yoga, or an art book on Catholic architecture in a white evangelical-run regime could be considered as subversive as a text written by Charles Darwin, so collecting a copy for ourselves would be worthwhile. Nothing should be regarded as unworthy or insufficiently atheist, as freedom of thought is at the heart of this process.

The point is to choose what is meaningful to us, whatever it is we would feel at a loss without, collect it, and preserve it for ourselves, our children, and hopefully for the atheists in our families who will come after us. If we want to build a personal library to ensure we and our children have access to knowledge if a religio-fascist regime looks to curtail internet access, the news and library, or commercial access to certain books and music, there are several things we should consider:

1. **The books to include in our library:** The books we select should be, first and foremost, those that we and others who will be using our library will enjoy and value reading. Beyond that, choosing those that would otherwise be unavailable is essential if the current trend of book-banning by religious and social zealots continues. LGBTQ+ literature, anything on atheism or out-group religions, socialist and left-lean-

ing politics, and literature by people of color are sure bets for censorship, as are books on dystopian societies, democracy, and history books. A sample reading list is included in *Appendix I* at the end of this book to help get started.

2. **The format of our library:** Will it be physical, digital, or both? If it's physical, we'll need to consider whether we have the money to acquire it, space to maintain and hide it, adequate security to protect it, and a temperature and humidity-controlled environment optimal for preserving the materials. If it's digital, we must consider accessibility, digital security, and backups.
3. **The purpose of our library:** What kind of information and resources do we want to include? Are we focusing on ensuring access to children's educational materials, scientific data, historical events, or fiction? Will it include just the written word or music and art as well?
4. **The audience of our library:** Who is the library for? Are we just building it for ourselves, our families, or a broader group of underground atheists? Different uses will dictate accessibility, security protocols, and inventory controls.
5. **The riskiness of our library materials:** Different types of books and materials will draw different levels of condemnation from religio-fascist authorities. Will we include materials considered blasphemous, call into question the dominant religion, or just litera-

ture that may be discouraged? If it is high risk, how will we segregate it from the rest of our collection and keep it from detection?

6. **Preservation of our materials:** How will we ensure that the materials endure? Will we seek out archival-quality publications or include multiple copies of essential publications, possibly in different formats?
7. **The security of our library:** How will we protect it and its contents from potential threats, such as fire, theft, natural disasters, and unwanted detection?
8. **The funding and maintenance of our library:** How will we fund its building and maintenance? Who will be responsible for maintaining it and its contents?

Way #29

Aim for Success, Prepare for Blowback

Many critics are born of envy.

Wayne Gerard Trotman

I'VE ALWAYS BEEN fascinated by the Japanese idiom, "the nail that sticks out gets hammered down." It conveys that those who are different or conspicuous, especially in their success, will get criticized or sanctioned by others, so it is best to remain unassuming and unremarkable. While this notion is bemusing to anyone outside of Japanese or some other Asian cultures that have historically valued humility and conformity over self-expression and aggrandizement, it is something quite alien to our Western celebrity and fame-obsessed culture. I've always felt that it holds, with some modifications, particular relevance for those of us who are atheists. With success or perceived success among even a tiny minority of any out-group, especially if the broader community considers success unearned or unwarranted, comes increased potential for the out-group to be vilified.

The ascent of the Rothschilds serves as a prime example, one that profoundly shaped the perception of Jewish communities in Europe on the eve of the Second World War. This storied family, rising from the Frankfurt ghetto to become a powerful international banking dynasty in the nineteenth century, inadvertently catalyzed a legend, one that served well those aspiring autocrats who sought to insinuate that Jewish people nefariously dominated the world of finance and manipulated political events across the continent and must therefore be eradicated or disempowered. Yet, this narrative, which primarily centered around a singular family's success as well as ancient myths that Jewish people were responsible for the evils and greed of rapacious capitalism, obscured a more complex and sad reality. The broader Jewish population, far from the echelons of power and wealth attributed to them, witnessed a decline in their economic and political fortunes as the nineteenth century waned and the twentieth century dawned. Yet amidst this decline, a pernicious belief took root, fueled more by myth than fact, that Jewish people as a whole, not just the Rothschilds and other banking families, possessed unearned power, wealth, and privilege. This belief, distorting the socioeconomic realities of the time, contributed significantly to the persecution of Jewish communities by the Nazis, who drew on the perennial scapegoating of Jewish communities for every calamity that befell them, from war and famine to the severe economic depression that convulsed Germany after the First World War, to legitimate their extermination and the expropriation of their wealth.

The fate of Black communities after the Civil War provides another cautionary tale. These communities frequently experienced rapid economic prosperity, at times even exceeding the success of their white neighbors, which more often than not triggered violent retaliatory responses, even though the vast majority of Black families as a whole experienced far more deprivation than most whites. One notable catastrophe was the *1921 Tulsa Race Massacre*, where white supremacists orchestrated a brutal onslaught on the prosperous *Black Wall Street*, resulting in the eradication of $200 million in Black wealth and the killing or injuring of over a thousand individuals. To this day, white apologists often try to minimize the horror of such events or deny their racial motivations.[148]

Perhaps more pernicious but equally devastating was the systematic disruption of thriving Black communities across the United States. Infrastructural projects such as highways and bypasses in the 1950s through the 1970s were often strategically designed to run right through the middle of Black neighborhoods, splitting them in two and effectively diluting their economic and political potency.[149]

Historically, atheists have held a somewhat inconspicuous role in economic and political spheres due to our limited numbers. However, this has begun to change. As wealth increasingly concentrates in urban areas, often associated with secularism, over the past twenty-five years, there has been growing discontent in the more religious rural areas. These communities view the accumulation of wealth by "godless" urbanites as an insult, contradicting their belief in divine favor for the devout, a narrative often echoed in the prosperity gospel. They are also usually at a loss to understand the value of many urbanites' technical jobs, which can breed a sense that they haven't worked for their wealth.

One of my school friends once attacked me with the idea that the world consists of "makers" and "takers." But unlike those who see makers as those who work and support themselves and takers as those who are lazy and unemployed, he, as a contractor who builds houses, had a unique take that makers were only those people who labor to make things like houses, cars, and bridges, or provide tangible services. In contrast, takers include the overpaid mind workers like me, who he and I suspect many blue-collar white Americans on the right believe to be the takers. If that is the case, then the masters of high-tech have become the Rothschilds of atheism, lending credence to the myth that all atheists, regardless of station, possess unearned wealth and power and must be brought to heel.

Indeed, the primary potential trigger of a massive religio-fascist backlash is the economic success, or at least perceived success, of atheists with the rise of the high-tech industry. Complaints against the monopolistic tendencies of companies like *Apple* and *Microsoft* and the predation by *Amazon* against mom-and-pop stores that are thought to be contributing to the business blight experienced in downtown America are non-partisan. Yet the most vociferous detractors have been from the right, especially the Christian right.

As mentioned earlier, the algorithms that power *X*,

Facebook, and *Instagram* typically favor the incendiary, conspiratorial, and provocative over the mundane, unhinged ideas that have found the most fertile ground and been most successfully propagated by the right. Nevertheless, the dominant perception among those on the right, including religionists, is that these companies are founded and run by liberal atheists hostile to conservative politics and religious values, and perception is often far more potent than reality. The notion that radical liberalism has come to dominate the media, culture, and education has become a pervasive narrative, and the backlash we are currently experiencing will only become more swift and violent as long as it serves the narrative of religionists who hope to seize control over these very aspects of society.

We, atheists, are spawned by the cultures in which we live rather than introduced from the outside, so we don't maintain a foreignness to the white Christian majority that holds most of the levers of power to the same degree as Jewish or Black people. Nevertheless, we are ideological outsiders relative to the community that surrounds us, especially in countries where Islam, Christianity, or other religions hold sway over a majority of the population. Perhaps more than any other group, atheists, particularly ethical ones, call into question the notion, core to any faith, that religion is the only source of morality and truth and, therefore, the only path to leading a meaningful life. We are like the winter ice that forms in the cracks of the road year after year, eventually creating gaping potholes and fissures in religionists' tidy conception of atheists and morality until they can no longer continue on the path of their lives without acknowledging that they don't hold a monopoly on morality.

As we increase our profile and influence within our respective cultures, politics, and economies, the chances of virulent oppression increase. Some recommendations to mitigate the backlash include:

1. **Remaining humble as our success grows:** To avoid attracting negative attention from those who are envious, approach success with modesty, acknowledge that others have played a role in our success, and recognize that there is always room for growth and improvement. Libertarian claims that "I alone built that" are debatable, but they land poorly with those who have failed in life and who may have a propensity for blaming those who are more successful for their failure. This goes double if we are atheists who, according to the prosperity gospel, should be at the bottom of the social ladder.
2. **Emulating the philanthropic rich:** With growing income disparity, it is a miracle that the rich and famous don't regularly face a firing squad with their backs against the wall. Their secret? Philanthropy and giving back to the community that they are robbing blind. Andrew Carnegie and Steve Jobs were awful human beings. Still, the public overlooked their violent tempers and worker mistreatment because they brought the world both economic and technical advances, as well as hefty endowments and

charitable foundations. A successful atheist can buy a lot of goodwill by giving back to the society that scorns them.

3. **Maintain strong relationships with those around us:** Treat people respectfully and avoid any actions or behaviors that are exclusionary or elitist. That is, don't be like a religionist. Being approachable, friendly, and inclusive can help build strong relationships with others that can support our success. It's hard to hate someone we know and like, even if their beliefs don't correspond to ours. One of my most intriguing professors at university was a preening peacock who regularly spewed insensitive and politically incorrect nonsense. His wit, humor, and avuncular nature, however, enabled him to thrive in a progressive environment where few like him could.
4. **Be mindful of our success's impact on others, particularly those who may have yet to achieve similar success.** Be sensitive to others' feelings and avoid dismissive and condescending actions or behaviors. Empathy can help foster an environment of mutual respect and support and is especially important in dispelling the notion that atheists are self-serving and lack empathy.
5. **Maintain a positive outlook, even in the face of adversity and criticism:** Conservatives and traditionalists love to "own the libs" and lap up their snowflake tears. As I mentioned before, since we are atheists, we are liberals in the minds of many reli-

gionists. Being negative and fearful only invites their ire. By maintaining a positive attitude and not letting ourselves appear bothered by their abuse, they will be more likely to leave us be. My wife was bullied daily at school in the United States for being an Iranian during the hostage crisis. A particularly large male student slammed her head into her locker daily at lunch. After a few weeks, she turned to him and said, "Next time, please let me know in advance so I can take an aspirin since you seem to enjoy giving me a headache." The other kids laughed, and the bully stopped his attacks, realizing he couldn't get a rise from her.

Section V
Fight Back

Choose to fight only righteous fights, because then when things get tough — and they will — you will know that there is only one option ahead of you: Nevertheless, you must persist.[150]

Elizabeth Warren

IN A WORLD under assault by increasingly politicized religious movements, maintaining neutrality during every struggle with them is an exercise in futility. Ideological battlefields, especially religious ones, offer no demilitarized zones. There are no bystanders in these struggles, only degrees of involvement. Of course, we can choose to do nothing and retreat into apathy or indifference. However, this inaction only strips us of our agency and renders us victims, placing us at the mercy of zealots who wield their convictions like cudgels and bludgeon all who fail to fall in line. Even if we survive, in the end, we must face the shame of letting others fight and die for us.

Alternatively, we might opt for collaboration, nodding in agreement while privately dissenting, playing the role of the silent assenter. We may buy temporary respite from the zealots' enthusiasm. Still, at best, it is a stalling tactic, postponing the inevitable day when even the complicit are called to account for their lack of religious belief or adherence.

Another path offers hope for those who value intellectual freedom and individual agency. It is the path of resistance, varying in form but consistent. As we discussed in *Way #1*, it ranges from passive resistance as a "crypto atheist" covertly challenging religious dogma while outwardly conforming to diplomatic negotiation, the realm of the "diplomatic atheist" striving to build bridges of understanding, tempering critique with empathy; to the aggressive challenge of the "firebrand atheist" openly and unapologetically taking ideological adversaries to task. Our resistance is critical to building the pluralistic world we desire, regardless of its form. The choice to go underground, actively resist, challenge the status quo, or some combination of the three is not merely about opposing particular religious doctrines; it is a reaffirmation of the value of intellectual freedom and the right to personal belief.

Fortunately for atheists, we have typically had to struggle constantly against an often hostile religious majority all our lives, or at least since our atheist awakening, which has battle-hardened us to mount an effective defense despite our relatively small numbers. Religion, of course, is often inextricably intertwined with the dynamics of power, dominance, and violence. From religious wars to sectarian strife, from ideological purges to the persecution of heretics, history is awash with instances where religion has been weaponized to exert control and enforce conformity. Such is the language that zealots understand, the language of force and enthusiasm, of unyielding conviction and uncompromising demands, and that is the language we atheists must learn to speak.

To counter the forces of religious absolutism with equal and opposite force, to fight fire with fire, is not to mirror their zealotry but to refuse to be cowed by it. It is to reject the premise that ideological struggles are won solely by the loudest or the most zealous and to assert every individual's right to question, doubt, and dissent.

The notion of remaining neutral amid ideological struggles is a fanciful illusion. The tides of religious and political zealotry will sweep away those who stand idle or feign ignorance. Resistance, whether as a crypto atheist, a diplomat atheist, or a firebrand atheist, is the clarion call for those who value the principles of intellectual freedom and individual belief. In the face of dogma, doubt is our shield; in the face of zealotry, reason is our sword. The struggle may be arduous, but it is a battle worth fighting.

WAY #30

TRANSFORM CRYPTO-RELIGIOUS INSTITUTIONS

Hegemony refers to the control of the ideology of a society. The dominant group maintains power by imposing their ideology on everyone.[151]

SENSOY AND DIANGELO

THE SUBTLE AND not-so-subtle imprints of religion are woven throughout our linguistic fabric; they underpin the foundations of our civic institutions and are written into the fine print of our laws.

In the domain of language, for example, I, as an atheist, find the words "In God We Trust" on U.S. currency and "Under God" in our Pledge of Allegiance alienating and offensive — that is, if I think about them at all, which is seldom. Of course, I don't carry much paper money anymore, and having completed grade school, I have been spared those daily recitations of the pledge. The unfortunate fact is, however, that our society is dripping with a tremendous amount of Christian symbolism and pageantry so ubiquitous that I and I suspect most Americans, have grown almost oblivious to it as one would a foul smell that has been wafting from under the house for a month.

Unbeknownst to most, the Western mind and the societies we've forged remain ensnared by the tendrils of institutionalized religion. This all-encompassing embrace secretly stretches as far as nations proudly championing secular ideals to philosophers striving to transcend religious boundaries. Such entanglement hinders our capacity to perceive history with clarity and envision a future free from the shackles of spiritual residue that has spawned suffering, inequality, and discord over centuries, even when overt religiosity has been in retreat. In the here and now, it also helps to ensure that minority voices, including those of atheists, go unheard and that our political power and rights remain subordinate to those of the dominant religion, regardless of our growing ranks.

Linguistic Imprints

Even as Crypto-religious words seem to linger innocuously, tucked deep and hidden in our lexicon, there exists a disquiet in their origin. Basic terms like *atheism*, *nonbeliever*, or *non-religious* exist relative to religion and religionists rather than in their autonomous right. Such language invokes Orwellian undertones, as language manipulation molds thought, enabling those in power to maintain control. In George

Orwell's *1984,* Syme, who worked with Winston in the Ministry of Truth, explained:

> "…what justification is there for a word, which is simply the opposite of some other word? A word contains its opposite in itself. Take 'good' for instance. If you have a word like 'good' what need is there for a word like 'bad'? 'Ungood' will do just as well — better, because it's an exact opposite, which the other is not."[152]

The term *atheism* merely reflects the opposite of *theism,* devoid of individual significance, not to mention that it implies it is a religion or cohesive ideology when, in fact, it is the negation of such notions. Related terms like *non-religious* amount to negating the word *religious.* Crafted by religionists, these labels strip us of actual agency, confining our minds and actions within a realm of systemic religion. Our conversations, shaped by their language and logic, form a continuous loop. In their framework, if theism is virtuous, atheism and any act we perform become inherently tainted.

Religious terminology also infiltrates our discourse, not only with overtly religious words that we toss about colloquially today like *grace*, *sacrifice,* or *holiday*, but subtly camouflaged and secularized ones like *inspiration*, *vestige, trivial,* and *vocation* all of which have religious etymologies, among thousands of others. These seemingly innocuous words reveal the historical imprint of religion throughout our culture. Yet, beyond acknowledging this influence, they serve as points of manipulation that religious authorities can wield to tighten their grip on society.

It is no coincidence that the religio-fascist right wing in the United States has honed its skills at linguistic *jiu-jitsu*, transforming positive words like *equity*, *diversity*, and *progressive* into virtually unutterable epithets. Conversely, they are steadily rehabilitating and reinvigorating once repugnant terms like *Christian nationalism* or replacing the scientific term "fetus" with "baby" to transform the legal and logical debate about bodily choice into a hysterically emotional one. Linguistic manipulation is a powerful tool most effectively wielded by authoritarians and authoritarian movements that know how to resurrect and evoke ancient imagery and emotion from commonly used words.[153]

By using their religion-laden language, we become entangled in the religionists' intellectual constructs. Attempting to disprove religious dogma from within their theological boundaries is futile. While I, constrained by linguistic limitations, may utilize some of their language here, I strive to remain vigilant against their traps and resist surrendering to their linguistic and theological entanglements.

Ideological Frameworks

A subtle yet undeniable trace of religiosity often remains in the expansive corpus of intellectual thought, from philosophical doctrines to academic paradigms. I've traversed the landscape of medieval history, a realm steeped in the sacred, wrestling with these frameworks. A seemingly simple task like dating exposes the problem. BC (Before Christ) and AD (*Anno Domini*, or in the year of our Lord) delineate human history, anchoring it to the life of a Middle Eastern figure shrouded in myths and dubious historical truths.. This imposition extends into our scholarly conversations, even when adopting BCE (before the common era) and CE (common era). These modifications fail to sever our ties to that Jesus-centric reference, imperceptibly shaping our narratives and debates. They aren't merely dates; they mold our everyday dialogues. And here's where the fabric of academia frays. These seemingly innocuous abbreviations, even the sanitized ones, are seized by the unlearned and the misinformed as proof of the existence of Jesus and to validate the Bible. Their echoes ripple through social media conversations and encounters with devout believers, wielded as tokens of certainty, proof through letters and time that we can't easily dismantle.

Beyond these temporal designations, a host of ideologies and philosophies, even those purporting to be secular like Marxism or capitalism, maintain echoes of Christianity. Early Christian communities shared a kinship with Marxism's collectivism, advancing principles of communal ownership. Acts 4:35 records that in the early Christian Church in Jerusalem, "[n] o one claimed that any of their possessions was their own, but shared everything in common," which is echoed in Karl Marx's "From each according to his ability, to each according to his needs" expounded in his Critique of the Gotha Programme.[154]

While devoid of inherent religious mechanics, capitalism also thrives on power dynamics echoing the medieval Christian hierarchy. Extracting profit from labor hinges on business owners subduing the workforce and absconding with a portion of the value of their labor. The ideal worker accepts diminished control over their labor, time, and remuneration. Borrowing a notion from the genius scientist in the adult cartoon *Rick And Morty*, the owner-laborer hierarchy is just the medieval serf-lord relationship with a bit more worker freedom and a few extra steps.

Next, let's take the seemingly innocuous notion of the American Dream. The dream itself, a central part of our national ethos and identity for generations, has its roots in the Calvinist work ethic, which emphasizes the spiritual value of hard work and diligence. Wealth is the mark of divine favor, while poverty reflects sloth and moral failing. On the surface, whether religiously inspired or not, its effects seem like an overall positive for society (with some collateral damage among the "undeserving poor"), driving us to tackle challenges, build world-straddling industries, and make life-changing scientific breakthroughs. Such success is not the sole province of Protestants, given the economic successes in Pre-Reformation Catholic communities, which arose then, according to historians Fernand Braudel and Hugh Trevor-Roper. Also, Muslim nations created extensive and highly lucrative trade routes throughout much of Europe, Northern Africa, and Asia while building empires that eclipsed the West at the time. However, Calvinist values have made the United States the economic behemoth that it is today.

Unfortunately, the *American Dream* is also intertwined with other notions, some equally supported by Christianity, that tie it to our worst bigotries and biggest moral and historical blunders. The American Dream promotes the idea that anyone, regardless of background or social status, can succeed through hard work and perseverance. The prosperous post-war period propagated that myth, claiming anyone who worked diligently could achieve the *Leave it to Beaver* dream that persists among many to this day: economic security, working dad and homemaker mom, a house and 2.3 children, with the children destined for an even better, more prosperous life when they grew up.

All of this is well and good until it isn't. The flip side of the dream is that those who haven't achieved success have only themselves to blame. Calvinist theology, much like the prosperity gospel today, holds that success is a sign of their god's grace. Naturally, those who aren't successful are considered to have been denied or haven't earned that grace, even if acknowledged only subconsciously. The dream has historically excluded and marginalized people who face systemic barriers to success, such as people of color and those who are living in poverty who are, *de facto*, considered to be outside the pale of divine favor.

The truth is that the religious underpinnings of the dream have some nasty side effects. These metastasized when, starting in the 1970s and extending through globalization, wage stagnation, the growing income gap, and the Great Recession of subsequent decades, Americans began to see the prospects for their future and their children's dim no matter how hard they worked. As good Christians, it couldn't have been their shortcomings, nor could it be their god's oversight. This assumption triggered a search for those responsible for the retraction of the grace that America had received since its inception. Immigrants, minorities, the irreligious, and the undeserving poor became the scapegoats.

Joel Osteen and other Prosperity Gospel merchants now peddle the idea that Jesus and copious and frequent monetary "seed offerings" can enable followers to regain divine grace and recapture the American Dream. At the same time, those seen as poor and struggling are beneath contempt. Read J.D. Vance's memoir *Hillbilly Elegy*, and we find a stark fissure between the salt-of-the-earth blue-collar Americans who extoll Christian faith and duty to country versus the undeserving poor and those who have fallen on bad luck who are perceived as lazy, immoral, and given to vice.[155]

American exceptionalism is also similarly tainted. Our supposed exceptionalism rests on the belief that the United States is alone among nations, with a unique political system and values in human history. French writer, historian, and philosopher Alexis De Tocqueville, upon his return from his travels to the United States in 1831, was the first to describe it as exceptional in *De la démocratie en Amérique* (1835).[156] And perhaps at the time, it *was* exceptional relative to the illiberal and undemocratic government that ruled De Tocqueville's France. The implication is that the United States is destined and entitled to play a distinct and positive role on the world stage. It falls flat because it necessitates the maintenance of in-group/out-group division to ensure a sense of cohesion. Not only do non-Americans fall into the out-group camp, but so does anyone whose identity doesn't conform to the image of what an American should be, including minorities and those whose religious belief differs from the majority.

Further, religious Americans often believe their exceptionalism is divinely inspired. Many Puritans embraced the theology of *Divine Providence,* where their god had made a covenant with his people and chosen them to provide a model for the other nations of the Earth. Before his first group of Massachusetts Bay colonists set sail on the *Arbella,* the Puritan leader John Winthrop delivered a lecture, *A Model of Christian Charity,* on March 21, 1630, at Holyrood Church in Southampton. Quoting Matthew's Gospel (5:14), he declared that the Puritan community of New England should serve as a beacon of hope for the rest of the world. Americans, in general, eventually adopted the Puritans' moralistic values, which have remained a component of the national identity for centuries. The implication among many Americans is that if the nation strays from its Christian theological and moral roots, then The American Dream and Divine Providence will be withdrawn. Current calls to return prayer to schools, religion to politics, and traditional values to the family are symptomatic of this fear.

We may ask ourselves why any of this matters. The point for atheists is that the religious systems of oppression that negatively impact us and any other religious, ethnic, and racial minority run more deeply than just rank bigotry. Deeply rooted Crypto-religious words, beliefs, and institutions are entrenched and dangerous, and we must challenge them. Society may currently be outwardly transforming to be more non-religious and secular, but the underlying Crypto-religious structures could be used in times of crisis or discomfiting change to yank us as a nation back into overt religiosity.

Legal and Political Frameworks

The rule of law serves as a critical thread running through democratic nations, weaving together a system that steadfastly safeguards our rights over time and across often vast geographies and diverse peoples. It stands as a bulwark against the whims of capricious authorities, ensuring that both the governors and the governed adhere to a standard set of principles. Within this framework, disputes find resolution through a legal process that prides itself on fairness and impartiality, hallmarks of a civilized society. Likewise, political forms dictated by national Constitutions bring predictability and stability to the political process, establishing, for instance, in the United States, how and when people vote for representatives, how representation is distributed among states, how powers and responsibilities are allotted to the different branches of government, and so on.

This steadfast adherence to the law harbors within it a paradox. The immutability of these laws and political processes, designed to offer consistency, can also emerge as a formidable roadblock to progress, particularly within longstanding democracies with deep-rooted histories. The legal system, unable to evolve organically with the society it oversees, often grows through a process akin to accretion, layering new laws and amendments upon the old in a complex sedimentary process of legal formation. This approach, while pragmatic, often leaves behind anachronistic laws such as the Comstock Act, not actively repealed but simply overshadowed by newer regulations more attuned to the zeitgeist, though always having the potential to be resurrected for political purposes.

This sedimentation of legal layers has its complications. It can lead to a labyrinthine legal system, weighed down by overlapping and sometimes contradictory statutes. Judges in this landscape, especially when governments become gridlocked as it currently is in the United States to the point that new, necessary legislation rarely gets passed, are often forced to find novel, frequently controversial interpretations of laws to accommodate the ever-shifting cultural and societal sands. These attempts at workarounds to the law represent a challenge today as our society changes at breathtaking speed, especially regarding science and technology unanticipated by the nation's founders.

It can also lead to constitutionally mandated political structures, originally designed to enhance democracy, becoming anti-democratic over time. The U.S. Electoral College and congressional apportionment that favors smaller, less populated states over larger ones, violating the one-person, one-vote ideal, are prime examples. Again, we must do more than amend these due to political inertia and dysfunction.

Most importantly, laws often leave residue behind, even when technically rendered obsolete. In the United States, for instance, the abominable laws that enabled slavery and Jim Crow were not so much uprooted as mooted by monumental shifts such as the passage of the 14th Amendment and the Civil Rights Act of 1964, respectively. Yet, even slave and Jim Crow laws linger like relics that nonetheless clutter the legal system and leave behind vestiges of racial bias. Redlining and unequal treatment concerning arrests and sentencing of Black people and other minorities have lingered long after they were deemed equal citizens under the law. Indeed, these remnants continue to cast long shadows, subtly influencing the present.

For atheists, this means that many laws that disadvantaged us in the past, such as those that forbid nonbelievers from holding office or anti-blasphemy laws, although since rendered unconstitutional, can at least continue to color our profoundly religious society's perception of atheists as being unfit to hold office, as evidenced by the fact that most people would be averse to voting for us and many call into question our patriotism.

Critical Religious Theory

Given this linguistic, ideological, and legal Gordian knot, the Western mind and the societies we have built are bound by institutionalized religion for the most part without our being aware. Even those Western European nations that purport to have restructured their society according to secular principles have populations that have only nominally thrown off the yoke of religious superstition. Such entanglement complicates our pursuit of untainted perspectives on history, making it arduous to both view the past clearly and imagine a future unsullied by the religious taint that has fostered so much pain, inequity, and discord. It is this structural religionism, much like structural racism, that needs to be recognized and dismantled if we are ever to extract the bootheel of religion from our necks.

Critical Race Theory (CRT), the academic discipline not the catch-all for Right-wing white grievance, was developed to identify systemic racial biases perpetuated through the legal system. Similarly, we must formulate a concept of Critical Religious Theory to help us unveil and catalog the religious biases woven into the fabric of our language, culture, and jurisprudence. It can also help identify gaps that allow for unequal treatment of atheists even as society gives lip service to plurality and religious freedom.

Yet, neither religion nor atheism are standalone factors in social dynamics. Critical Race Theory, Critical Religious Theory, Critical Gender Theory, and other critical theories intersect to shape experiences of oppression and privilege. An intersectional approach can help uncover how different forms of discrimination compound and influence each other. By understanding where the vestiges of racial bias remain in our legal and political systems, we may gain clues as to where the shadow of anti-atheist or pro-religious bias lurks.

Aligning our plight with other out-groups also works to our practical benefit. By understanding the divisions in religious groups that deny leadership positions and equality to women and racial minorities and vilify non-heteronormative sexuality, we can make the case that these groups should not remain in the religionist camp but should ally themselves with those of us who are seeking to eliminate all structural bias.

To get practical benefits from Critical Religious Theory, we must:

1. **Make sure Critical Religious Theory doesn't become just another academic framework:** It's also a call to action. Theories are useless until they are tested, continually updated, and revised through practice in the real world. Such activism could include working to challenge negative stereotypes and biases against atheists in media portrayals, politics, and the workplace and advocating for increased inclusion of atheist voices. Also, fighting for voting rights, healthcare, housing access, and employment and labor rights not only for atheists but those in out-groups that often intersect with atheists is critical. As much as protecting our lives is essential, so too is protecting fellow atheists from anything that may place us at an economic, social, or political disadvantage. For those who are more academically or activism-inclined, we should be scouring our laws and customs for signs of anti-atheist bias and working on challenging them legislatively.
2. **Ensure the centrality of marginalized voices that intersect with atheists:** Keep front and center the perspectives and experiences of marginalized communities, including sexual and racial minorities, in addition to those of atheists, and seek to understand where their challenges intersect with those of atheists. By valuing these voices, we can better uncover hidden biases throughout our linguistic, political, and social institutions.

WAY #31

BE HONEST ABOUT WHY YOU RESIST

Your beliefs become your thoughts, your thoughts become your words, your words become your actions, your actions become your habits, your habits become your values, your values become your destiny.[157]

MAHATMA GANDHI

SIMILAR TO THE pointless arguments about politics with our Ultra-MAGA, Pentecostal uncle from rural Alabama during holiday dinners, geopolitical conflicts rooted in ideology or religion tend to be senseless, exhausting, and dehumanizing, offering no real benefits. These disputes stem from disagreements over subjective, artificially constructed principles rather than concrete issues like resources or territory, much like family arguments over who gets the last serving of stuffing at holiday gatherings.

In religious conflicts, neither side can objectively claim

the moral high ground. Consider, for example, the Muslim conquest of the Levant and Europe during the seventh and eighth centuries or the Christian crusades from the eleventh to the thirteenth centuries, which saw religious factions embroiled in violent struggles under the guise of a holy war between Cross and Crescent. In reality, these conflicts were nothing more than political power plays driven by two rapacious politicized religious traditions seeking to expand their spheres of influence, each committing morally reprehensible atrocities against the other.

On the opposite end of the spectrum, some conflicts pit oppressive ideologies against the forces of freedom and resistance. The struggle between the Axis and Allied powers in World War II is a prime example, with the Japanese and Germans both seeking national expansion, with the former seeking the subjugation and humiliation of the Chinese and the latter the extermination of Jewish people and other undesirables and domination of Europe. We could also cite the armed resistance of Africans, Native Americans, and South Americans against European and U.S. colonizers driven by notions of white superiority and Christian chauvinism.

In the ongoing struggle between atheism and Religio-fascism, which combines both religious and secular dynamics, how can we ensure that we remain aligned with justice and human rights rather than succumbing to mere religious prejudices and naked power plays? While atheism itself is not an ideology or political force, it's crucial to ensure that it never becomes such and that we remain transparent about our motivations when resisting Religio-fascism. This clarity will help us maintain humane methods and a just cause, even as we challenge the oppressive and dehumanizing aspects of religious extremism.

What does this mean? Implicit in defending our right to disbelieve should be our commitment to the broader concept of religious pluralism. Ensuring the right of the religionist to maintain their right to worship as they wish is necessary, even as they work to snuff out our right not to worship or our rights in general. We should do this not solely out of idealism but out of practical necessity. Religion, especially Christianity, thrives on resistance and oppression. The myth of martyrdom and the brutal oppression of Christian communities dominates the history of early Christianity. Candida Moss, in her book *The Myth of Persecution,* puts it best, "The myth of Christian martyrdom and persecution needs to be corrected because it has left us with a dangerous legacy that poisons the well of public discourse. We cannot use the mere fact that we feel persecuted as evidence that our cause is just or as the grounds for rhetorical or actual war. We cannot use the supposed moral superiority of our ancient martyrs to demonstrate the intrinsic superiority of our modern religious beliefs or ideological positions. Once we recognize that feeling persecuted is not proof of anything, then we have to engage in serious intellectual and moral debate about the actual issues at hand."[158] The notion that Christianity not only survives but thrives in the face of incredible odds and persecution sustains the belief in the power of their faith to triumph over adversity. As atheists, it's incumbent upon us to disabuse society of that notion by emphasizing that this victim-mentality is a cover for religio-fascist bigotry and oppression.

It is for us to realize that the religious outnumber us. The goal of warfare is to vanquish our enemy and make it so that they can no longer fight, but that assumes that we are of greater or equal strength to them. Rarely does a smaller force prevail. The colonial troops didn't exhaust Britain's ability to wage war during the American Revolution. They just made maintaining their colonial grip over the colonists more trouble than it was worth and ensured that their logistics and planning could not be sustained at such a great distance, much like the wars in Vietnam or Afghanistan where a more powerful American military was worn out by inferior armies. In that respect, we should style ourselves as rebels fighting an asymmetrical guerilla war of liberation against an occupying force. Rather than a war of weapons, it's a war of ideas where we aren't trying to defeat or destroy religion, only carve out a space where we can exist on equal footing with religionists. But how do we achieve this detente?

In the ongoing struggle for reason and rationality, we must occasionally pause to reflect upon the motivations and convictions driving us in our quest for a world free from religious oppression. This self-examination is crucial, as it can strengthen our resolve and sharpen our focus, ensuring that our efforts are well-directed and impactful:

1. **Consider the origins of our motivations:** Do personal experiences of religious coercion drive us, or are we propelled by a broader understanding of religion's

detrimental impact on society? While individual experiences can be powerful catalysts for change, a more comprehensive grasp of the issue ensures that our fight is rooted in rationality and evidence rather than solely in emotion.

2. **Scrutinize the depth of our convictions:** To what extent are we willing to dedicate ourselves to the cause of dismantling religious oppression? Are we prepared to endure the resistance and backlash that inevitably accompany such endeavors? A steadfast commitment is vital, as fighting for reason often requires tremendous persistence and resilience in the face of adversity.
3. **Acknowledge our potential biases and blind spots:** As champions of rationality, we must guard against dogmatism or intolerance. While we may critique religious beliefs and their consequences, we must maintain a respectful and empathetic approach. Dismissing or belittling believers' experiences and emotions will only hinder our cause, as it breeds animosity rather than fostering constructive dialogue.
4. **Be mindful of our methods in pursuing change:** Are we utilizing evidence-based arguments and fostering critical thinking, or are we resorting to *ad hominem* attacks and emotional appeals? Our cause will be most persuasive when grounded in logical reasoning and solid evidence. By consistently striving for intellectual rigor, we can ensure that our arguments resonate with those open to reevaluating their beliefs.

5. **Periodically evaluate the progress and impact of our efforts:** Are our methods effectively dismantling the structures of religious oppression, or are they inadvertently reinforcing them? By assessing the outcomes of our actions, we can refine our strategies and optimize our impact.

Way #32
Champion Sexual Diversity

All religions have something to say about sex, and it rarely coincides with scientific knowledge of sex and sexuality.[159]

Darrel Ray

WHEN MY WIFE and I first stumbled into each other's lives, we were at a point where logic and long-standing customs held no sway. Both in our thirties, our paths were marked by their fair share of turmoil, yet our coming together felt like a wild, youthful whirlwind, a rush of emotions akin to a high school romance. I was still reeling from a sudden breakup, and she was threading her way out of the legal and emotional labyrinth of a messy marriage, a blend of circumstances that seemed both reckless and explosive.

Our first encounter was far from the traditional script. We connected through *Yahoo Personals*, a digital wasteland of oddballs, fetishists, and losers (ourselves, the obvious exceptions, of course). We spent countless hours engaged in virtual backgammon battles and typed conversations. After a handful of live, frequently X-rated live dates, she moved into my tiny duplex. We had no discussions of our vastly different cultures and backgrounds. It was a spontaneous, almost mindless act, marked by exchanging a key, a makeshift wardrobe cobbled together for her belongings, and an extra pillow. It was all rather absurd, and we knew it.

More than two decades later, we stand together, having weathered a journey that defied conventional norms. Our bond wasn't forged in the traditional crucible of religion or societal timelines of romance, cohabitation, and matrimony. Instead, we've navigated the challenges and victories accompanying any enduring partnership, from career upheavals and family losses to the exhilaration of overseas adventures. The secret to our enduring connection has been our mutual commitment to growth and adaptability, which are vital components in an ever-evolving world, not religion.

For those whose romantic and sexual explorations and gender identities extend into even less traditional realms like polyamory, pansexuality, non-binary identities, and beyond, our story might appear almost conventional, even tame. But it's all relative. Anyone's deviation from the so-called "ideal" paths laid down by religious norms doesn't necessarily diminish the health and strength of the relationship. Often, it might even be a boon compared to those strictly adhering to these norms.

As someone who honors the inherent wisdom and diversity in love and sexuality, I find the religious antagonism towards human sexuality perplexing. Abrahamic faiths, in particular, propagate a rigid, hierarchical worldview, advocating for order and conformity as bulwarks against what they perceive as unpredictable and potentially destructive human passions. In their doctrine, stringent regulations around sex, procreation, gender expression, and marriage are upheld as the sole avenue to a stable, moral relationship and, by extension, a well-ordered society. This worldview posits that religious edicts provide the only safeguard against chaos, an idea I've always found to be more suffocating than comforting, especially as it doesn't reduce the true horrors of illicit sexuality such as rape, pedophilia, and sexual coercion. Often, it exacerbates or covers them up.

It's a peculiar thing, this deep-seated dread of change that clings to the fabric of religious thought, a fear that clutches at the heart of social structures. Those who follow religion see in the fluid, natural dance of human sexuality, particularly in those relationships and gender roles that color outside their scriptural lines, a force potent enough to send the walls of civilization tumbling down. But it's not the world that quivers on the brink of upheaval; it's the brittle foundations of religious institutions, rooted in unyielding roles, hierarchies, and moral codes, which threaten to fracture under the weight of progress.

In their grasp for control, religious gatekeepers weave chilling tales, and myths spun to uphold bans on life's most natural expressions, be it the love that dares not speak its name, the solitary comfort of one's own touch, or the joy of love unburdened by the sanctity of marriage. These are the narratives that bind, that seek to confine the expanse of human connection within the narrow corridors of doctrine, denying the simple truth that intimacy, in all its myriad forms, needs no validation from on high to flourish.

Recently, in many Republican-controlled regions in the United States, prohibitions on teaching about same-sex attraction and gender dysphoria in schools, participating in drag performances, denying gender-affirming health care to trans individuals, and so on have exploded in the last several years, a reactionary response to the gains that these issues have made legally and socially and the fear that it has struck in the hearts of religious authorities. Similar moves have been made by reactionaries in Europe and elsewhere as the fictions propping up the spiritual world order crumble. It is the dying gasp of old social forms desperately struggling to maintain relevance.

Ultimately, what religio-fascists don't want people to know is that rigid hierarchy and social control are not necessary for a well-run society and that there is a working alternative every bit as robust and successful as their own, again more so since society increasingly demands flexibility and resilience in all things, including relationships, as society becomes more just and inclusive. Every non-religionist whose relationship is healthy and functional proves the viability of this alternative.

My relationship with my wife, though not aligning with the Christian ideal, is largely tolerated and doesn't significantly challenge Christian dominance. The LGBTQ+ community's diversity, however, poses a continuous threat to religious authority, undermining not just the religious norms around sex and relationships but also traditional views on gender roles and identities.

Atheists and the LGBTQ+ community share a deep bond characterized by mutual support and understanding. This connection goes beyond mere identity; it's a rejection of religious strictures and judgmental attitudes, offering a safe space for LGBTQ+ individuals free from religious scrutiny. However, the atheist community is not free from prejudice, with some members still influenced by the biases of spiritual teachings we've left behind. This serves as a reminder of our ongoing journey towards solidarity, requiring self-reflection and a commitment to personal and collective growth.

In *Way #30*, we discussed the need to deconstruct the language and organizations perpetuating religion. We need to look no further than the trans community for a blueprint to make that happen. The adoption of they/them pronouns by transgender individuals represents a significant challenge to religion-defined linguistic frameworks, as it allows them to assert their identity and reclaim control over the language and mental constructs traditionally used to erase their existence or reduce them to vile epithets. This act of self-definition disrupts the rigid gender roles and expectations that many religious teachings have imposed, questioning the authority of religious institutions to define personal and societal morality based on gender.

Similarly, we atheists have the opportunity to reclaim language and narratives that are deeply infused with religious undertones. By consciously selecting words that reflect secular values and the principles of humanism, we can challenge the dominion religion holds over language. This deliberate act of choosing and crafting our language is a powerful statement of independence and self-identification, starkly contrasting identities defined by religion. It serves as a source of motivation, pushing us to determine our own ethical and moral frameworks without the constraints of religious doctrine, and underlines the significance of personal freedom and the right to select our own beliefs. Just as the transgender community has resisted the imposition of religious norms on gender and identity, atheists too can scrutinize and question the role of religious institutions in shaping language, societal norms, laws, and education. In doing so, we advocate for secular options that respect the individual's autonomy and celebrate the richness of human diversity.

Together, atheists and the LGBTQ+ community challenge the traditional moral order, with devoutly religious individuals viewing the affirmation of same-sex relationships, gender fluidity, and non-binary identities not as progress but as moral decay. These expressions of human diversity are wrongly attributed to a lack of religion rather than being recognized as natural variations within humanity.

This philosophical kinship extends into a practical alliance, forming a united stand against the rise of Religio-fascism and a shared commitment to upholding secular values.

The LGBTQ+ community has been at the vanguard of societal transformation. Their relentless pursuit of recognition, their fight for the right to love and live openly, has not only chipped away at the monolithic structures of gender norms but also loosened the grip of religious orthodoxy. This erosion of spiritual authority is a beacon of hope for atheists, for whom questioning and skepticism are not just intellectual exercises but integral to their very existence.

On the flip side, atheists, often perceived as the challengers of faith and questioners of the divine, stand as inadvertent allies to the LGBTQ+ community. Our presence, our questioning of the sacred narrative, affirms the right to exist beyond the confines of religious dogma. In challenging the status quo, in daring to imagine a world unshackled from celestial decrees, atheists inadvertently pave the way for a society where being different isn't just accepted but celebrated.

Together, these two groups, each distinct in their journey yet united in their cause, represent a powerful force. They are not just resisting an old order; they are architects of a new world where the freedom to be oneself is not just a right but a central aspect of human existence.

To expand secularism, these two groups must work together:

1. **Atheists must support the LGBTQ+ community by speaking out:** Actively advocating for the community, undermining the influence of religious institutions that foster intolerance and bigotry, and exposing the often prevalent hypocrisy among religious adherents, contribute to dismantling structural and deep-seated prejudices against the LGBTQ+ community. We should also advocate for policies that promote equality and inclusion for all, regardless of sexual orientation or gender identity.

2. **Atheists should ensure that all secular institutions are welcoming, not just tolerant:** It's not enough to break down religious institutions and their hold on society if there are no alternatives to replace them. As we build and reinforce secular institutions to provide a sense of community free of religious coercion, they must arise as places of inclusion for the LGBTQ+ and minority communities. Growth within these groups necessitates the inclusion of community members into leadership positions, which will have the bonus of helping to grow our overall numbers.
3. **The LGBTQ+ community can help to expand the reach of secularism:** non-religious members of the LGBTQ+ community should publicly embrace atheism or at least explicitly voice their solidarity with the non-religious. As I mentioned, they are often associated with the absence of religion anyway. We can build a formal alliance between the two movements by openly embracing the connection, as we should do with every social and religious out-group.

Way #33
Acknowledge That Religion Is Here to Stay

I'm an atheist myself, but religion is here to stay. Live with it. Do you want to get rid of religion? Good luck to you![160]

Richard Dawkins

LIKE ALMOST EVERY atheist, I cheer every time I see news headlines like *"Losing their Religion: Why US Churches are on the Decline"*[161] and *"America's Christian majority could end by 2070."*[162] Yes, nones are rising in the United States and Europe, especially among Gen Z, which is starting to flex its enormous progressive cultural and political influence, but don't break out the champagne just yet. Christianity and Islam are like the world's spiritual *Coke* and *Pepsi.* They, as with other major religions, are ubiquitous, highly addictive, and deeply ingrained in global cultures, ensuring they will probably be around for a long time.[163]

Worldwide, both Christianity and Islam and, to a lesser degree, every religion, except for Buddhism, is expected to grow through the end of the century.[164] At the same time, the proportion of the religiously unaffiliated will shrink due to low birth rates relative to religionists. Indeed, despite predictions of accelerating secularization in Western countries, religious populations around the world continue to proliferate. Growth is fastest in developing countries, where poverty and lack of education and opportunities make people more dependent on religious organizations for emotional and financial support. They also tend to have much higher birth rates than more secular societies. These trends ensure that religious beliefs, practices, and dependencies are effectively passed down from one growing generation to the next. Conversion plays a much smaller part, though it is responsible for much of the growth in China and the rest of Asia.

Larger extended family units in poorer, more religious societies are critical to maintaining religion's persistence. Parents, grandparents, and other family members shape children's religious upbringing, instill values, and enforce religious belief as a core component of family and community. Growing up in the United States and Europe, I remember visiting my grandparents perhaps once or twice a year and aunts and uncles even less frequently. We often lived thousands of miles away, which is not atypical in Western nations. Living in the same home as extended relatives is as unthinkable to me as living separately is to many in much of the developing world, even if they had the financial resources to choose another alternative.

As many ex-religionists in the West reading this guide can

attest, only a tiny percentage of people have the fortitude to ultimately decide to leave their faith even in the wealthy and geographically mobile West, often losing their families, homes, and communities in the process. People in poorer countries and communities need more resources and a cultural desire to separate from their families. A sense of family duty and cultural identity typically win out over selfish religious doubts, prompting them to stay and continue their family's spiritual traditions.

One of the stickiest aspects of religion is that religious institutions play a significant role in many aspects of society. In this case, the spiritual and the practical are intimately intertwined. Impoverished nations often rely on food and medical aid from religious groups for survival, as well as schools, community wells, and public works. They provide essential services and support to communities, fostering a sense of social cohesion and unity even under the yoke of patronizing and sometimes abusive missionaries. Unfortunately, in the West, too, many of the hospitals, private K-12 schools, universities, and programs for the homeless are controlled by churches and other religious entities. These then avail themselves of their captive and dependent audiences to proselytize and promote their religious views, such as forbidding abortions at Catholic hospitals, gay teachers in schools, and insurance coverage for contraception at Christian-owned businesses since bigotry and hatred are central parts of their catechism that we must not infringe.

I don't quite understand the need or desire many, if not most, people to seek, and will continue to pursue, meaning and purpose not just in their personal lives but cosmically as well, but it is not mine to judge. The fault in human programming is the propensity for teleological thinking, which compels many to seek meaning and causation, two very human-centric notions when there is none in an infinite universe. Even when formal religion is, for the most part, extracted from daily life as is increasingly common in the West, we see the need for meaning continue in the popularity of such practices as mindfulness, meditation, and yoga, as well as the continued interest in traditional forms of spirituality and mysticism, even among the unchurched.

Religious beliefs and practices will continue to persist in many societies, particularly those with relatively low levels of education, those that are susceptible to economic, political, and environmental uncertainty, as well as those that have a high proportion of its population that is having difficulty adapting to the fast pace of technological and social change. Rural communities are a prime example where tradition, conformity, and in-group identity are ingrained survival mechanisms. Through religious teachings, rituals, and communities, people can cope with life's challenges and establish a moral framework. For many, religion is an essential source of comfort and guidance in times of crisis, making it unlikely to fade away as long as we have challenges and hardships to overcome.

Finally, religion continues to play a growing role in shaping public discourse and informing public policy in the United States despite its decreasing importance among the population. Politicians, who still need to burnish their bona fides among members of the faithful, are compelled to regularly pander to religious groups and leaders who have deep pockets and highly effective lobbyists that gain them access.

It is crucial to recognize that the grip of religion on society is tenacious and deeply rooted. Nevertheless, we can strive to minimize its power and social impact through various methods, emphasizing reason, education, and open dialogue:

1. **Promote critical thinking and scientific literacy:** By fostering a society that values evidence-based reasoning and skepticism, we can equip individuals with the tools to question dogmatic beliefs and the supernatural claims often perpetuated by religious institutions. Education should emphasize the importance of examining, evaluating, and seeking evidence before accepting any claim, spiritual or otherwise.
2. **Advocate for secular education, free from religious indoctrination:** Children should learn about the diversity of religious beliefs and the historical contexts from which they arose without promoting any one faith. This unbiased approach would enable future generations to make informed decisions about their beliefs rather than unquestioningly adhering to the faith of their upbringing. As many atheists can confirm, the more one learns about religion, especially approaching it in an academic and evidence-based way, the more likely it will produce a non-religious adult.
3. **Challenge the privilege granted to religious institutions, particularly in the political and legal spheres:** We must uphold secularism at all costs, ensuring that the government bases its decisions on reason and evidence rather than religious doctrine. Tax exemptions for

religious organizations should also be reconsidered, as they perpetuate their power and influence over society and advantage them over their non-religious analogs, discouraging their establishment.

4. **Work to provide a sense of community and belonging to replace religious organizations:** Numerous people turn to religious institutions for comfort, support, and a sense of community. While houses of worship often meet the need for a tight-knit, like-minded group, religion's capacity to provide this is not inherently unique. The sense of compelling community found within religions plays a significant role in reinforcing and perpetuating beliefs. Additionally, religions' structured organization and tax-exempt status contribute to their sustainability.

Some like-minded atheists have begun creating alternatives to Sunday service that slake people's thirst for fellowship. These include *Oasis communities*[165] and *Sunday Assembly*,[166] which have chapters nationwide. Several annual conventions, like Skepticon, have also sprung up. Alternatives are out there. We just need to look for them or establish our own.

Way #34

Handle Proselytizers With Care

"The act of bell ringing is symbolic of all proselytizing religions. It implies the pointless interference with the quiet of other people."[167]

Ezra Pound

I ATTENDED AN Episcopalian boarding school that was only nominally religious. In fact, like a European country with a state-sponsored religion, its nominal affiliation probably did more to dissuade spiritual belief than to encourage it. Combined with the fact that the school was religiously mixed, overt expressions of religiosity beyond the invocation at our weekly assembly were non-existent, save for a pair of identical twins a year or two behind me. The duo, "Bill" and "Todd," regularly accosted me, sauntering across the main quad side-by-side in lockstep. How I dreaded seeing them coming! Their ongoing mission: to engage me in some tiresome conversation about Biblical inerrancy and, I assume, gain a convert who might join the odd Jews-for-Jesus kid who sometimes tagged along with them. At the time, I rarely discussed my atheism with anyone unless asked, but I must have emitted some sort of secularist vibe, or perhaps my social ineptitude made me appear an easy mark.

Bill and Todd were like characters straight out of a horror movie, a modern-day version of the Children of the Corn. They stood out on campus, tall, blond, and always dressed in dark trousers and polo shirts. Ok, so maybe they weren't quite that bad. Both were prodigious violinists who once tutored me, and I am grateful for their help in transforming me from a horrendous, tone-deaf violinist into a merely awful one. So, I probably annoyed them as much as they did me. But that doesn't negate the fact that the more assertive of the two would carry a black briefcase filled with religious tracts, Bibles, and what I assume was a home exorcism kit. A reflexive sigh would reverberate through my body every time they approached. The only small consolation was that they weren't Scientologists.

Whenever they tried to engage me in a conversation, I would typically brush them off with a dismissive, "I don't believe in that nonsense," hoping to avoid getting entangled in their web of religious fervor. However, they persisted, and after months of this, I'd had enough. During one particularly heated discussion, Bill, the more extroverted brother, gave me the perfect opening when he challenged me to explain the meaning of "INRI." Without skipping a beat, I replied, "Of course, it's an acronym for *Iesus Nazarenus Rex Iudaeorum*, a

Latin phrase supposedly inscribed on the cross as a Roman mockery." Bill's shock was evident as he had only known the English translation, and he mumbled something, turned heel, and left. From that point on, Bill and Todd's attempts to convert me were a thing of the past.

According to various surveys, atheists are often more knowledgeable about religion than many of the faithful. This paradox poses a problem for evangelists and missionaries when they find themselves at the doorstep of an ex-Catholic, invigorated by his first cup of coffee that's unlocked his Jesuit-trained brain. He is ready to quote scripture and deftly wield exegesis like a cudgel.

Ironically, the reason many atheists leave religion behind in the first place is because they have delved deeply into the Bible, Koran, or other religious texts and found them to be rife with contradictions, illogic, and even immorality. I have heard this countless times, particularly from those raised in extreme forms of religion, such as Pentecostalism and Islam, both of which, unfortunately, are on the rise. Forcing children to memorize verses or shun modern society in hopes of brainwashing them frequently has the opposite effect.

As atheists, we may feel compelled to engage in verbal sparring with religious believers, using our scriptural or scientific knowledge to challenge their faith. However, such exchanges rarely change anyone's mind. My response to the twins, while effective in getting them to stop engaging with me, did nothing to challenge their commitment to their religion or prevent them from harassing others. In fact, except in situations where those who are targets of missionaries are either forced or bribed with food, medicine, and education to convert, proselytizing and missionary work are rarely effective. They are designed more to reinforce the beliefs of the proselytizer than to convert. If a wicked nonbeliever resists or abuses them as the persecuted believer expects, it proves their path must be correct.

In retrospect, my efforts would have likely backfired if I had gone beyond mere polite conversation and launched into openly hostile verbal attacks or refutation. Open hostility often reinforces Christians' ever-present persecution complex and kills any chance of an honest and open dialog or can provoke them to redouble their proselytization efforts. The twins would have definitely grown more animated or possibly turned hostile. As is typical of religionists, particularly devout Christians, they thrive on their identity as a persecuted group, even when they are in the majority and wield tremendous political power. Christianity, as practiced in the United States particularly, also demands the right to proselytize, and its followers see any resistance to their attempts at doing so or their right to insinuate their beliefs into every conversation, legislative act, and facet of life as anti-Christian. Many genuinely believe they have the right to share the "Good news," even when it is terrible news to us and violates our right to remain unmolested.

Proselytizing is possibly one of the most irritating aspects of religionists. Yet it also has a broader impact by injecting religion into the public sphere beyond the closed doors of the church, where almost every atheist wishes it would remain. Fighting it only serves to invigorate its perpetrators.

Minimizing interaction can help to reduce religion's further insinuation into the social fabric.

When proselytizers accost us in the Walmart parking lot or pound on our front doors at all hours, the best responses to consider:

1. **Call it like it is and set clear boundaries:** We should courteously inform them that we are not interested in hearing their proselytizing and would appreciate their respect for our boundaries by leaving. This approach serves two purposes. Firstly, the term "proselytizing" carries negative implications and a troubled history of coerced conversions among colonized populations. Despite Christians' efforts to distance themselves from this term, their actions still align with it. Subtly addressing this serves as a reminder that such behavior is considered abusive and inappropriate. Secondly, it establishes clear boundaries. We can further clarify that just as their right to practice their religion is acknowledged, they should also respect our right to privacy and to be left alone.
2. **Simply say, "No, thank you.":** Declining their message politely and directly without entering into a debate is achievable by saying, "Thank you for your offer, but I am not interested in discussing religion right now." This approach is the least aggressive, although it might not always ensure they leave immediately.

3. **Use humor to diffuse the situation:** A well-timed humorous remark can often diffuse the situation and allow the proselytizer to save face, which is critical, while also getting their message across. Losing face, especially when multiple missionaries flock together, will likely provoke a negative group response, so avoid sarcasm, as it involves conveying contempt to the recipient.
4. **Close the door or walk away:** If engaging with a proselytizer makes us uncomfortable, we have the right to walk away. While this may seem rude and doesn't ensure these missionaries won't persist and return later, it can temporarily remove them from our doorstep.

Way #35

Embrace Gen Z, Our Greatest Hope

Gen Z'ers (born after 1997) focus a significant amount of energy on determining what matters to them and what they can contribute.[168]

Anna Long

THE MARCH 23, 2023, House Energy and Commerce Committee hearing on *TikTok* was just the usual DC spectacle, a confusing circus of Boomers and Gen X Luddites, Conservative Karens, and redneck Congresspersons, most of whom, from their lines of questioning, struggle with simple internet and email usage, let alone understanding the complexities of social media and cybersecurity. And it showed. The company's CEO, Shou Zi Chew, was bombarded with inaccurate information about the Chinese cybersecurity threat and inflammatory accusations about TikTok's business operations. The fact that his interrogators cut him off before he could answer was the real kicker, but I can't say I'm surprised. Such grandstanding is par for the course in such hearings.[169]

What was genuinely incomprehensible was the Democrats' complicity in this kangaroo court and their persecution of TikTok. Desperate to appear tough on China and perhaps placate American tech giants like Facebook, threatened by the innovative TikTok juggernaut, they ignored the needs of the young constituents they represent. Although 57% of Gen Z gets its news from TikTok (a considerable portion of them generate income from the platform), Democrats joined in the pile-on. Gen Z and millennials are among the few groups that lean Democrat, with 77% and 56%, respectively, voting blue.[170]

As of now, the House has passed a bill giving ByteDance, TikTok's parent company, six months to find a buyer for the social media platform, or else it will be banned from the Apple and Android app stores.[171] Although President Biden has signaled he will sign the bill into law if it reaches his desk, its fate is not assured in the Senate. Even so, it's hard to imagine a better way for Democrats to alienate such a key voting demographic than cutting off their primary source of news and information and an essential income-generating platform and guaranteeing they sit on their hands come the next election cycle.

As atheists, we must learn from this and heed the voices of this vital demographic, on whose shoulders both atheists' and the Democratic party's futures rest. Much of what we have said about gender and race, where atheism tends to be the province of privileged white men, begins to bend toward a more diverse, potentially less religious future when we look at Gen Z, as long as we don't blow it.

When examining Gen Z's faith, I find it heartening to observe the growing numbers of that cohort who now embrace nonbelief. A remarkable 17% of Gen Z already identifies as atheist or agnostic, a rate twice as high as any other age group. An additional 31% fall into the category of "nothing in particular," demonstrating a detachment from organized religion.

Even more intriguing is the notable shift in religiosity among women born after 2000. In *Way #3*, we talked about how women have historically been more religious than men, but this is not the case for Gen Z. For the first time in recorded history, women exhibit lower levels of religious affiliation than their male counterparts within Gen Z. Among this cohort, 49% of women identify as "nones," while men lag slightly behind at 46%. This departure from the historical trend, where young men now display higher religiosity, signals a significant transformation in societal attitudes and the growing agency of women.

The racial aspect of the religious landscape is also a cause for optimism. Surprisingly, Black women stand out as the most likely group within Gen Z to identify as "nones," with a substantial 53% embracing non-religious affiliations. White women follow closely behind at 51%.[172]

However, we must remain cautious and address trends and factors that could sway Gen Z back into the religious fold. As with previous generations, we can expect that Gen Z will likely become more conservative as they mature. Additionally, the convergence of Right-wing politics and radical religion poses a concerning risk. Gen Z may be non-aligned religiously, but there is a large cohort that is taken in by megachurches and their Christo-tainment allure, as well as their growing Right-wing political radicalization. The angry young incels, *Unite the Right* marchers, Andrew Tate groupies, and Ashbury Revivalists are not drawn from the ranks of Boomers or Gen X. We're too busy enjoying the wealth, homes, families, and American Dream that is so often denied to the younger generations. The allure of extreme religious ideologies, coupled with the pull of Right-wing political forces, may nudge young individuals toward radicalized religious beliefs as part of their future political alignment. We must take the new generation seriously and provide proper mentorship.

As a Gen Xer, I don't know much about what's new with Gen Z, and my humor is probably a little beyond eye-roll-worthy dad jokes. Yet, being authentic and committed to ideals is fundamental to them, perhaps more than any other generation. To combat any natural rightward shift, we must champion, where our interests align, issues important to that demographic, such as racial, gender, and sexual diversity and equity, school safety, affordable education and healthcare, and fighting environmental degradation and climate change. These values span the social and political spectrum among Gen Z and are vital reasons most have found political and religious conservatism repellent. Each of these is indirectly part of the fight against religious intolerance, given that these are typical religio-fascist bugbears. As such, we must become champions of millennial and Gen Z needs and aspirations, not try to tell them what they should or shouldn't want. The atheism of the future must be defined and redefined by the new generations, not by those of us whose time is much closer to the eternal dirt nap.

To avoid alienating Gen Z and millennials and to appeal to those who may be reticent about embracing the atheist moniker, atheists of older generations need to:

1. **Be a mentor:** For an older nonbeliever like me, being a good atheist doesn't mean standing firm or pure in our convictions but being willing to teach those young atheists who would follow us. Millennials and Gen Z have lost the heroes, role models, and mentors that previous generations were fortunate enough to have. Many, especially young men, are angry, disillusioned, and adrift.[173] It takes a mentor to embrace them for who they are. For atheists, it means telling them that their growing religious disbelief is ok and that they are not freaks, immoral, or alone, and ushering them into membership in one of the fastest growing worldviews: atheism, or at least healthy skepticism.
2. **Speak inclusively, even when talking about religionists:** Both Gen Z and millennials are the most diverse generations in U.S. history, so atheists and atheist organizations should strive likewise to be inclusive of all people, including those from religious communities. While these younger cohorts tend to be more likely to embrace atheism, they are not typically as intolerant of religionists as those of us who are older. They can separate believers as people from their religious behavior and politics more than

older generations. Stereotyping and making sweeping generalizations or using offensive language toward religionists or any other group will likely not go down well, as younger people are typically more attuned to all types of prejudice.

3. **Be open-minded about talking about religious topics:** We should learn to be more open-minded and willing to engage in thoughtful conversations about religion and spirituality. This does not mean compromising our beliefs or becoming religious; instead, we should be ready to learn about different spiritual beliefs and perspectives and avoid dismissing them. Such openness will enable us to nudge those on the fence toward pluralism. Few young people want to join closed-minded groups, especially those that openly mock others' beliefs.
4. **Always be authentic regarding atheism:** It is often tempting, even for me, to sometimes dismiss the notion of being authentic as a trite neologism or an insult to older people who are often wrongly seen as fake and inauthentic. For millennials and Gen Z, however, being authentic just means being true to oneself and expressing one's true beliefs and values, something that should come naturally to us atheists who have had to buck the majority to embrace our convictions openly. Younger generations prioritize honesty, transparency, and sincerity in their personal and professional lives. So we should push even further with the notion of authenticity by being honest

about both the benefits and challenges of embracing atheism, as well as acknowledging that some atheists, for example, can be extreme in their views, which may turn off some people. We need to recognize our whole selves, warts and all.

In the age of TikTok and other social media, being authentic means being genuine in our online presence. Millennials and Gen Z are keenly aware of the curated nature of social media, and they value individuals who are willing to share their flaws and struggles in addition to their successes in a genuine fashion. They will appreciate atheists who stand up for what they believe in, even if it is unpopular, and share their candid perspectives and advice.

CONCLUSION

Standing at the precipice of a rapidly changing world, where entrenched fears and superstitions collide with the enlightening forces of progress, we atheists must illuminate a path forward. Our mission is to safeguard our rights, freedoms, and opportunities in an era increasingly shadowed by the rise of religiously intolerant movements. This guide is not an instrument of combat against religion or an endeavor to dismantle faith-based beliefs. Instead, it is a proactive, comprehensive blueprint for navigating these times as nonbelievers committed to preserving secular democracy and cultivating mutual respect and tolerance. I hope this guide is only a start, not an end, with others expanding on my writing. Your efforts can help extend its reach, accelerating enlightenment globally and promoting tolerance, secularism, pluralism, and inclusivity.

Our activism as atheists must center on preserving and enhancing our rights to live free from organized religion's impositions and the politicization of faith, which clash with our values. We must immerse ourselves in learning about the history, strategies, and objectives of religio-fascist movements to understand their stories, fears, and motivations and recognize the social and economic forces driving their emergence.

Building a resilient and supportive community among atheists and those of similar mindsets is crucial. We need to foster safe spaces, both in the virtual and physical realms, where atheists can find comfort, share experiences, and strategize. Our community should know no borders, welcoming atheists and secularists worldwide, particularly those in areas most affected by religious extremism.

Political activism is a vital element of our strategy. We must engage in the democratic process, supporting only candidates who uphold secular values and advocate for the separation of church and state. Additionally, we should advocate, contribute to public discourse, and educate policymakers about the perils of religious extremism, aiming to influence legislation.

In our defense of secular democracy's principles, we must challenge laws and policies that favor religious perspectives and combat discrimination against atheists and other minorities. Advocating for a secular education system that nurtures critical thinking and scientific literacy is equally important.

Our struggle, however, extends beyond external threats. We must confront internal biases and prejudices, striving for inclusivity and forging alliances with other marginalized groups. We should examine our assumptions and beliefs through self-reflection and critical analysis, always remaining receptive to new ideas and viewpoints.

Finally, we must be ready to counter the encroachment of Religio-fascism through legal and moral means, including peaceful protests, civil disobedience, and other forms of nonviolent resistance. Our aim is not to defeat religion but to uphold the secular, democratic values that enable all beliefs to coexist peacefully. We must stand firm in our resolve to fight but only resort to such measures as a last recourse.

Our battle against religious intolerance is a quest for a world where love and knowledge prevail over fear and ignorance. It is a struggle not solely for atheists but for all who value freedom, reason, and the dignity of every human being.

APPENDIX I

RECOMMENDED ATHEIST LIBRARY BOOKS

The following is a small sampling of recommended books for an atheist library that may become difficult to acquire under a religiously authoritarian government:

Atheism

Carrier, Richard, *Sense and Goodness without God: A Defense of Metaphysical Naturalism*, Bloomington: AuthorHouse, 2005.

Dawkins, Richard, *The God Delusion*, New York: Mariner Books, 2006.

Dawkins, Richard, *The Blind Watchmaker: Why the Evidence of Evolution Reveals a Universe without Design*, New York: W. W. Norton & Company, 1996.

Dennett, Daniel, *Breaking the Spell: Religion as a Natural Phenomenon*, New York: Penguin Books, 2006.

Harris, Sam, *Letter to a Christian Nation*, New York: Vintage Books, 2006.

Harris, Sam, *The End of Faith: Religion, Terror, and the Future of Reason,* New York: W. W. Norton & Company, 2004.

Hitchens, Christopher, *God is Not Great: How Religion Poisons Everything,* New York: Twelve, 2007.

Hitchens, Christopher, *The Portable Atheist: Essential Readings for the Nonbeliever,* Philadelphia: Da Capo Press, 2007.

Russell, Bertrand, *Why I Am Not a Christian*, London: Routledge, 1957.

Smith, George H., *Atheism: The Case Against God*, Buffalo: Prometheus Books, 1979.

Religion

Ali, Abdullah Yusuf, *The Holy Qur'an: Text, Translation and Commentary*, Brentwood: Amana Corporation, 1934.

Confucius, *The Analects*, Translated by D. C. Lau, London: Penguin Classics, 1997.

Confucius, *The Doctrine of the Mean*, Translated by A. C. Muller, Beijing: Foreign Language Press, 2003.

Confucius, *The Great Learning*, Translated by James Legge, North Charleston: CreateSpace Independent Publishing Platform, 2013.

Easwaran, Eknath, trans. *The Bhagavad Gita*, Tomales: Nilgiri Press, 2007.

King James Version, *The Holy Bible: Containing the Old and New Testaments*, London: Robert Barker, 1611.

Dystopia

Atwood, Margaret, *The Handmaid's Tale*, Toronto: McClelland and Stewart, 1985.

Atwood, Margaret, *The Testaments*, New York: Doubleday, 2019.

Bradbury, Ray, *Fahrenheit 451*, New York: Ballantine Books, 1953.

Collins, Suzanne, *The Hunger Games*, New York: Scholastic Press, 2008.

Huxley, Aldous, *Brave New World*, London: Chatto & Windus, 1932.

Orwell, George, *1984*, London: Secker & Warburg, 1949.

Subversive Literature

Alderman, Naomi, *The Power*, London: Viking, 2016.

Alexander, Michelle, *The New Jim Crow: Mass Incarceration in the Age of Colorblindness*, New York: The New Press, 2010.

Awad, Mona, *Bunny*, New York: Viking, 2019.

Ballard, J. G., *Crash*, London: Jonathan Cape, 1973.

Banks, Iain, *The Wasp Factory*, London: Macmillan, 1984.

Bataille, Georges, *Story of the Eye*, Paris: Jean-Jacques Pauvert, 1928.

Bulgakov, Mikhail, *The Master and Margarita*, Moscow: YMCA Press, 1967.

Ellis, Bret Easton, *American Psycho*, New York: Vintage Books, 1991.

Frost, Mark, *The Secret History of Twin Peaks*, New York: Flatiron Books, 2016.

Frost, Mark, *Twin Peaks: The Final Dossier*, New York: Flatiron Books, 2017.

Hendrix, Grady, *We Sold Our Souls*, Philadelphia: Quirk Books, 2018.

Herman, Edward S., and Chomsky, Noam, *Manufacturing Consent: The Political Economy of the Mass Media*, New York: Pantheon Books, 1988.

Hoban, Russell, *Riddley Walker*, London: Jonathan Cape, 1980.

Jemisin, N.K., *The Fifth Season*, New York: Orbit, 2015.

Kadare, Ismail, *The Palace of Dreams*, Tirana: Naim Frashëri Publishing House, 1981.

Kingsolver, Barbara, *The Lacuna*, New York: Harper, 2009.

Lanagan, Margo, *Red Spikes*, Australia: Allen & Unwin (Little Ark Books), 1991.

Lawrence, D. H., *Lady Chatterley's Lover*, Florence: Tipografia Giuntina, 1928.

Lee, Harper, *To Kill a Mockingbird*, Philadelphia: J.B. Lippincott & Co., 1960.

Marquez, Gabriel Garcia, *One Hundred Years of Solitude*, New York: Harper & Row, 1967.

McEwan, Ian, *The Cement Garden*, London: Jonathan Cape, 1978.

Morrison, Toni, *Beloved*, New York: Alfred A. Knopf, 1987.

Moshfegh, Ottessa, *My Year of Rest and Relaxation*, New York: Penguin Press, 2018.

Murakami, Ryū, *Piercing*, Tokyo: Kodansha, 1994.

Nabokov, Vladimir, *Lolita*, Paris: Olympia Press, 1955.

Nutting, Alissa, *Tampa*, New York: Ecco, 2013.

Orwell, George, *Animal Farm*, London: Secker & Warburg, 1945.

Palahniuk, Chuck, *Damned*, New York: Doubleday, 2011.

Palahniuk, Chuck, *Fight Club*, New York: W. W. Norton & Company, 1996.

Salinger, J.D., *The Catcher in the Rye*, Boston: Little, Brown and Company, 1951.

Thomas, Angie, *The Hate U Give*, New York: Balzer + Bray, 2017.

Thompson, Hunter S., *Fear and Loathing in Las Vegas*, New York: Random House, 1971.

Vonnegut, Kurt, *Breakfast of Champions*, New York: Delacorte Press, 1973.

Vonnegut, Kurt, *Slaughterhouse-Five*, New York: Delacorte Press, 1969.

Walker, Alice, *The Color Purple*, San Diego: Harcourt Brace Jovanovich, 1982.

History

Arendt, Hannah, *The Origins of Totalitarianism*, San Diego: Harcourt Brace Jovanovich, 1951.

Brown, Dee, *Bury My Heart at Wounded Knee: An Indian History of the American West*, New York: Holt, Rinehart and Winston, 1970.

Frank, Anne, *The Diary of Anne Frank*, New York: Doubleday, 1947.

Shirer, William L., *The Rise and Fall of the Third Reich: A History of Nazi Germany*, New York: Simon & Schuster, 1960.

Law

Holt, J.C., ed., *Magna Carta*, Cambridge: Cambridge University Press, 1992.

Constitution of the United States, Washington D.C.: National Archives and Records Administration, 1787.

Hamilton, Alexander, James Madison, and John Jay, *The Federalist Papers*, New York: J. and A. McLean, 1787-1788.

Politics and Political Fiction

Alexander, Michelle, *The New Jim Crow: Mass Incarceration in the Age of Colorblindness*, New York: The New Press, 2010.

Marx, Karl, and Friedrich Engels, *The Communist Manifesto*, Translated by Samuel Moore. London: Penguin Classics, 2002.

Sinclair, Upton, *The Jungle*, New York: Doubleday, Page & Company, 1906.

Zinn, Howard, *A People's History of the United States*, New York: Harper & Row, 1980.

Most Banned

Kobabe, M., *Gender Queer: A Memoir*, St. Louis: Lion Forge, 2020.

Johnson, G. M., *All Boys Aren't Blue: A Memoir-Manifesto*, New York: Farrar, Straus and Giroux (BYR), 2020.

Morrison, T., *The Bluest Eye*, New York: Holt, Rinehart and Winston, 1970.

Curato, M., *Flamer*, New York: Henry Holt and Co. (BYR), 2020.

Green, J., *Looking for Alaska*, New York: Dutton Books, 2005.

Chbosky, S., *The Perks of Being a Wallflower*, New York: MTV Books, 1999.

Evison, J., *Lawn Boy*, Chapel Hill: Algonquin Books, 2018.

Alexie, S., *The Absolutely True Diary of a Part-Time Indian*, New York: Little, Brown and Company, 2007.

Perez, A. H., *Out of Darkness*, Minneapolis: Carolrhoda Lab, 2015.

Maas, S. J., *A Court of Mist and Fury*, New York: Bloomsbury USA Children's Books, 2016.

Hopkins, E., *Crank*, New York: Margaret K. McElderry Books, 2004.

Andrews, J., *Me and Earl and the Dying Girl*, New York: Amulet Books, 2012.

Dawson, J., *This Book Is Gay*, London: Hot Key Books, 2014.

Appendix II

Atheist Organizational Resources

Organizations

American Atheists
(https://www.atheists.org/)

American Humanist Association
(https://americanhumanist.org/)

Atheist Republic
(https://www.atheistrepublic.com/)

Center for Inquiry
(https://centerforinquiry.org/)

Freedom from Religion Foundation
(https://ffrf.org/)

Secular Coalition for America
(https://secular.org/)

Social Media Groups

Atheist Underground
(https://www.tiktok.com/@atheistunderground)

Atheism United
(https://www.facebook.com/groups/atheismunited)

Atheism World
(https://www.tiktok.com/@atheism_world)

Atheist Community
(https://www.facebook.com/
groups/2888067768096708/)

Atheist Republic
(https://www.linkedin.com/company/atheist-republic/)

Atheists
(https://www.facebook.com/groups/185348921846461)

The Sarcastic Atheist
(https://www.facebook.com/groups/182377446358063)

Church Alternatives

Oasis Network (https://www.oasisnetwork.com/)

Sunday Assembly (https://www.sundayassembly.org/)

Endnotes

1 AP, "Father Sues Air Force Academy," *LA Times*, October 7, 2005, accessed March 22, 2023, https://www.latimes.com/archives/la-xpm-2005-oct-07-na-academy7-story.html.

2 Colin Bertram, "Tammy Faye and Jim Bakker: Inside Their Relationship and the Scandals That Brought Down Their Empire," *Biography*, September 15, 2021, accessed July 18, 2023, https://www.biography.com/crime/tammy-faye-jim-bakker-relationship-scandals.

3 Maggie Astor, "How the Politically Unthinkable Can Become Mainstream," *NYT*, February 26, 0219, accessed August 24, 2023, https://www.nytimes.com/2019/02/26/us/politics/overton-window-democrats.html.

4 Tim Dickenson, "These Christian Nationalists Want to Stone Adulterers to Death." *Rolling Stone*, July 29, 2023, accessed July 29, 2023, https://www.rollingstone.com/politics/politics-features/execution-stoning-christian-nationalism-1234797127/.

5 Laura Ansley, "Don't Say Gay, Stop Woke, Banned Books, And Anti-Trans Laws: the AHA's Teaching Through the Backlash Webinar." *Perspectives On History*, February 10, 2023, accessed July 14, 2023, www.historians.org/research-and-publications/perspectives-on-history/february-2023/dont-say-gay-stop-woke-banned-books-and-anti-trans-laws-the-ahas-teaching-through-the-backlash-webinar.

6 Melissa Gira Grant, "The Mysterious Case of the Fake Gay Marriage Website, the Real Straight Man, and the Supreme Court," *The New Republic*, June 29, 2023, accessed July 1, 2023, https://newrepublic.com/article/173987/mysterious-case-fake-gay-marriage-website-real-straight-man-supreme-court.

7 Amy Howe, "Supreme Court rules website designer can decline to create same-sex wedding websites," *SCOTUSblog*, June 30, 2023, accessed July 1, 2023, https://www.scotusblog.com/2023/06/supreme-court-rules-website-designer-can-deny-same-sex-couples-service/.

8 Nina Totenberg and Meghanlata Gupta, "The Supreme Court rules against USPS in Sunday work case," *NPR*, June 29, 2023, accessed July 1, 2023, https://www.npr.org/2023/06/29/1182121772/supreme-court-religious-freedom-postal-worker-decision.

9 Jon Henley, "How Europe's far right is marching steadily into the mainstream," *The Guardian*, June 30, 2023, accessed July 1, 2023, https://www.theguardian.com/world/2023/jun/30/far-right-on-the-march-europe-growing-taste-for-control-and-order.

10 Gregory A. Smith, Michael Rotolo, and Patricia Tevington, "45% of Americans Say U.S. Should Be a 'Christian Nation,'" *Pew Research*, October 22, 2022, accessed March 19, 2023, https://www.pewresearch.org/religion/2022/10/27/45-of-americans-say-u-s-should-be-a-christian-nation/.

11 Gregory A. Smith, "About Three-in-Ten U.S. Adults Are Now Religiously Unaffiliated," *Pew Research*, December 14, 2021, accessed March 22, 2023, https://www.pewresearch.org/religion/2021/12/14/about-three-in-ten-u-s-adults-are-now-religiously-unaffiliated/.

12 Chris Stokel-Walker, "Behind the Rise of the Online 'Tradwife' Movement," *Vice*, March 10, 2023, accessed July 21, 2023, https://www.vice.com/en/article/3ak8p8/online-rise-of-trad-ideology.

13 Matt Stieb, Chas Danner, and Benjamin Hart, "Why Did Fox News Fire Tucker Carlson? The host's misogyny is a leading theory," NY Magazine Intelligencer, April 28, 2023, accessed October. 7, 2023, https://nymag.com/intelligencer/2023/04/tucker-carlson-has-left-fox-news.html.

14 Lucy Williamson & George Wright, "Andrew Tate charged with rape and human trafficking," BBC, June 21, 2023, accessed October 7, 2023, https://www.bbc.com/news/world-europe-65959097.

15 Nicole Karlis, "Tucker Carlson hawks 'testicle tanning' to boost testosterone. Experts say it may do the opposite," *Salon*, April 21, 2022, accessed July 22, 2023, https://www.salon.com/2022/04/21/tucker-carlson-testicle-tanning/.

16 Cameron Easley, "U.S. Conservatives Are Uniquely Inclined Toward Right-wing Authoritarianism Compared to Western Peers," *Morning Consult*, June 28, 2021, accessed June 17, 2023, https://pro.morningconsult.com/trend-setters/global-Right-wing-authoritarian-test.

17 Dalia Fahmy, "Americans are far more religious than adults in other wealthy nations," *Pew Research*, July 31, 2018, accessed July 15, 2023, https://www.pewresearch.org/short-reads/2018/07/31/americans-are-far-more-religious-than-adults-in-other-wealthy-nations/.

18 Sarah Crawford and Virginia Villa, "Religiously Unaffiliated People Face Harassment in a Growing Number of Countries," *Pew Research*, Jan. 27 2023, accessed March 12, 2023, https://www.pewresearch.org/short-reads/2023/01/ 27/religiously-unaffiliated-people-face-harassment-in-a-growing-number-of-countries/.

19 Campbell Robertson, Christopher Mele and Sabrina Tavernise, "11 Killed in Synagogue Massacre; Suspect Charged With 29 Counts," *The New York Times*, October 27, 2018, accessed March 12, 2023, https://www.nytimes.com/2018/ 10/27/us/active-shooter-pittsburgh-synagogue-shooting.html.

20 Maureen Groppe, "With more than 800 antisemitic acts since October 7, Jewish student groups plead for Biden's help," *USA Today.* November 21, 2023, accessed December. 2, 2023, https://www.usatoday.com/story/news/politics/ 2023/11/20/rising-antisemitism-campus-federal-investigation/71579893007/.

21 Staff, "India: Surge in Summary Punishments of Muslims Discriminatory Demolitions of Property, Public Flogging," *Human Rights Watch*, October 27, 2022, accessed March 12, 2023, https://www.hrw.org/news/2022/10/07/india-surge-summary-punishments-muslims.

22 Hanibal Goitom, Foreign Law Specialist (Coordinator), with the Staff of the Global Legal Research Center, "Laws Criminalizing Apostasy in Selected Jurisdictions," May 2014, accessed March 12, 2023, https://tile.loc.gov/storage-services/service/ll/llglrd/2014434112/2014434112.pdf.

23 Zack Beauchamp, "It Happened There: How Democracy Died in Hungary," *Vox*, September 13, 2018, accessed March 12, 2023, https://www.vox.com/policy-and-politics/2018/9/13/17823488/hungary-democracy-authoritarianism-trump.

24 Julian Coman, "Family, Faith, Flag: The Religious Right and the Battle for Poland's Soul," *The Guardian*, October 5, 2019, accessed March 12, 2023, https://www.theguardian.com/world/2019/oct/05/family-faith-flag-catholic-religious-right-battle-polands-soul.

25 Ihsan Yilmaz, "The AKP's Authoritarian, Islamist Populism: Carving out a New Turkey," *European Center for Populism Studies*, February 5, 2021, accessed March 12, 2023, https://www.populismstudies.org/the-akps-authoritarian-islamist-populism-carving-out-a-new-turkey/.

26 William A. Galston, "The Populist Challenge to Liberal Democracy," *Brookings Institute*, April 17, 2018, accessed March 12, 2023, https://www.brookings.edu/research/the-populist-challenge-to-liberal-democracy/.

27 Norman Hepburn Baynes, "The Speeches of Adolf Hitler, April 1922–August 1939," New York: H. Fertig, 1969, p. 378.

28 David Niose, *Fighting Back the Right: Reclaiming America from the Attack on Reason* (New York: St. Martin's Press, 2014)

29 Sergey Gavrilets and Peter J. Richerson, "Collective Action and the Evolution of Social Norm Internalization," *PNAS*, May 22, 2017, accessed March 9, 2023, https://www.pnas.org/doi/10.1073/pnas.1703857114.

30 Psychology Today Staff, "Conformity," *Psychology Today*, accessed March 12, 2023, https://www.psychologytoday.com/us/basics/conformity.

31 David Niose, *Nonbeliever Nation: The Rise of Secular Americans* (St. Martin's Griffin, 2013), p. 9.

32 Bishop McNeil, "Wait, You're an Atheist AND a Conservative?," *The Humanist*, March 10, 2014, accessed March 12, 2023, https://thehumanist.com/commentary/wait-youre-an-atheist-and-a-conservative/.

33 Bradbury, Ray (New York: Ballantine Books, 1953), p. 178.

34 Kevin Ingram, ed., *The Conversos and Moriscos in Late Medieval Spain and Beyond: Departures and Change* (Brill, 2009), p. 1-12.

35 Barbara O'Brien, "When the U.S. Supreme Court Didn't Ban School Prayer," *Patheos*, November 10, 2022, accessed July 22, 2023, https://www.patheos.com/blogs/thereligioushistorynerd/2022/11/when-the-u-s-supreme-court-didnt-ban-school-prayer/.

36 Pew Research, "The Gender Gap in Religion Around the World: Women are generally more religious than men, particularly among Christians," March 22, 2016, accessed March 16, 2023, https://www.pewresearch.org/religion/2016/03/22/women-more-likely-than-men-to-affiliate-with-a-religion.

37 Elizabeth Dias and Ruth Graham, "Southern Baptists Move to Purge Churches With Female Pastors," *New York Times,* June 13, 2023, accessed July 22, 2023, https://www.nytimes.com/2023/06/13/us/southern-baptist-movement-women-pastors.html.

38 Emile P. Torres, "Godless grifters: How the New Atheists merged with the far right," *Salon*, June 5, 2021, accessed July 22, 2023, https://www.salon.com/2021/06/05/how-the-new-atheists-merged-with-the-far-right-a-story-of-intellectual-grift-and-abject-surrender/.

39 Ali, Ayaan Hirsi, *Infidel: My Life* (New York: Free Press, 2007), p. 320.

40 Charles C.W. Cooke, "Yes, Atheism and Conservatism Are Compatible," *National Review*, February 26, 2014, accessed June 22, 2023, https://www.nationalreview.com/2014/02/yes-atheism-and-conservatism-are-compatible-charles-c-w-cooke/.

41 Pew Research, "Religious Landscape Study: Party affiliation among atheists," 2014, accessed March 15, 2023, https://www.pewresearch.org/religion/religious-landscape-study/religious-family/atheist/party-affiliation/#social-and-political-views.

42 Shibley Telhami and Stella Rouse, "American Public Attitudes on Race, Ethnicity, and Religion," *University of Maryland Critical Issues Poll*, May 6-16, 2022, accessed March 15, 2023, https://criticalissues.umd.edu/sites/criticalissues.umd.edu/files/American%20Attitudes%20on%20Race%2C Ethnicity%2CReligion.pdf.

43 R. Buckminster Fuller Quotes. BrainyQuote.com, BrainyMedia Inc, 2024, accessed April 10, 2024, https://www.brainyquote.com/quotes/r_buckminster_fuller_ 151688.

44 Morgan Quinn, "Rich people and psychopaths tend to have 7 distinct traits in common," *Business Insider*, March 17, 2015, accessed July 22, 2023, https://www.businessinsider.com/here-are-the-7-distinct-traits-many-rich-people-have-in-common-with-psychopaths-2015-3.

45 Jack McCullough, "The Psychopathic CEO," *Forbes*, December 9, 2019, accessed July 4, 2023, https://www.forbes.com/sites/jackmccullough/2019/ 12/09/the-psychopathic-ceo/?sh=3987ab31791e.

46 Dr. R. Albert Mohler Jr., "Not Even Close? — Is America Becoming a Post-Christian Culture?" April 27, 2009, accessed July 17, 2023, https://albertmohler.com/2009/04/27/ not-even-close-is-america-becoming-a-post-christian-culture.

47 Pew Research, "In U.S., Decline of Christianity Continues at Rapid Pace," October 17, 2019, accessed March 15, 2023, https://www.pewresearch.org/religion/2019/10/17/in-u-s-decline-of-christianity-continues-at-rapid-pace/.

48 Frank Newport, "Slowdown in the Rise of Religious Nones," Gallup, December 9, 2022, accessed July 4, 2023, https://news.gallup.com/opinion/polling-matters/406544/slowdown-rise-religious-nones.aspx.

49 Pew Research, "Key Findings From the Global Religious Futures Project," December 21, 2022, accessed August 24, 2023, https://www.pewresearch.org/religion/2022/12/21/key-findings-from-the-global-religious-futures-project/.

50 Greta Thunberg, Twitter post, August 31, 2019, 8:03 a.m., https://twitter.com/GretaThunberg/status/1167916177927991296?lang=en.

51 Catherine Caldwell-Harris, Caitlin Fox Murphy, Tessa Velazquez, et al., "Religious Belief Systems of Persons with High Functioning Autism," Boston University, accessed March 15, 2023, https://escholarship.org/content/qt6zh3j3pr/qt6zh3j3pr_noSplash_45688aea088dae92fc3c0777d699502e.pdf.

52 Douglas Adams, *The Hitchhiker's Guide to the Galaxy* (New York: Del Rey, 2017). P. 181.

53 Brendan C. Walsh, "Gabriele Amorth conducted over 60,000 exorcisms and believed Hitler was possessed. Meet the man who inspired *The Pope's Exorcist*," *The Conversation*, April 5, 2023, accessed July 22, 2023, https://theconversation.com/gabriele-amorth-conducted-over-60-000-exorcisms-and-believed-hitler-was-possessed-meet-the-man-who-inspired-the-popes-exorcist-201383.

54 Ben Gilliam, "Abingdon theater pulls film from pastor who compares autism to demonic possession," *WJHL*, March 3, 2023, accessed July 22, 2023, https://www.wjhl.com/dont-miss/abingdon-theater-pulls-film-from-pastor-who-compares-autism-to-demonic-possession/.

55 Catherynne M. Valente, *The Girl Who Fell Beneath Fairyland and Led the Revels There* (New York: Feiwel & Friends, 2012). p. 8.

56 Leslie A. Anderson, Margaret O'Brien Caughy, and Margaret T. Owen, "'The Talk' and Parenting While Black in America: Centering Race, Resistance, and Refuge," *Journal of Black Psychology*, accessed June 11, 2023, https://doi.org/10.1177/00957984211034294.

57 Sally C. Curtin and Matthew F. Garnett, "Suicide and Homicide Death Rates Among Youth and Young Adults Aged 10–24: United States, 2001–2021." *CDC*, June 15, 2023, accessed July 4, 2023, https://stacks.cdc.gov/view/cdc/128423.

58 Amy Howe, "Justices side with high school football coach who prayed on the field with students." *SCOTUSblog*, June 27, 2022, accessed July 4, 2023, https://www.scotusblog.com/2022/06/justices-side-with-high-school-football-coach-who-prayed-on-the-field-with-students/.

59 James Baldwin, *Notes of a Native Son* (Boston: Beacon Press, 1955), p. 15.

60 Phil Zuckerman, *What It Means to Be Moral: Why Religion Is Not Necessary for Living an Ethical Life* (Berkeley: Counterpoint, 2020).

61 Christine Tamir, Aidan Connaughton, and Ariana Monique Salazar, "The Global God Divide," *Pew Research*, July 20, 2020, accessed July 3, 2023, https://www.pewresearch.org/global/2020/07/20/the-global-god-divide/.

62 Will M. Gervais et al. "Global Evidence of Extreme Intuitive Moral Prejudice Against Atheists," *Nature*, Aug 7, 2017, accessed July 7, 2023, https://www.nature.com/articles/s41562-017-0151.

63 Gregory S. Paul, "Cross-National Correlations of Quantifiable Societal Health with Popular Religiosity and Secularism in the Prosperous Democracies," *Journal of Religion & Society*, Vol. 7 (2005), accessed July 6, 2023, https://cdr.creighton.edu/server/api/core/bitstreams/f1441b64-ec3f-47db-a563-f383124d825c/content.

64 Jennifer Schuessler, "Philosophy That Stirs the Waters," *New York Times*, April 29, 2013, accessed June 24, 2023, https://www.nytimes.com/2013/04/30/books/daniel-dennett-author-of-intuition-pumps-and-other-tools-for-thinking.html.

65 Konner, Joan, *The Atheist's Bible: An Illustrious Collection of Irreverent Thoughts* (New York: HarperCollins, 2007), p. 4.

66 Juliana Menasce Horowitz, Ruth Igielnik, and Rakesh Kochhar, "Most Americans Say There Is Too Much Economic Inequality in the U.S., but Fewer Than Half Call It a Top Priority," *Pew Research*, January 9, 2020, accessed August 27, 2023, https://www.pewresearch.org/social-trends/2020/01/09/trends-in-income-and-wealth-inequality/.

67 Maxim Massenkoff and Nathan Wilmers, "Rubbing Shoulders: Class Segregation in Daily Activities," *SSRN*, August 21, 2023, accessed August 27, 2023, http://dx.doi.org/10.2139/ssrn.4516850.

68 Karl Marx, Critique of Hegel's '*Philosophy Of Right*', ed. Joseph O'Malley, Cambridge Studies in the History and Theory of Politics (Cambridge: Cambridge University Press, 1977).

69 Carlyle Murphy, "The Most and Least Educated U.S. Religious Groups," *Pew Research*, November 4, 2016, accessed July 2, 2023, https://www.pewresearch.org/short-reads/2016/11/04/the-most-and-least-educated-u-s-religious-groups/.

70 David Masci, "How Income Varies Among U.S. Religious Groups," *Pew Research*, October 12, 2016, accessed July 2, 2023, https://www.pewresearch.org/short-reads/2016/10/11/how-income-varies-among-u-s-religious-groups/.

71 Tzu, Sun, *The Art of War* (5th century BCE), chapter 3, verse 18.

72 Dawkins, Richard, *The God Delusion* (New York: Houghton Mifflin, 2006), p. 18.

73 David A. Roozen, *American Congregations 2015: Thriving and Surviving* (Hartford Institute for Religion Research, 2015), 12, accessed March 22, 2023, http://hirr.hartsem.edu/American-Congregations-2015.pdf.

74 Hemant Mehta, "Pastor Greg Locke whines after 'Shadowland' filmmaker quotes him accurately," *OnlySky*, September 22, 2022, accessed July 10, 2023, https://onlysky.media/hemant-mehta/pastor-greg-locke-whines-after-shadowland-filmmaker-quotes-him-accurately/.

75 Russell Gold, "The Billionaire Bully Who Wants to Turn Texas Into a Christian Theocracy," *Texas Monthly*, March 2024, accessed March 2024, https://www.texasmonthly.com/news-politics/billionaire-tim-dunn-runs-texas/.

76 Frank Newport, "Religious Group Voting and the 2020 Election," *Gallup*, Nov 13, 2020, accessed September 28, 2023, https://news.gallup.com/opinion/polling-matters/324410/religious-group-voting-2020-election.aspx.

77 Richard Rohr and John Bookser Feister, *Hope Against Darkness: The Transforming Vision of Saint Francis in an Age of Anxiety* (Cincinnati: Franciscan Media, 2002).

78 Colin Dwyer, "Charlottesville Rally Aimed To Defend A Confederate Statue. It May Have Doomed Others," *NPR*, August 14, 2017, accessed March 19, 2023, https://www.npr.org/sections/thetwo-way/2017/08/14/543471538/charlottesville-rally-aimed-to-defend-a-confederate-statue-it-may-have-doomed-ot.

79 Morgan Winsor, Ivan Pereira, and William Mansell, "4 dead after US Capitol breached by pro-Trump mob during 'failed insurrection'," *ABC News*, January 7, 2021, accessed March 19, 2023, https://abcnews.go.com/Politics/capitol-breached-protesters/story?id=75081629.

80 Rich Schapiro and Michael Kosnar, "Capitol rioter in horned hat gloats as feds work to identify suspects," *NBC News*, January 7, 2021, accessed March 19, 2023, https://www.nbcnews.com/news/us-news/capitol-rioter-horned-hat-gloats-feds-work-identify-suspects-n1253392.

81 Manji, Irshad, *The Trouble with Islam Today* (New York: St. Martin's Press, 2004), p. 103.

82 Pew Research, "The 'Zeal of the Convert': Is It the Real Deal?," October 28, 2009, accessed July 7, 2023, https://www.pewresearch.org/religion/2009/10/28/the-zeal-of-the-convert-is-it-the-real-deal/.

83 Ross Douthat, *Bad Religion: How We Became a Nation of Heretics* (New York: Free Press, 2012). p. 3.

84 Scott, Donald, "Divining America: Evangelicalism, Revivalism, and the Second Great Awakening," Queens College / City University of New York. National Humanities Center, October 15, 1999, accessed July 7, 2023, https://nationalhumanitiescenter.org/tserve/nineteen/nkeyinfo/nevanrev.htm.

85 Noah Hendrix, "Effects of Postmillennialism during the Second Great Awakening," *The Alexandrian X*, no. 1 (2021), accessed July 7, 2023, https://journals.troy.edu/index.php/test/issue/view/64/1.

86 Stefanie M. Vaught, "Religious Intolerance in the Second Great Awakening: The Mormon Experience in Missouri," December 18, 2013, accessed September 25, 2023, https://scholarworks.gsu.edu/cgi/viewcontent.cgi?article=1080&context=history_theses.

87 Jonna Marcaida Calagui, "Evangelical Author Hits Big Tech's Anti-Christian Bias, Warns Christians To Be 'Wise' In Social Media," *Christianity Daily*, February 22, 2021, accessed March 18, 2023, https://www.christianitydaily.com/news/evangelical-author-hits-big-tech-s-anti-christian-bias-warns-christians-to-be-wise-in-social-media.html.

88 *VOA News*, "Iran's Basij Force: Specialists in Cracking Down on Dissent," September 22, 2022, accessed March 18, 2023, https://www.voanews.com/a/iran-s-basij-force-specialists-in-cracking-down-on-dissent-/6759796.html.

89 Rebeka Castor, "'Proud Boys' provide security at pro-America rally in Milton," *Wear TV*, October 23, 2020, accessed March 15, 2023, https://weartv.com/news/local/proud-boys-provide-security-at-pro-america-rally-in-milton.

90 Michaels, Jon and Noll, David, "We Are Becoming a Nation of Vigilantes," *NY Times*, September 4, 2021, accessed March 3, 2023, https://www.nytimes.com/2021/09/04/opinion/texas-abortion-law.html.

91 Adrian Vermeule, "Beyond Originalism," *The Atlantic*, March 31, 2020, accessed March 18, 2023, https://www.theatlantic.com/ideas/archive/2020/03/common-good-constitutionalism/609037/.

92 Jeffrey M. Jones, "How Religious Are Americans?" *Gallup*, December 23, 2021, accessed March 15, 2023, https://news.gallup.com/poll/358364/religious-americans.aspx.

93 Justin Nortey, "Most White Americans who regularly attend worship services voted for Trump in 2020," *Pew Research*, August 30, 2021, accessed March 15, 2023, https://pewrsr.ch/2WyjkLJ.

94 Pew Research, "The Future of World Religions: Population Growth Projections, 2010-2050," April 2, 2015, accessed March 15, 2023, https://www.pewresearch.org/religion/2015/04/02/religious-projections-2010-2050/.

95 Virginia Villa, "Four-in-ten countries and territories worldwide had blasphemy laws in 2019," Pew Research, January 25, 2022, accessed March 15, 2023, https://www.pewresearch.org/short-reads/2022/01/25/four-in-ten-countries-and-territories-worldwide-had-blasphemy-laws-in-2019-2/.

96 Barbara Kingsolver, "Creeping Sharia Has Nothing On The Woke Mob," *New York Times*, June 16, 2023, accessed June 16, 2023, https://www.nytimes.com/2023/06/16/opinion/conservatives-muslims-lgbtq.html?smid=nytcore-ios-share&referringSource=articleShare.

97 Christina Cauterucci, "Ron DeSantis Is Betting the Farm on Trans Hate: The era of tepid acceptance is over," *Slate*, July 10, 2023, Accessed July 11, 2023, https://slate.com/news-and-politics/2023/07/ron-desantis-lgbtq-video-trump-2024-presidential-campaign.html.

98 W. Gervais, D. Xygalatas, R. McKay et al., "Global evidence of extreme intuitive moral prejudice against atheists," *Nat. Hum. Behav.* 1, no. 6 (2017): 0151, accessed March 15, 2023, https://doi.org/10.1038/s41562-017-0151.

99 Justin McCarthy, "Less Than Half in U.S. Would Vote for a Socialist for President," *Gallup*, May 8, 2019, accessed March 25, 2023, https://news.gallup.com/poll/254120/less-half-vote-socialist-president.aspx.

100 Pew Research, "Religious Landscape Study," 2017, accessed March 25, 2023, https://www.pewresearch.org/religion/religious-landscape-study/.

101 Pew Research, "Jewish Americans in 2020," May 11, 2021, accessed March 25, 2023, https://www.pewresearch.org/religion/2021/05/11/u-s-jews-political-views/.

102 George Bernard Shaw, *Man and Superman* (London: Archibald Constable and Company, 1903), Act II, line 407.

103 AJ Willingham,"A nonstop worship gathering at a Kentucky school echoes an old Christian tradition," *CNN*, February 18, 2023, Accessed July 8, 2023, https://www.cnn.com/2023/02/18/us/asbury-revival-christian-what-is-cec/index.html.

104 Laiken Neumann, "'Scripture don't pay the bills': Server says customers who came in after church left her a scripture instead of tip," daily dot, April 20, 2022, Accessed July 8, 2023, https://www.dailydot.com/irl/customers-after-church-scripture-tip/.

105 Darcy, Oliver, "How Twitter's algorithm is amplifying extreme political rhetoric," *CNN Business*, March 22, 2019, accessed July 17, 2023, https://www.cnn.com/2019/03/22/tech/twitter-algorithm-political-rhetoric/index.html.

106 Deborah Solomon, et al. "Mark Zuckerberg Testimony: Senators Question Facebook's Commitment to Privacy," *New York Times*, April 10, 2018, accessed July 8, 2023, https://www.nytimes.com/2018/04/10/us/politics/mark-zuckerberg-testimony.html.

107 Sean Illing, "Why conservatives are winning the internet," *Vox*, June 3, 2019, accessed March 18, 2023, https://www.vox.com/policy-and-politics/2019/6/3/18624687/conservatism-liberals-internet-activism-jen-schradie.

108 Katie Paul, "Meta's 'friendly' Threads collides with unfriendly internet," *Reuters*, July 7, 2023, accessed July 8, 2023, https://www.reuters.com/technology/metas-friendly-threads-collides-with-unfriendly-internet-2023-07-07/.

109 Theresa Riley, "Margaret Atwood Reflects on 'The Handmaid's Tale'," *BillMoyers.com*, April 14, 2017, accessed February 4, 2024, https://billmoyers.com/story/margaret-atwood-on-the-handmaids-tale/.

110 Matt Lewis, "Evangelicals Worshiping Trump Is as About as Unchristian as It Gets," *Daily Beast*, October 3, 2023, accessed February 4, 2024, https://www.thedailybeast.com/evangelicals-worshiping-trump-is-as-about-as-unchristian-as-it-gets.

111 Ron Allen, "Ron DeSantis' "God ad" invokes God 10 times in 96 seconds," Axios, November 5, 2022, accessed February 4, 2024, https://www.axios.com/2022/11/05/ron-desantis-god-ad-florida-governor.

112 Jack Jenkins, "Mike Johnson suggests his election as House speaker ordained by God," *Washington Post*, October 27, 2023, accessed February 4, 2024, https://www.washingtonpost.com/religion/2023/10/27/house-speaker-mike-johnson-evangelical/.

113 Guthrie Graves-Fitzsimmons, "About Project 2025," *MSNBC*, September 8, 2023, accessed September 30, 2023, https://www.msnbc.com/opinion/msnbc-opinion/project-2025-heritage-foundation-christian-nationalism-rcna103510.

114 Amandine Barb, "'An atheistic American is a contradiction in terms': Religion, Civic Belonging and Collective Identity in the United States." *European Journal of American Studies*, Spring 2011, accessed July 8, 2023, https://journals.openedition.org/ejas/8865.

115 Chris Hedges, *American Fascists: The Christian Right and the War On America* (New York: Vintage, 2008). p. 24.

116 "Chametz Law Banning Bread in Israeli Hospitals Violates 'Freedom From Religion,' AG Says," *Haaretz*, February 23, 2023, accessed March 12, 2023, https://www.haaretz.com/israel-news/2023-02-19/ty-article/.premium/chametz-law-banning-bread-in-israeli-hospitals-violates-freedom-from-religion-ag-says/00000186-691f-d3ca-a3e7-ef9f7fc50000.

117 Carrie Keller-Lynn "Israel's judicial overhaul: What is the coalition planning and where does it stand?" *The Times of Israel*, March 4, 2023, accessed March 12, 2023, https://www.timesofisrael.com/israels-judicial-overhaul-what-is-the-coalition-planning-and-where-does-it-stand/.

118 Bill Chappell & Joe Hernandez, "Why Iranian women are burning their hijabs after the death of Mahsa Amini," *NPR*, September 21, 2022, accessed September 30, 2023, https://www.npr.org/2022/09/21/1124237272/mahsa-amini-iran-women-protest-hijab-morality-police.

119 Shane Harris, Greg Miller and Josh Dawsey, "CIA concludes Saudi crown prince ordered Jamal Khashoggi's assassination," *Washington Post*, Nov 16, 2018, accessed September 30, 2023, https://www.washingtonpost.com/world/national-security/cia-concludes-saudi-crown-prince-ordered-jamal-khashoggis-assassination/2018/11/16/98c89fe6-e9b2-11e8-a939-9469f1166f9d_story.html.

120 "Elliot Rodger: How misogynist killer became 'incel hero'," *BBC*, April 26, 2018, accessed March 22, 2023, https://www.bbc.com/news/world-us-canada-43892189.

121 Avishay, Artsy, "How Andrew Tate sells men on toxic masculinity," *Vox*, January 10, 2023, accessed March 22, 2023, https://www.vox.com/culture/2023/1/10/23547393/andrew-tate-toxic-masculinity-qa.

122 BBC, "What is India's caste system?" June 19, 2019, accessed April 9, 2023, https://www.bbc.com/news/world-asia-india-35650616.

123 Jack Butler, "An Unsettling Glimpse at CPAC Texas," *National Review*, August 12, 2022, accessed March 22, 2023, https://www.nationalreview.com/corner/an-unsettling-glimpse-at-cpac-texas/.

124 Russell, Bertrand *Unpopular Essays* (London: George Allen & Unwin Ltd. 1950), p. 38.

125 Jeff Diamant, "Faith on the Hill," *Pew Research Center*, January 3, 2023, accessed March 18, 2023, https://www.pewresearch.org/religion/2023/01/03/faith-on-the-hill-2023/.

126 Milton Ezrati. "China's Economic Base Is Shrinking, And Dramatically So," *Forbes*, March 13, 2023, accessed March 13, 2023, https://www.forbes.com/sites/miltonezrati/2023/03/13/chinas-economic-base-is-shrinking-and-dramatically-so/?sh=7e6b303f1e51.

127 Peter L. Berger, *The Heretical Imperative: Contemporary Possibilities of Religious Affirmation* (New York: Anchor Press, 1979).

128 Daniel Silliman. "'No Celebrities Except Jesus': How Asbury Protected the Revival." *Christianity Today*, February 23, 2023, accessed March 22, 2023, https://www.christianitytoday.com/news/2023/february/asbury-revival-outpouring-protect-work-admin-volunteers.html.

129 Nickel Terry Ellis. "Gov. DeSantis' conservative takeover of a liberal arts college could silence diversity, critics say," *CNN*, February 17, 2023, accessed March 22, 2023, https://www.cnn.com/2023/02/15/us/desantis-new-college-inclusion-reaj/index.html.

130 D'Angelo, Anthony J. *The College Blue Book.* (Pittsburgh: Dangelo International Publishing, 1994), p. 230.

131 Statista Research Department, "Reported violent crime rate in the United States from 1990 to 2022," *Statista*, October 20, 2023, accessed January 9, 2024, https://www.statista.com/statistics/191219/reported-violent-crime-rate-in-the-usa-since-1990.

132 CDC, "An Update on Cancer Deaths in the United States," 2021, accessed March 16, 2023, https://www.cdc.gov/cancer/dcpc/research/update-on-cancer-deaths/index.htm.

133 US Department of Commerce, "News: Unemployment is at its Lowest Level in 54 years," February 3, 2023, accessed March 16, 2023, https://www.commerce.gov/news/blog/2023/02/news-unemployment-its-lowest-level-54-years.

134 Jonathan Friedman, PhD, Nadine Farid Johnson, "Banned in the USA: The Growing Movement to Censor Books in Schools," *Pen America 100*, September 19, 2022, accessed March 16, 2023, https://pen.org/report/banned-usa-growing-movement-to-censor-books-in-schools/.

135 Shawna Mizelle, "Republicans across the country push legislation to restrict drag show performances," *CNN*, February 5, 2023, accessed March 16, 2023, https://www.cnn.com/2023/02/05/politics/drag-show-legislation/index.html.

136 Martha Stout, *Outsmarting the Sociopath Next Door: How to Protect Yourself Against a Ruthless Manipulator* (New York: Harmony Books, 2005).

137 Elizabeth Perry, "Grey rocking: Why this method works for a minute (and when it doesn't)," *Betterup Blog*, March 22, 2022, accessed May 7, 2023, https://www.betterup.com/blog/grey-rocking.

138 Hall, Alvin. *Driving the Green Book: A Road Trip Through the Living History of Black Resistance.* (New York: Amistad, 2024)

139 Ducharme, Madeline. "We Are Everywhere," *Slate*, August 27, 2020, accessed February 25, 2024, https://slate.com/human-interest/2020/08/mapping-gay-guides-project.html.

140 Confucius, *The Analects*, trans. D.C. Lau (Penguin Classics, 1979), 6.30.

141 Vicky Baker, "The preachers getting rich from poor Americans," *BBC*, May 29, 2019, accessed March 26, 2023, https://www.bbc.com/news/stories-47675301.

142 BBC, "Catholic Church Child Sexual Abuse Scandal," October 5, 2021, accessed March 26, 2023, https://www.bbc.com/news/world-44209971.

143 Karen Swallow Prior, "Why Are Christians Such Bad Tippers?" *Christianity Today*, February 5, 2013, accessed March 26, 2023, https://www.christianitytoday.com/ct/2013/february-web-only/why-are-christians-such-bad-tippers.html.

144 Klepic, Jure. *Twitter for Authors: Social Media Book Marketing Strategies for Shy Writers.* (New York: CreateSpace Independent Publishing Platform, 2015), p. 50.

145 Eric Siegel, PhD, "When Algorithms Infer Pregnancy or Other Sensitive Information About People," *NAIEI*, November 2, 2020, accessed July 22, 2023, https://montrealethics.ai/when-algorithms-infer-pregnancy-or-other-sensitive-information-about-people/.

146 White, E.B., *Quotable E.B. White*, edited by Martha White. (Ithaca: Cornell University Press, 2012).

147 James T. Keane, "How does a book reading turn into an attempted murder? The threat against Salman Rushdie has been decades in the making," *America Magazine*, August 12, 2022, accessed May 11, 2023, https://www.americamagazine.org/arts-culture/2022/08/16/cbc-column-salman-rushdie-243563.

148 Josh Marcus, "Oklahoma superintendent sparks outrage with claim Tulsa massacre wasn't about race." *Independent*, July 8, 2023, accessed July 24, 2023, https://www.independent.co.uk/news/world/americas/us-politics/tulsa-massacre-ryan-walters-race-b2371449.html.

149 Farrell Evans, "How Interstate Highways Gutted Communities — and Reinforced Segregation," *History.com*, May 23, 2023, accessed July 24, 2023, https://www.history.com/news/interstate-highway-system-infrastructure-construction-segregation.

150 Warren, Elizabeth. *This Fight Is Our Fight: The Battle to Save America's Middle Class* (New York: Metropolitan Books, 2017), p. 333.

151 Özlem Sensoy , Robin DiAngelo, et al., *Is Everyone Really Equal?: An Introduction to Key Concepts in Social Justice Education (Multicultural Education Series).* (New York: Teachers College Press, 2017).

152 George Orwell, 1984 (New York: Signet Classics, 1977) Pg. 51.

153 John Blake, "How conservatives use 'verbal jiu-jitsu' to turn liberals' language against them," CNN, August 20, 2023, accessed August 28, 2023, https://www.cnn.com/2023/08/20/politics/conservatives-verbal-combat-blake-cec/index.html.

154 Karl Marx, "Critique of the Gotha Programme," (Moscow: Progress Publishers, 1977).

155 J.D. Vance, *Hillbilly Elegy: A Memoir of a Family and Culture in Crisis* (New York, NY: Harper, an imprint of HarperCollins Publishers, 2016).

156 Alexis de Tocqueville, *De la Démocratie en Amérique* (First edition, 1835).

157 Fischer, Louis, ed. *The Essential Gandhi: An Anthology of His Writings on His Life, Work, and Ideas.* (New York: Vintage Books, 1962), p. 392.

158 Candida R. Moss, *The Myth of Persecution: How Early Christians Invented a Story of Martyrdom* (HarperOne, 2013), p. 256.

159 Darrel Ray, *Sex & God: How Religion Distorts Sexuality* (Bonner Springs: IPC Press, 2012).

160 Richard Dawkins, *The God Delusion* (1st Mariner Books ed. Boston, Houghton Mifflin Co, 2008.), p. 19.

161 Adam Gabbatt, "Losing their religion: why US churches are on the decline," The Guardian, January 22, 2023, accessed March 16, 2023, https://www.theguardian.com/us-news/2023/jan/22/us-churches-closing-religion-covid-christianity.

162 Kavya Beheraj, "America's Christian majority could end by 2070," *Axios*, September 21, 2022, accessed March 16, 2023, https://www.axios.com/2022/09/21/pew-religion-christian-majority-2070.

163 Mordi Miller, "Jewish Law Above All: Recordings Reveal Far-right Knesset Member's Plan to Turn Israel Into a Theocracy," *Haaretz*, January 19, 2023, accessed March 19, 2023, https://www.haaretz.com/israel-news/2023-01-19/ty-article-magazine/.highlight/jewish-law-above-all-recordings-reveal-far-right-mks-plan-to-turn-israel-into-theocracy/00000185-cae1-da66-a1bf-fbfb32560000.

164 Pew Research, "The Future of World Religions: Population Growth Projections, 2010-2050," April 2, 2015, accessed March 17, 2023, https://www.pewresearch.org/religion/2015/04/02/religious-projections-2010-2050/.

165 Isaac Anderson, "A Less Lonely Way to Lose Your Faith," *The Atlantic*, September 11, 2016, accessed September 30, 2023, https://www.theatlantic.com/politics/archive/2016/09/oasis-secular-groups/499148/.

166 Adam Lee, "Atheist churches: A new type of secular community," Salon, December 3, 2013, accessed September 30, 2023, https://www.salon.com/2013/12/03/atheist_churches_a_era_of_secular_community_partner/.

167 Ezra Pound, *ABC of Reading* (New York: New Directions Publishing Corporation, 1960), p. 37.

168 Anna Long, Milennials and Gen Z'ers Redefine Their Stereotypes, The Height, December 3, 2018, Accessed April 10, 2024, https://www.bcheights.com/2018/12/03/millennials-and-gen-zers-redefine-their-stereotypes/.

169 Cathy McMorris Rodgers et al., "Full Committee Hearing: TikTok: How Congress Can Safeguard American Data Privacy and Protect Children from Online Harms," *Energy & Commerce*, March 23, 2023, accessed July 18, 2023, https://energycommerce.house.gov//events/full-committee-hearing-tik-tok-how-congress-can-safeguard-american-data-privacy-and-protect-children-from-online-harms.

170 Morley Winograd, Michael Hais, and Doug Ross, "How younger voters will impact elections: Younger voters are poised to upend American politics," *Brookings*, February 27, 2023, accessed March 26, 2023, https://www.brookings.edu/blog/fixgov/2023/02/27/younger-voters-are-poised-to-upend-american-politics/.

171 Allyn, Bobby. "The House Passed a TikTok Ban Bill. But Is the App Really a National Security Threat?" *NPR.* March 14, 2024, accessed March 16, 2024, https://www.npr.org/2024/03/14/1238435508/tiktok-ban-bill-congress-china.

172 Ryan P. Burge, "Gen Z and Religion in 2021," *Religion in Public: exploring the mix of sacred and secular*, June 15, 2022, accessed July 18, 2023, https://religioninpublic.blog/2023/04/03/gen-z-and-religion-in-2022/.

173 Christine Emba, "Men are lost. Here's a map out of the wilderness," *Washington Post*, July 10, 2023, accessed July 20, 2023, https://www.washingtonpost.com/opinions/2023/07/10/christine-emba-masculinity-new-model/.

www.ingramcontent.com/pod-product-compliance
Lightning Source LLC
Chambersburg PA
CBHW062045270326
41931CB00013B/2954

* 9 7 9 8 2 1 8 4 2 1 6 2 5 *